THE
EGG
PROJECT

THE
EGG
PROJECT

Gary Null's Complete Guide to Good Eating

Drawings by Judith Lerner

FOUR WALLS EIGHT WINDOWS
NEW YORK

Library of Congress Cataloging-in-Publication Data

Null, Gary.
   The egg project.

   1. Reducing diets.   2. Food allergy—Diet therapy.
3. Nutrition.   4. Food, Natural.   5. Menus.
I. Title.
RM222,2.N85   1987   613.2   87-21101
ISBN 0-941423-05-0
ISBN 0-941423-06-9 (pbk.)

Four Walls Eight Windows
P.O. Box 548
Village Station
New York, N.Y. 10014

Designed by Hannah Lerner
Printed in the U.S.A.

To Dr. Herbert Shelton

Acknowledgements

With thanks to some of the men and women whom I have known and communicated with over the years and who inspired me, especially Dr. Herbert Shelton, Adelle Davis, Paavo Airola, Herb Baley, Albert Szent-Gyorgyi, Robert and J.I. Rodale, Bob Hoffman, Broda Barnes, Nathan Pritikin, Linda Clark , John Lust, Lelord Kordel, H.E. Kirschner, John Christopher, Wilfrid Shute, Linus Pauling, Ralph Nader, Irwin Stone, Fred Klenner, Carlton Fredericks, Paul Bragg, Gayelord Hauser and Bernard MacFadden. I would also like to thank Max Friedman, Trudy Gobbic, Adria Eisenmeyer, and Philip J. Hodes, Ph.D. for their invaluable research and editing assistance.

Contents

PART ONE: WHAT IS FOOD?

1 · *CARBOHYDRATES*

Why You Need Carbohydrates 4.   Complex and Refined
Carbohydrates 4.   Danger: Sweets Can Quickly Sour 5.
How Many Carbohydrates Do You Need? 6.   Sources of
Complex Carbohydrates 8.   Preparing Complex Carbohydrate
Foods 9.   Facilitating Digestion of Carbohydrates 9.   A Word
or a Few about Fiber 11.

2 · *FATS*

Why You Need Fat 16.   Saturated and Unsaturated Fats 16.
How Much Fat Do You Need? 17.   Hydrogenation 18.   Fats
and Dieting 18.   The Dangers of Fat 19.

3 · *PROTEIN*

Why You Need Protein 22.   How Much Protein Do You
Need? 23.   Complete Proteins: The Eight Essential Amino
Acids 23.   Preparing Protein Foods 24.   Too Little
Protein 25.   Too Much Protein 27.   Protein and
Dieting 28.   Protein and Disease 29.   Protein and
Athletics 30.

4 · *VITAMINS*

Vitamin A 34.   The B-Vitamin Complex 34.   Vitamin B_1
(Thiamine) 35.   Vitamin B_2 (Riboflavin) 35.   Vitamin B_3
(Niacin) 36.   Vitamin B_5 (Pantothenic Acid) 36.   Vitamin B_6
(Pyridoxine) 37.   Vitamin B_{12} (Cyanocobalamin) 37.   Folic
Acid 37.   Para-aminobenzoic Acid (PABA) 38.
Choline 38.   Inositol 38.   Biotin 39.   Vitamin C 39.
Vitamin D 40.   Vitamin E 40.   Vitamin K 41.

PART TWO: GETTING TO GROUND ZERO

RECIPES

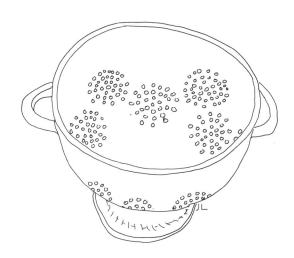

PROCEDURES AND TESTS

PROGRAMS AND PLANS

TO THE READER

No one aspect of good nutrition can be applied in isolation; all must be considered together.

What do I mean? Take food combining, for example. The approach has been developed and refined during this century by Dr. Herbert Shelton and many others and forms an essential part of this book. But to try and apply the tenets of food combining without an understanding of your individual nutritional needs is, quite simply, futile. First you must understand what food is, how it works and how it interacts with your body. You must also understand what is wrong with your present diet. If you are American and follow the typical American diet, you may want to know some facts about how food is produced and prepared here, especially animal products and grain foods. Then you must take into consideration the issue of detoxification. In order to pass from an inferior diet to a superior one, you will have to detoxify. Or else you will fail.

Next there is the problem of food allergies. They affect a far greater proportion of the population than is generally acknowleged. Proper testing is important. Low-potency vitamin and mineral supplements may also be appropriate for people seeking proper nutrition, especially in an urban environment. And we cannot ignore the importance of combining enhanced nutrition with regular exercise; the two are inseparable aspects of good health. Finally, you must know how to integrate these changes into your daily life and also how to find an alternative health practitioner for help if and when you need it.

What is *The Egg Project?* It is the shape of things to come, first in this book and then in your life. The various points raised here all come together and form a circle – or should I say, an ovoid. Other books may attempt to inform you of one or another of them. But only when you bring them all together will you be in a position to really apply them in your life. Food combining alone is of no value, unless joined with a basic understanding of nutrition and health, an appreciation of the importance of regular exercise, and an acute awareness of the environment in which we now find ourselves, late in the 20th century. With access to the right information and the right health professionals, it can be the start of something new.

What is *The Egg Project?* It is the realization that complete well-being is not beyond our grasp, but does not depend on fads or simple answers either. And it may be the only complete, well-rounded, clear, readable guide there is.

Gary Null
July 1987

INTRODUCTION

FORTY YEARS AGO, roughly a third of the grocery store was devoted to natural fresh produce. Today, it is a small fraction of that, and even what appears to be natural has been altered. Fruits and vegetables are routinely grown with artificial fertilizers, sprayed with pesticides, treated with hormones and chemicals to control the time of ripening to facilitate mechanical harvesting, dyed, sprayed with chemicals to prevent them from ripening during shipping or to induce ripening after shipping, and coated with waxes to give a glossy appearance.

Modern bread fares no better. The Western world is built on wheat, which, for thousands of years, has been prepared as bread and known as the staff of life. Wheat (and other whole grains) provides a rich source of nutrients: complex carbohydrates, protein, oils, roughage, and an excellent balance of dozens of vitamins and minerals. Grinding wheat with stone rollers blends these ingredients together, providing a product so nutritionally rich that it is prone to spoilage and attacks by vermin and fungi if not immediately used. In order to make a product that could be transported over long distances and stored indefinitely, a product incapable of sustaining life was necessary. White flour was born.

White flour begins with steel rather than stone rollers, thereby flattening and separating the bran and germ, which carry most of wheat's nutrients and are sold as animal feeds, from a chalklike dust. Chlorine gases are used to bleach out any remaining sustenance. The product is then "enriched" with synthetic versions of some of the vitamins removed earlier in the processing. The vitamins considered necessary for this "enrichment" are, not coincidentally, those which are most easily synthesized. These are the ingredients commonly listed on loaves of bread made from enriched flour: barley malt, ferrous sulfate, niacin, thiamine mononitrate, riboflavin, corn syrup, partially hydrogenated vegetable shortening, yeast, salt, calcium sulfate, sodium stearoyl lactylate, mono- and diglycerides, whey dicalcium phosphate, calcium propionate, and potassium bromate.

Some of the flour additives and processing chemicals that need not, according to the Code of Federal Regulations, be listed on the package include: oxides of nitrogen, chlorine, nitrosyl chloride, chlorine dioxide, benzoyl peroxide, acetone peroxide, azodicarbonamide, and plaster of Paris.

One of the most common additives in processed foods is sugar. The average American eats 120 pounds of sugar a year. After processing, many foods are so lacking in taste that there would be no taste at all without adding large quantities of sugar or salt.

Sugar is ideal for the processed food industry because many people like its taste and it is cheap, but primarily because it is addictive. Sugar in large quantities is concealed in many foods; not only in candy, cake, and soft drinks, but in bread, breakfast cereals, cheeses, condiments, and canned or packaged foods. Most processed foods have large amounts of sugar, and those that do not have large amounts of salt. It is not easy to eliminate sugar from your diet.

Americans have grown accustomed to the excellence of their water supplies. Since the turn of the century, treatment of municipal water with chlorine disinfectants has provided protection against disease-causing microorganisms, and private wells are usually tested periodically to assure quality standards. Massive programs to build sewage treatment plants are in effect throughout the country, and standard operating procedures maintain the strict control of disease-causing microorganisms, since much of the water we drink is someone else's sewage. However, even as the problem of human wastes is being controlled, a larger problem is looming: the industrial pollution of drinking-water supplies. Hundreds of thousands of industrial plants discharge grit, asbestos, phosphates, nitrates, mercury, lead, caustic soda, sulfur, sulfuric acid, oils and petrochemicals into many of the waterways from which we eventually drink. Treatment plants designed to handle human wastes are unable to handle many of these more toxic, chemically complex and sometimes unstable substances. Ironically, one of the carcinogens identified as occurring in water results when chlorine mixes with organic matter.

Nationwide, over 700 chemical pollutants have been identified in public water supplies. Most of these are carcinogenic, cause birth defects, or are otherwise toxic. Over 20 scientific studies have documented a consistent link between consumption of trace organic chemical contaminants in drinking water and elevated cancer mortality rates. In spite of mounting evidence, existing United States public health standards reflect virtually no acknowledgement of toxic and carcinogenic substances in drinking water. As a result, no concerted effort has been made to remove them from public water supplies. Parallel failures to protect drinking water quality and to regulate massive discharges of non-biodegradable industrial wastes forecast a grim future for the American public. Toxic contamination has already forced many communities to find alternative sources of water supply. Still, the overwhelming majority of the nation's drinking water systems have never been tested for the presence of toxic pollutants. The response to this dual environmental and health dilemma has been woefully inadequate.

Most of us picture farms as being like those we remember from childhood, or those we have seen in pictures or on television. We imagine farm animals in their pens, or even roaming around a farmyard. Such farms may exist, but they are not the source of the meat we buy and eat today. Chickens are raised by the tens of thousands in giant buildings where they never see the light of day. They are kept in cages in which they cannot move, with conveyor belts bringing them food and water and carrying away their waste. When they do move about, they often slide around on their breasts, as some modern breeds grow too fast for their legs to support them. They are constantly sprayed and their food doused with chemicals, hormones, and medicines. Attempts also are being made to breed featherless chickens.

Many pigs are also raised in cages, without ever seeing daylight. Such conditions are particularly cruel for pigs, which are close to dogs in intelligence and sensitivity. Steers spend most of their lives out of doors, but are no less exposed to chemicals in their upbringing. Today, a steer is born, taken from its mother and put on a diet of powdered milk, synthetic vitamins, minerals and antibiotics. Drugs in its food reduce its activities to save on feed. Next, it is actually allowed to eat some pasture grass, but this is supplemented with processed feed premixed with antibiotics and growth-promoting drugs. At six months, it weighs 500 pounds and is ready for the feed lot. Here it is doused with pesticides and then placed in a pen that is lit around the clock to change natural sleep rhythms and encourage continuous feeding. Food consists of grains, urea, carbohydrates, ground-up newspaper, molasses, plastic pellets, and, most recently, reprocessed manure, a high protein source. After four months in the feed lot, the steer weighs 1,200 pounds. A few more doses of pesticides, antibiotics and hormones to pretenderize it while it is still alive, and it is ready for slaughter. Nearly all poultry, pigs, and veal calves and 60 percent of cattle get antibiotics added to their feed. Seventy-five percent of pigs eat feed laced with sulfa drugs. Cattle feeders use a variety of hormones and other additives to promote rapid weight gain in their animals.

While farmers rely more and more on chemistry to shore up animal health under factory conditions, dangerous residues are showing up in meat and poultry products. Fourteen percent of meat and poultry sampled by the Agriculture Department in the mid and late 1970s contained illegally high levels of drugs and pesticides. According to a recent General Accounting Office report, "of the 143 drugs and pesticides G.A.O. identified as likely to leave residues in raw meat and poultry, 42 are known to cause or are suspected of causing cancer, 20 of causing birth defects and six of causing mutations."

The average American ate two pounds of chemical additives in food in 1960 and ten pounds in 1978, a fivefold increase in less than 20 years. Most of these additives were not put in foods to preserve shelf life or retard spoilage, as is usually claimed; instead, more than 90 percent of the additives (both by weight and by value) were there to deceive—that is, to make the agribusiness product look, taste, feel and nourish more like the real thing.

No one questions the fact that there are a lot of chemicals in our food. Manufacturers contend, however, that these chemicals are safe, that they have been tested and approved by the Food and Drug Administration. Are all these chemicals really safe? The answer is no.

If food additives can be dangerous, why are we told otherwise? The answer lies in the complex interrelations of the food industry, media, government and medical research. The food industry is very big business, with annual sales well over $200 billion. Each year, well over $500 million worth of chemicals are added to foods. The food industry is a major advertiser in consumer magazines and on television, so magazines and television too often are careful of being critical. Food industries are major sources of grants for university research departments. Government agencies have close relationships with the industries they are supposed to regulate. Many research scientists and government management personnel eventually enter the industry they previously regulated—and at much higher paying jobs.

There are literally thousands of chemicals added to food. Few of these have been adequately tested, and none have been tested in combination with others. Many that have been tested have been known to be dangerous for 30 years or more. DES, a synthetic hormone used to fatten cattle, has been known for decades to cause cancer. Industry fights attempts to ban such chemicals every step of the way. When, as in the case of DES, a ban is finally achieved, some producers continue to use it anyway. And by the time the ban is obtained, there are a dozen similar chemicals to replace the one banned, some of which may be worse.

Agribusiness encourages a way of eating that disrupts our physical health and erodes the sense of fulfillment that comes from preparing and eating real food. A fast-food rationale enters the community and the home, with deleterious effects. Agribusiness also undermines small local farmers, who lend economic and ecological stability to the country. And industrialized foods simply do not taste as good as food should. They are dependent on salt, sugar, chemicals, and billions of dollars in advertising. The fact is, most of us simply have forgotten what real food tastes like.

This book talks about real food and how to make the most of it in living a more healthful life.

Part One

What Is Food?

BASIC NUTRITION BEGINS WITH six major nutrients: carbohydrates, proteins, fats, vitamins, minerals, and water. Along with an understanding of these basic nutrients, for good health you also need to be aware of the air you breathe, the balance of enzymes in your body, and the function of antioxidants in helping your body to combat disease and degenerative processes. Your body needs all of these nutrients every day. How much you need of each depends on your health as well as your energy needs.

Energy may be why we need food, but it isn't necessarily why we eat—sometimes a great deal, sometimes too little, all too often the wrong things in the wrong amounts. When it comes to nourishing our bodies, many of us follow the dictates of myths, fads or bizarre and exotic diets. We all know the proper kind of gas for a car and the best kind of food for our cat or dog. We may know our carburetors and our Siamese, but we don't know ourselves.

Information about good nutrition abounds. Yet many people don't bother to find out more about good nutrition. Some simply don't know where to look or what to trust. These chapters—on our six basic nutrients—should help point the way and begin that journey.

1 · CARBOHYDRATES

"Buy produce in season, buy it fresh,
and eat it raw when possible."

UNTIL RECENTLY, CARBOHYDRATES HAVE gotten a bad press. Highly sugared and refined carbohydrates such as candy, soft drinks, pastries, sugared cereals, as well as refined breads and pastas, have been lumped together with complex carbohydrates such as fruit, nutritious starchy vegetables, whole grains, and tubers. When we have thought—carbohydrates—we have tended to think "calories and fattening."

Most people don't understand that there is a distinction between two forms of carbohydrates: the refined starches and sugars that have given carbohydrates their reputation as food for fat, and the complex carbohydrates whose health benefits are finally beginning to be appreciated. Carbohydrates are vital in a proper diet.

3

WHY YOU NEED CARBOHYDRATES

Carbohydrates are everywhere. In fact, they are one of the most abundant compounds in living things. The nutrient group includes nondigestible cellulose (the fibrous material that helps give plants their shape) as well as starches and sugars, two of the storable fuels that supply living things with immediate energy. Each gram of carbohydrates supplies the body with four calories of energy when it is burnt up in our cells. In the U.S., half the calories we get—half of our energy—come from these carbohydrate foods. Many carbohydrate-rich foods also contain substantial amounts of amino acids—the building blocks of protein.

We need carbohydrates. They are the most important source of energy for all our activities. The foods in which they are found—fruits, cereals, seeds and nuts, vegetables, and tubers—also are important sources of the vitamins, minerals, and other nutrients we need to live.

COMPLEX AND REFINED CARBOHYDRATES

Carbohydrate foods come in two forms: complex or refined. *Complex carbohydrates* are starches and fibers in foods like cereals, legumes, seeds, nuts, vegetables, and tubers. They exist in these foods just as they are found in nature, having undergone minimal or no processing.

Refined carbohydrates, on the other hand, have been substantially tampered with. "Refined" may in fact be an overly refined way of putting it. Having been processed by machinery and industry, they are merely skeletons of the complex carbohydrates found in nature.

While the starches and sugars of all carbohydrates supply energy, complex carbohydrates also offer the fiber necessary for good digestive functioning, to supply B and C complex and other vitamins, and/or protein, the building blocks of our bodies. In addition, our bodies tolerate and absorb complex carbohydrates best and most effectively.

Refinement, on the other hand, is a recent innovation in our long history of evolution, food consumption, and food delivery.

When carbohydrates are refined, they are stripped of both their outer shell (the bran layer that contains most of the fiber) and their oil and B vitamin-rich germ (found at their cores). Refined carbohydrates may also be bleached, milled, baked (bread), puffed (some cereals), or otherwise processed (sugar).

Unfortunately, these refined carbohydrates predominate in our diet. Breakfast cereals generally are made from wheat, corn, oats, or rice. But they (with the exception of real oatmeal and a few hot whole wheat cereals) are rarely served in their natural forms. Instead they are dried, refined, bleached, steamed, puffed, flaked, or sugared; occasionally a small percentage of the recommended daily allowance of certain minerals and (usually synthetic) vitamins are added. The cereals can then be labeled "enriched."

But most of the nutrients available from such breakfasts come from the milk that people add rather than from the cereal itself. Our breads (even "rye" and "whole wheat") are usually produced from refined flour and are often loaded with chemical additives. The white rice that graces our plates may look pretty, but it lacks the fiber, vitamins, and minerals found in whole brown rice. Even the potato chips we crunch are a far cry from the vitamin- and fiber-rich whole potatoes from which they are made. Refined carbohydrates may not be good for you. What's worse, they may harm you. They contain little or no fiber, so overreliance on them as a source of energy can lead to poor intestinal health and a myriad of digestive disorders. Also, overconsumption of refined sugar is linked to obesity, hypoglycemia, diabetes, and other blood-sugar disorders.

Complex carbohydrates are closer to their natural state.

Refined carbohydrates are highly processed foods, depleted of nutrients and fiber, and contain little more than pure starch or sugar, which are energy sources of no practical use to anyone.

DANGER: SWEETS CAN QUICKLY SOUR

As we said, you need carbohydrates for energy, especially to fuel your brain. But you don't really need refined sugar. Too much glucose in your bloodstream, an aftereffect of a typical high-sugar coffee and doughnut break, for example, may actually worsen fatigue and overburden your vital organs rather than picking you up. If you have a well-balanced diet, you should be relying on your liver to send forth new energy from its reserves to your working muscles, not on candy bars or doughnuts. Sugar also has been implicated in cardiovascular problems and diabetes.

We know that anyone with hypertension (or high blood pressure) should avoid salt. They should also avoid refined sugar. Animal studies suggest that high blood pressure may even lead to blood-sugar disorders.

Another bonus you receive when you aviod refined sugars is improved resistance to infections. The protective functions of your cells are depressed by all forms of sugar, but especially by sucrose. Also, sugar seems to provoke and worsen skin conditions such as acne. Withdrawing it often results in visible healing. Omiting refined sugar from your meals will also keep the various acids and other digestive juices in your stomach at normal levels.

Your brain must have a constant supply of glucose (blood sugar) in order for its "circuits" to communicate and function properly. Hypoglycemia or low blood sugar, often caused by overconsumption of refined sugars and flour, can distort perception and alter behavior.

If you suspect you are one of America's hypoglycemia victims, don't take this blood sugar disorder lightly. Consult your doctor for the necessary lab tests. Hypoglycemia not only may lead you to snack too often or to nap too often because of the fatigue and hunger it causes, it could also lead to diabetes or obesity. Remember, if you follow a poor diet high in refined carbohydrates—especially sugars—you are inviting hypoglycemia's damage to your brain and nervous system. But at the same time you need a constant supply of glucous in your bloodstream. A proper diet can help.

Too much refined sugar could be a contributing factor in causing children to become hyperkinetic or learning-disabled. It may also cause young adults to be learning-disabled or delinquent. Some studies even suggest that too much sugar is a causative factor in adults who behave criminally or antisocially.

Even naturally occurring sugars can pose problems. Gastrointestinal complaints, for example, can be caused by a sensitivity to the milk sugar lactose in dairy products. Cultured dairy products, including yogurt, which are more easily digested, can provide a substitute for this as well as providing the vitamins and minerals you would miss if you avoided milk.

Fructose (the form of sugar predominant in fruits and honey) has been much praised recently as being superior to sucrose (cane sugar) or glucose (corn sugar). Not always true. It may be sweeter, so you may use less of it—but a simple sugar is sugar to your body. Watch out for any simple or concentrated sugar!

HOW MANY CARBOHYDRATES DO YOU NEED?

Half the calories Americans consume come from carbohydrates. Unfortunately, most of these are refined carbohydrates. The breads most people eat are 55 percent carbohydrate, since the refined flour from which they are made is 75 percent refined carbohydrate. Most flour cereals are 80 percent refined carbohydrate; our spaghettis and pastas are 75 percent refined carbohydrate. Jams, candies, and some pastries may be 90 percent refined carbohydrate.

In contrast, fresh fruit is only 15 percent carbohydrate; dry legumes, even before being doubled in size by the addition of water in cooking, are just 60 percent carbohydrate; and uncooked whole grains, before the absorption of water, are 70 percent carbohydrate. Green leafy vegetables average 8 percent carbohydrate or less; starchy vegetables such as potatoes or corn, 20 percent or less. The point is, by eating vegetables, grains, legumes, seeds and some fruits, with moderate to low carbohydrate content, we are actually reducing calories and sugars in our diet.

The ideal diet gets most (85 to 90 percent) of its calories and protein from complex carbohydrates, and 10 to 15 percent from fats found in nuts, seeds and oils. This ratio allows complex carbohydrates to be the mainstay of the diet, with fewer calories from fats and fewer from complete protein foods. But, in most cases, that is not what happens.

Our bodies are factories—processing foods, making chemicals , storing materials, and producing energy. Just as plants do, your body factory stores much of its energy in the form of simple sugars and starches. Our backup energy reserve is stored as fat. The form of stored energy immediately available and most easily converted into action comes from carbohydrates. The sugars we absorb from our food may be converted into energy, starch, or fat, by the body. At any given time, we usually have available about a 13-hour supply of glycogen (starch) and glucose (a simple sugar). Our blood levels of glucose are supposed to remain stable, with about 15 grams circulating at all times. Each gram of glycogen or glucose, when oxidized by the cells, provides four calories of energy for all the body's needs.

Despite what our backgrounds, palates, or emotions may tell us, supplying energy remains the number one purpose of food. Carbohydrates yield immediately available energy; if they are oversupplied, the body builds up its muscle and liver glycogen reserves or converts the extra amount into fat. High-protein diets, on the other hand, can be dangerous. Protein is mainly a building material—not a primary energy source. It can be burnt up as fuel, but this is an inefficient way to provide energy to our systems; it requires extra energy, and it results in a waste product called urea, which must be disposed of through the kidneys. Over the long term, eating too much protein and burning protein as fuel can overstress and even weaken the kidneys.

Tip: To keep our bodies in balance and get proper supplies of complex carbohydrate, try to have three or four servings a day of fruits or vegetables, and three servings daily of whole grains or legumes. In later chapters you'll see how to combine those foods to get the best possible kinds of proteins from them.

SOURCES OF COMPLEX CARBOHYDRATES

Complex carbohydrates are not hard to find. You just have to know where to look. Basic whole grains, for example, include whole wheat (to which, unfortunately, too many people have became allergic because they have consumed so much refined wheat flour in breads, cakes, pastas, and packaged, processed foods), rye, triticale (a cross between rye and wheat you may be able to tolerate if you are allergic to real whole wheat), corn, barley, brown rice, oats, millet, and buckwheat. All these can be served whole, as cereals or side dishes, mixed in soups and casseroles, ground into whole grain flour and baked into bread, or rolled into whole grain pastas.

Legumes, an excellent source of complex carbohydrates, are also more varied then most people realize. Among the common varieties are soybeans and soy products such as tofu, tempeh, and miso, mung beans, lentils, aduki beans, split peas, black-eyed peas, kidney beans, navy beans, red beans, pink beans, pinto beans, black beans, turtle beans, fava beans, chick-peas (garbanzos), and peanuts.

Seeds such as sunflower, pumpkin, chia, and sesame are high in both protein and carbohydrates; alfalfa, chia and flax seeds (those grown organically for food, not for fabrics, to avoid pesticide contamination) are highly nutritious when sprouted. Most nuts are mainly fat, but almonds, cashews, pistachios, and pine nuts are high in carbohydrates as well.

The entire vegetable family is a rich source of carbohydrates. Those lowest in calories, such as celery, broccoli, and mushrooms, contain mostly water and fiber; the starchier, root vegetables like carrots, beets, potatoes, and yams, tend to be higher in unrefined starches and sugars as well as in fiber.

Fruits are excellent sources of complex carbohydrates, natural sugars, minerals, vitamins, and fiber. Choose from apples, pears, peaches, nectarines, plums, grapes or citrus fruits. Although the sugar content of these fruits is fairly high, it is diluted with water and released relatively slowly into your system as you chew and digest the cellulose-encased cells of the pulp. Your body doesn't get the kind of sudden jolt it receives from refined, pure sugar. Bananas and other tropical fruits should be eaten in moderation by those sensitive to sugar, since their sugar content is higher. Similarly, dried fruits, including figs, prunes, raisins, dates, apricots, pears, and apples contain three times the sugar dose of fresh fruit; like refined sugar, they are highly concentrated carbohydrates, which should only be eaten occasionally. *Hypoglycemics and diabetics should take special note of this precaution.*

Eating too much fruit can add extra calories, but as long as you don't eat fatty foods as well, fruit will not make you fat. An apple indeed may contain the equivalent of three teaspoons of sugar and the calories that go with that. But it is much harder to down three whole apples than nine teaspoons of sugar. Some people consume as much sugar in one cup of coffee, one mug of cocoa, or one doughnut—without getting all the beneficial vitamins, minerals, fiber, and enzymes of the apple.

PREPARING COMPLEX CARBOHYDRATE FOODS

Grains should be rinsed before use, and the larger legumes—such as beans—should be soaked overnight before cooking. Cooking time can be shortened by using pressure cookers.

People who eat meat and wish to switch to a more complex-carbohydrate-oriented, vegetarian diet often worry that eating will become a boring, asensual experience, limited in variety and taste. Pilgrims, seek no more. There are vegetarian recipes and menus to satisfy every palate and taste. The vegetarian recipes included in later chapters will provide a sampling of their variety and set you on the right nutritional track.

For those who must restrict their sodium intake, a variety of other herbs and spices are available that are even livelier than salt. They include leeks, dill, oregano, cumin, curry, and chili peppers. Vegetables may be mixed with legumes for stews and casseroles as well as soups; seasoned grains, such as millet (perhaps combined with soy granules or lentils for protein enhancement), are delicious stuffed into peppers, tomatoes, or hollowed-out zucchinis.

FACILITATING DIGESTION OF CARBOHYDRATES

Cooked starches are easier to digest than uncooked ones, since heat ruptures the cell walls of plants and allows certain chemicals, called enzymes, to convert the starches to sugars more easily in the mouth and the intestines. These sugars are then used by the body for energy.

Normally, carbohydrates are digested quickly. The carbohydrates in fruit juice may be digested in as little as 40 minutes; starchy foods, such as beans or grains, may take up to $1^1/_2$ hours. Cooked and eaten properly, the digestion time of a carbohydrate meal may be only 80 to 90 minutes. The more fiber you consume with your meals, the faster the digestion process, since fiber absorbs water and stimulates the actions of the digestive tract.

Animal proteins and fats take much longer to digest, and if sweet or starchy foods are eaten at the same time as meat and fish, they can remain in the stomach for much of the time the protein foods take to digest (up to six hours). This can cause gas and indigestion, since the sugar from the carbohydrates may begin to ferment in the warm acid environment of the digestive tract. For this reason, it's a good idea if you eat meat, fish, or fowl to serve your meal with only a salad and vegetables, saving primary carbohydrate foods for other meals. Also, as we age we may lose some of our digestive capacities, which increases digestion time. This may vary widely, depending on the size of the animal protein portion, how long it was cooked, how thoroughly the food was chewed, and the age as well as the mental and physical condition of the individual.

If you begin your meal with a beverage, you can briefly dilute the acid in your stomach and slow digestion. Cold beverages can suspend initial digestion for a short time, since the acids and enzymes of your digestive system usually operate at body temperature.

Some people complain that they have trouble digesting beans, and that flatulence is a problem. Partly, this is because these products may ferment in the large intestines, producing gas. Beans should be soaked for at least 15 hours before cooking. Cook them slowly to avoid altering the protein, and thoroughly so that their fiber is completely softened. Digestion will then be easier.

Bean sprouts also may be easier to digest than cooked dried beans. Sprouting increases the nutrient content as well as the digestibility of beans, grains, and seeds. Alfalfa and mung beans are two of the most popular types. Alfalfa sprouts are a nutrition powerhouse, containing five times the amount of vitamin C of alfalfa seeds. Two ounces of sprouts a day will supply you with vitamins and live, raw enzymes you might not otherwise obtain from your diet, as well as chlorophyll, which is considered an intestine and blood cleanser. Always steam soy bean sprouts briefly before serving them, since the raw beans contain digestion inhibitors, trypsin, and other natural toxins that can only be neutralized by heating.

The typical American dinner, consisting of meat, potatoes, vegetables, and perhaps a salad, with dessert afterwards, mixes up all four digestive processes at once, weakening them all. The acid from the meat's protein neutralizes the enzyme in your mouth that breaks down starches into sugars, so starch digestion is limited and extended. When a sugary dessert is added, its simple refined sugars start fermenting, resulting in too much acid in the stomach. If you then take an antacid, this plays additional havoc with the digestive process. Such habits eventually can lead to chronic indigestion and too much stress for the gastrointestinal tract.

It would be best to eat complex carbohydrates at one meal, protein at another, and fruits as snacks between meals. Protein meals take a long time to digest, and can leave you with less energy for several hours after eating them, since, ironically, much of your energy is used just to digest the protein, with blood channeled from other parts of the body to the digestive organs to help with the work.

If you eat some fruit 10 to 15 minutes before such a meal, you can also prevent your blood-glucose levels from declining during the time you are digesting your meal. The glucose in the blood has also been diverted to help in the digestive process. Someone who eats complete protein at every meal may spend the whole day with part of his or her energy involved in digestion—a strange way to spend a day!

If, on the other hand, you eat three or four small meals that include complex carbohydrates, your energy levels are likely to be higher and more constant throughout the day. What's more, your intestines will be spared the somewhat exhausting, though necessary, process of prolonged digestion.

There are some people who are allergic to one or more grains, legumes, seeds, or nuts; however, most people who in the past have been diagnoised as "carbohydrate intolerant" can actually benefit from complex instead of refined carbohydrates. (For fuller discussion of allergies, see Chapter 8, "Food Allergies.")

A WORD OR A FEW ABOUT FIBER

Fiber, quite simply, is made up of carbohydrates that the human body cannot digest. But just because they are nondigestible does not mean they serve no useful purpose. Fiber substances such as cellulose are in the cell walls, giving plants the power to grow structurally strong. Fiber does a great deal for us, too.

In the late 1980s, fiber has been rediscovered both by the physician and the nutritionist. More and more researchers—at the National Cancer Institute, the America Cancer Society and elsewhere—are jumping on the fiber bandwagon of digestive health. They have pinpointed the value of fiber in our food to act as a kind of super janitorial service for our intestines, keeping them free of hazardous substances, including some powerful cancer-causing chemicals, that may enter our bodies.

Fiber is not found in meats, cheeses, refined carbohydrates or highly processed foods—that is, in the typical American diet, already too high in fatty meats, bleached breads, and sugary desserts.

Fibrous foods stimulate and exercise your mouth and gums, oral membranes and facial muscles. Fiber also scrubs the cell walls of your colon and bowels, cleaning and hastening transit time though the digestive system for the foods you eat, reducing the possibility that your body will harbor toxins longer than it should. Fiber also fills you up, so you don't have to snack so often.

When adequate amounts are missing from your diet, you may develop constipation, and are at risk of colorectal cancer, or one of the other common diseases that attack the gastrointestinal system. This risk becomes greater when your diet is low in fresh, nutritious whole foods and instead is high in fats and sugars.

By contrast, a diet emphasizing moderate amounts of protein, high intake of natural fiber foods, and low fat intake results in better health of the bowels and the whole body and provides protection against certain types of cancer. Fiber, for the most part, does not even contribute calories.

Fiber should be eaten in its natural form. Our bodies have evolved according to the foods our ancestors ate, and are adapted to derive the toal value of a food: protein, fats, carbohydrates, water, vitamins, minerals, trace minerals, and enzymes, along with the bulk necessary for good bowel movements. The processing of most supermarket cereals originally was based on several not necessarily healthful factors. One of these was profit, which continues to play a major role. Another was the erroneous belief that fiber serves no useful purpose. Now that we know better, processing and food industry methods and beliefs are changing. For example, whole-fiber breakfast cereals have begun to be distributed through supermarkets. Read the labels of "natural" cereals carefully to avoid sugar. Some are genuine whole foods, others contain large quantities of sugar in various forms, or are packaged with preservatives.

If you are in fairly good health, 20 to 30 grams, or about an ounce a day of fiber from natural souces should be adequate. If occasional periods of irregularity are a problem, a few extra tablespoons of untreated, unheated oat germ, wheat bran, or even a tasty variation such as rice or corn bran can be sprinkled over your morning cereal or evening salad and will provide extra benefits.

If you prefer to use fruits and salad foods to meet your roughage requirements, a raw salad for lunch and a partially cooked grain salad such as tabouli for dinner, plus a big puree of fresh fruit in season, would fill the bill nicely. Some researchers believe these absorb the most water in your intestines. Oat fiber will absorb up to six times its weight in water, and vegetables generally hold roughly half as much.

All vegetables weren't created equal in terms of fiber. Root vegetables such as carrots are at the top of the list: their crunchy quality and hardness indicate a high fiber yield. They also require beneficial exercise of your jaws and teeth. Buy produce in season, buy it fresh, and eat it raw when possible. Vegetables can be grated for uncooked salads. But do not neglect the less common tubers: yams, kohlrabi, parsnips, even eggplant can be eaten whole. Never peel away any vegetable skin if it isn't essential to your recipe to do so, since in and near the skin is stored much of the plant's roughage and nutrients.

The whole legume family deserves special attention. A good way to eat these and profit by the skins is to sprout your peas, chick-peas, mung beans, and lentils rather than cook them. Thus you are rewarded with the full value of the live food, including minerals, amino acids and carbohydrate energy. Remember to steam bean sprouts briefly before serving.

A little bran every day will improve your health and regularity, but there's no substitute for a well-balanced diet. And no two fibers are the same. Fiber in fruits and vegetables is different from that in grains. Include them all.

Take, for instance, the fiber in citrus fruits. If you've had a grapefruit or orange for breakfast, you've already had a beneficial two-carbohydrate food factor—protopectin. The pulp of all citrus fruits contains this combination of cellulose plus pectin.

The cellulose in the citrus fruit absorbs fluid from your intestines. So as it enlarges, it quickly pushes along any contents in the intestinal tract. Meanwhile, the pectin becomes gelatinous, and in counterpoint to the cellulose, it provides lubrication and ensures smooth passage for the food.

In addition, protopectin helps you get maximum value out of the other nutritious foods you eat, and enhances your system's use of dietary fats. This, in turn, helps provides some protection against the cardiovascular dangers that high cholesterol levels pose.

2 · FATS

"Fat is fine for fitness—in limited amounts."

AMERICANS RECEIVE NEARLY HALF (45 percent) of their total calories from fats. Our overindulgence in fatty foods has taken its toll by contributing to a high proportion of overweight Americans as well as to the degeneration of our heart and blood vessels, with fats reducing blood flow through our arteries and increasing blood pressure. Recently, the American Heart Association declared that we should reduce the amount of saturated fat and cholesterol in our diet to help prevent heart disease. By 1984, the government's National Heart, Blood and Lung Institute concluded a 10-year study and issued a report conclusively implicating cholesterol in individuals with an increased risk of heart attack. During the past four years, several other studies have confirmed the 1984 finding. We should not avoid fat completely. Reducing the fat in your diet doesn't mean eliminating it. People need not overreact, just act.

WHY YOU NEED FAT

Fat provides one of the body's primary nutrients. We need it in small amounts because it allows us to use the fat-soluable vitamins A, D, E, and K, which are essential for the health of our immune system. These vitamins only work when in the presence of fatty molecules or tissue. Fat helps prevent viral infections, protects our heart, blood vessels, and internal organs, slows down the aging process, and helps keep skin healthy. Most importantly, fats, like carbohydrates, are a usable and essential source of energy. They serve as a reserve supply of energy deposited in various parts of the body called adipose tissue.

Fat is a concentrated source of energy. It yields nine calories per gram when it is burned up or oxidized. Proteins and carbohydrates each yield only four calories per gram. Therefore, a little bit of fat goes a long way in carrying out normal body functions.

Body fat acts as an insulator and prevents excessive heat loss. It also acts as a shock absorber. You need some fat around your internal organs to prevent bruising, hemorrhage or rupture. It also is essential for the utilization of nutrients and the production of hormones. In fact, much of your body's chemistry revolves around the proper utilization of fat. Fat is fine for fitness—in limited amounts. But you don't want too much fat, because it may not only surround the organs but can also penetrate them. In excess it can lace itself through the organs, and through the muscle tissue, so your risk of disease (such as heart disease and diabetes) increases.

SATURATED AND UNSATURATED FATS

Not all fats are equal. They may be equal in calories, as the fat in margarine is no different in terms of its caloric count than the fat in olive oil or butter. But fats have unique properties. The omega 3 fatty acids, which are found in fish, for example, have been shown to be healthful to the heart. They also allow the body to use energy more efficiently. The essential fatty acids found in the oil from sesame seeds, sunflower seeds, safflower seeds, and soy beans are vital for the maintenance of health, growth, maturation, hormone production, and other functions. It is important, therefore, to have a variety of fats in the diet in small amounts. It is not necessary to add tablespoons of fat in the form of oil when grains, legumes, fish, seeds and nuts are plentiful sources, with a combination of long and short chain fatty acids found in each food.

There are two kinds of fats—saturated and unsaturated. *Saturated fats* are found in animal food sources such as meat and dairy products, constituting half of the USDA's dietary recommendations for the "basic four food groups." Technically speaking, fat is saturated if the carbon atom chain that makes it up is also saturated with hydrogen atoms. You can tell if fat is saturated if it turns solid at room temperature. Examples of saturated fats include butter, the fatty part of chicken, fish, veal, lamb, pork, and beef (the actual marbled fat that you can see), lard, and coconut oil.

Unsaturated fats are primarily found in grains, legumes, seeds, nuts, and the oils derived from them, including corn oil, safflower oil, sunflower oil, and soy oil—all of which are liquid at room temperature. These unsaturated oils should represent the majority of your fat intake. Unsaturated fats should be used because they provide us with certain essential fatty acids. These have several functions: controlling high blood pressure; helping form prostaglandins (important chemicals for a host of bodily functions); and regulating the ability of substances to enter and leave cells. The body can manufacture those fatty acids not considered "essential" if your diet doesn't provide them.

There are a variety of types of unsaturated fats. Most common are polyunsaturates—such as those found in corn or safflower oil. There are also monounsaturates—such as those in olive oil. There is new evidence suggesting that the latter type actually helps protect your heart by raising levels of certain types of cholesterols (high density lipoproteins), a blood fat in your body. The omega 3 fish fat mentioned above, for example, is also a monunsaturate.

All fats, however, are combinations of saturated and unsaturated, and we need both each day. But, primarily, the fats in our diet should be of an unsaturated quality. Not more than 25 percent should be saturated.

HOW MUCH FAT DO YOU NEED?

There is considerable disagreement regarding how much fat is necessary and appropriate in the diet. Estimates range from 10 to 30 percent of total caloric intake. To be safe, your consumption of calories from fat probably should be limited to 15 percent of your total calories. A quarter of these could be saturated. The rest should come from the unsaturated fats found in cooking and salad oils or, more beneficially, from those naturally occurring oils in vegetables, grains, legumes, nuts, and seeds. In their natural state, if they are unbleached, unadulterated, and have not been clarified or chemically altered to destroy their nutritional benefits, oils not only provide you with fat that the body can utilize, but also supply vitamin E, a substance that has powerful antioxidant properties, preventing the destruction of essential fatty acids and helping your body heal itself. Vitamin E promotes nerve growth and keeps our cells functioning normally.

HYDROGENATION

Once a vegetable oil has been hydrogenated (a process in which hydrogen is added to it to give it a longer shelf life) it becomes solid. It is therefore no longer a polyunstaurated fat (or liquid). It is now saturated.

Be wary of food labels that declare a product is made from polyunsaturates, including certain salad oils and margarines, as well as egg and cream substitutes. One part of the statement is true. What the labels may fail to mention is that now you are eating a saturated fat. The verdict on hydrogenated or partially hydrogenated oils, like margarines, is not yet conclusive concerning their harmful or beneficial effects.

FATS AND DIETING

One of the reasons doctors may prescribe high-fat, high-protein, low-carbohydrate diets is because of the ability of fat and protein to keep you feeling full after a meal, allaying between-meal hunger pangs. If, on the other hand, you eat a complex carbohydrate in the form of a grain or vegetable, it is digested and goes through your system in a matter of 30 to 80 minutes. You benefit from the energy and you're not taxing your digestive system. But it also means there will be a tendency to get hungry sooner.

After all, we tend to gain weight in large part because we get hungry and have in-between meal snacks. A fatty or high-protein food eaten at mealtime will require four to six hours of digestion just to empty out the stomach. As long as you have that much food in your stomach, your appetite is suppressed so you do not feel hungry. Snacks usually come in the form of high-sugar, refined carbohydrate foods like jelly rolls, candy bars and soft drinks. Bypassing the midmorning, midafternoon, and late evening snack, can mean eliminating 400 to 900 calories. In a period of a week you would be able to knock off a pound just by modifying your diet to reduce snacks and increase the protein and fat content.

THE DANGERS OF FAT

Many people like deep-fried foods such as french fries, onion rings, fried fish, potato chips, and doughnuts. These are prepared with fatty oils heated to high temperatures that alter the chemical structure of the fat, creating free fatty acids that can have an irritating effect upon the stomach and on the sensitive mucous linings of the intestines. Eating fried foods frequently can set into motion the ultimate dysfunction of your intestine. Colitis, spastic colon, or some other form of irritable intestine condition may be the result. Heated fats also slow down digestive time. The longer fat is cooked, the more difficult it is for the enzymes in the stomach and the intestine to break it down. Liquid fats are easier to digest. Oils (or unsaturated fats) go through the system much more rapidly than saturated fats.

As I've said before, when you have a lot of fat in your stomach after a meal, you will have less energy. Your energy is being diverted to facilitating the proper digestion, utilization, absorption, and elimination of your food—a lengthy process. Blood and oxygen, also, are diverted, to a degree, even from your brain, just for digestion.

Nearly 95 percent of the fat you consume is digested and utilized by the body. It is fine to have some amount of fat as reserve, but in the absence of regular, daily exercise the muscles begin to atrophy and fat infiltration into the muscle occurs. Fat then takes the place of unused, atrophied muscles. We lose our strength, endurance and stamina, and we become more susceptible to body injury, accident, and disease.

Fats are necessary nutrients. We need unsaturated fats from seeds, grains, legumes, and nuts. We don't need all of the oils from salad oil to cooking fats that is typically part of our diet now. Try to keep the fats in your diet to 15 percent. And be selective, choosing certain types of fish, like salmon, for their healthful fat content.

3 · PROTEIN

"Sprinkle brewer's yeast on your cereal or blend it with milk, combine tofu with algae in salads, add wheat germ to lentil burgers, and spread peanut butter on whole wheat bread to increase the usability of the protein in these excellent sources."

A THICK, RARE STEAK, a hamburger, or a platter of fried chicken—the joys of protein? For many of us, protein equals meat equals strength, endurance, growth, health. We have been misled! Meat is only one of several possible dietary sources of protein. Yet it has become the predominant and most expensive source in the average American diet. Our image of protein as the one most important nutrient ("protein" is derived from the Greek "protos," meaning first) has led us to eat so much meat that we often consume more than twice the protein we need each day.

On average, Americans eat nearly 100 grams or $3^{1}/_{2}$ ounces of protein every day when all most of us actually need is half of that. And despite the legends, even athletes are better off increasing their carbohydrate rather than their protein consumption if they want to increase their endurance and stamina. Eggs, dairy products, grain, legumes, nuts, and seeds are all excellent sources of protein that can supplement meat or replace it in the diet.

WHY YOU NEED PROTEIN

Proteins are the building blocks of life. They are the basic material from which all your cells, tissues, and organs are constructed. Only water represents a larger percentage of your total body weight than protein. Proteins are constantly being replaced, twenty-four hours a day, throughout your entire life, as your body uses and loses cellular materials. The optimal intake of high-quality proteins allows the body to grow and maintain healthy bones, skin, teeth, muscles, and nerves; it keeps the blood count correct; and it allows the metabolism—the body's ability to use food sources—to function at the highest level. Hemoglobin, the part of the red blood cells that provides oxygen to the cells, is made primarily of protein.

When we think of protein, we usually think of it as a body-building substance found in muscles. However, only one-third of our body's protein is concentrated in muscle tissue. Protein is part of every living cell in our body, from the hair on our heads to the nails on our toes. Skin, nails, hair, muscles, cartilage, and tendons all have fibrous protein as their main constituent.

And, with four calories per gram, it is also available as a source of heat and energy. When carbohydrates and fats are in short supply, protein can be converted to glucose, providing necessary energy to the brain and central nervous system.

Protein molecules called *enzymes* start the metabolic process; they must be present for hundreds of necessary chemical reactions and interactions in our body to occur. Enzymes allow energy to be stored and released in each cell; and they allow protein, fats, carbohydrates, and cholesterol to be synthesized by the liver. Protein is responsible for keeping your blood slightly alkaline, and it is the raw material out of which the antibodies that shield you from infection are created. Hormones, which regulate your metabolism, also contain some protein.

HOW MUCH PROTEIN DO YOU NEED?

Generally speaking, adults require .9 grams of protein per kilogram of body weight. (A kilogram is 2.2 pounds.) Thus, a 60-kilogram (132-pound) woman probably needs about 54 grams of protein a day. During spurts of growth, as in infancy, early childhood, and puberty, more protein is needed. Others with higher protein needs include pregnant women and lactating mothers; hypoglycemics; convalescents from surgery and certain types of infection, shock, or fever; and those under any kind of stress. Under certain conditions, such as kidney disease, lower protein intake for a period of time also may be in order.

COMPLETE PROTEINS: THE EIGHT ESSENTIAL AMINO ACIDS

The hundreds of proteins your body synthesizes are all made up of chains of only 23 smaller, basic protein substances, called *amino acids*— composed of nitrogen, carbon, oxygen, hydrogen, and in some cases, sulfur. Of these, the body can synthesize 15 on its own, leaving eight that must be present in your food to be used. These eight are called the essential amino acids. A ninth amino acid, histamine, is essential for children.

Amino acids, of which proteins are made, are necessary for certain vitamins and minerals to be utilized. The amino acid tryptophan, for example, initiates the production of the B vitamin, niacin. Proteins help transport fats through the bloodstream by combining with them to form lipoproteins. In fact, the only fluids in your body that do not normally contain protein are perspiration, urine and bile. It is possible to live without eating protein, but not for very long.

In order for your cells to make the proteins they need for growth, all the necessary amino acids must be present simultaneously in sufficient amounts. This means that if any one amino acid is not present, the protein cannot be constructed. Since protein cannot be stored (except, perhaps, by lactating mothers), it is necessary to eat complete proteins at each meal, or, if you are eating nonanimal products, to mix your protein sources to form complete proteins. To provide your body with only some of the amino acids it needs is like being a baker who buys 100 pounds of flour, 100 pounds of shortening, but only 1 ounce of yeast. Because of the yeast he still can bake only one or two cakes. What does he do with all that flour and shortening? In your body, unused amino acids might be excreted or broken down and oxidized for energy and other metabolic needs.

Protein deficiencies occur when we don't consume enough protein for our body's needs, or when the proteins we do consume lack one or more of the eight essential amino acids. These eight are threonine, valine, tryptophan, lysine, methionine, histidine, phenylalanine, and isoleucine. Foods that contain all eight of these essential amino acids are called complete protein foods. Eggs, meat, fowl, fish, and dairy products—all animal products—contain complete proteins.

For protein to be absorbed and used by the body, all eight essential amino acids must be present in a certain proportion, actually in about the same proportion in which they occur in eggs, nature's complete food package for chicken embryos. Partially complete proteins may contain all eight, but not in the correct proportions. Thus foods high in partially complete proteins, such as brewer's yeast (also called nutritional yeast), wheat germ, the soy food tofu, peanuts, and certain micro-sea algae, should be eaten in combination with other protein foods.

We have been led to believe that animal products—such as meats, poultry, fish, dairy products and eggs—are the only adequate sources of protein. This is based on misconceptions that originated over 40 years ago. If we can't thoroughly digest something, we can't utilize its protein—no matter how complete it is. In addition to digestibility, our ability to utilize protein may be influenced by the functioning of our digestive tract, the presence of any disease or infection, and age. Plant sources, once disparaged, are now starting to get higher ratings.

PREPARING PROTEIN FOODS

Protein digestion is improved by correct cooking practices. Moderate heating of most protein foods increases their digestibility, particularly in the case of beans, grains, and meat. Beans and other legumes contain several toxins (such as trypsin inhibitors) that can inhibit digestion, but that become harmless when they are cooked or sprouted.

Legumes should never be eaten raw: several of them contain even stronger toxins that must be neutralized by heat. All grains and some legumes contain phytic acid in their outer husks. In the intestines, these can form phytates that bind with zinc, calcium, and other minerals and can cause deficiencies in these minerals. Thus, grains should be sprouted, baked with yeast (unleavened breads contain more phytates than leavened), or cooked thoroughly, and vegetarians should supplement their diet with zinc and calcium or foods containing them. Zinc is present in seafood, peas, corn, egg yolk, carrots and yeast.

It is also very important to cook meat slowly but thoroughly, because of the microorganisms it contains. Pork harbors a parasite than can cause trichinosis if it is not thoroughly cooked. Other meats should be broiled or roasted. Excessive heating of any protein, whether of animal or plant origin, may cause what are known as cross-linkages (the same mechanisms that cause your hair to stay curled after a permanent wave). Cross-linkages make it difficult for protein-digesting enzymes to break protein down into simple amino acids so they can be absorbed. Therefore, it is best to stay away from deep-fried or overdone protein foods. Milk and milk products are especially sensitive to heat, and should not be heated above the boiling point.

If you have trouble digesting milk, you might try yogurt, buttermilk, or other cultured milk products. These contain live, healthy microorganisms that "pre-digest" lactose, the sugar in milk that many people cannot tolerate, changing it to more easily absorbed lactic acid.

On the average, about 90 to 93 percent of the amino acids in the foods you eat are absorbed after digestion commences.

Sprinkle brewer's yeast (if you are not allergic to it) on your cereal or blend it with milk, combine tofu with algae in salads, add wheat germ to lentil burgers, and spread peanut butter on whole wheat bread to increase the usability of the protein in these excellent sources.

TOO LITTLE PROTEIN

Eating an inadequate amount of high-quality protein forces our bodies to break down more tissue than it can build up, resulting in overall deteriorization. Some symptoms of protein deficiency are muscle weakness, loss of endurance, fatigue, growth retardation, loss of weight, irritability, lowered immune response, poor healing, and anemia. Pregnant women must be extra careful to avoid this deficiency, since it will not only affect their health but that of their unborn baby. A protein deficiency can promote a miscarriage, premature delivery, or toxemia. Its effects on the baby's development may set the stage for chronic diseases later in life.

The amino acids in grains are high quality and will maintain life and growth, but when supplemented with foods containing other amino acids, they may yield even higher quality protein in greater quantities. For example, wheat is a fairly good protein. It can maintain life, and millions of poor people have subsisted on bread or cereal alone for long periods of time. However, wheat alone cannot promote optimal growth, and even adults who restrict their protein to one or two food groups or types of foods (a mono-diet) run the very real risk of lowering their body's immune response. Remember, proteins also are needed for the body's natural disease fighters—the antibodies that combat infection. The poor quality of the hair and skin of those on mono-diets reflects their nutritional deficiencies. Their body functions much as a car does that runs on four cylinders when it was built for six or eight.

On the other hand, Americans have been led to think of meat, eggs, fish and milk as the only real suppliers of protein. They have been led to believe that any meat is a good protein source. Wrong! Cured ham has only 16 percent protein; hot dogs, only 7 percent, less than dried skim milk, which has over 34 percent, or sunflower seeds with 27 percent; lentils have more than 23 percent protein. And while all we need to satisfy our protein needs is a few ounces of complete high-quality protein a day, we are getting far more than that.

It is true that incomplete proteins alone do not provide an adequate diet. But one can create complete, or high-quality, proteins by combining foods so that those that are low in some amino acids are eaten together with ones that are high in those same acids. These complementary proteins—all from plant sources—are in this way completed and so can supply protein needs quite nicely. You just have to know how.

Soybeans, for example, are low in the amino acid tryptophan, but high in lysine. To enhance their biological values to you, combine them with complementary proteins like nuts, grains, and seeds, low in lysine but high in tryptophan. In countless combinations, they can make satisfying, delicious dishes.

Tofu, for example, made by curdling soybean milk and packing the solids in layers of cloth, has a protein value—in terms of completeness, digestibility and other factors—only slightly less than animal flesh. It can be made even higher in quality by combining it with grains such as brown rice. Soybean sprouts and soy flour, can also be used in cooking to enhance the complementary values of other foods.

Other legumes, like chick-peas, lentils, and various kinds of beans are low in certain amino acids, but high in others. They also can be combined with grains, nuts, and seeds to form complementary proteins of high nutritional values. Consider, after all, how the rest of the world, which has not had the luxury of high meat diets, subsists. Central American and Caribbean nations use beans and rice as staples. Middle Eastern countries combine sesame paste with chick-peas, while Italians mix lentils, chick-peas, and other beans with pasta.

Grains and cereals make ideal complements to legumes because they are generally high in tryptophan and low in isoleucine and lysine. Grains and cereals supply half the world's protein and are great sources of fiber, too. They do not need to be complemented with meat products to raise the protein values. The myth has been that cereals, grains, and seeds are incomplete, poor sources of protein even when combined. This is false. When you combine grains, seeds, and legumes, you can easily exceed animal protein quality. Consider breakfast cereals with soy milk, or macaroni and cheese, or tofu eggs—or real eggs if you prefer—served with whole grain breads. These sorts of combinations work well because they complement each other.

Why bother switching from what is easy, the protein found in animal products, to what may take some slight effort or change of habit, creating complementary proteins? Simply because health disadvantages of meats and other animal products should outweigh any slight discomfort in seeking new or improved sources of protein. And because our typical diet is based on an unhealthy protein excess.

TOO MUCH PROTEIN

Researchers now agree that American meat eaters and vegetarians alike are generally getting more protein than they need. A study done by the United States Department of Agriculture found that the average consumer of animal products gets over 165 percent of their Recommended Daily Allowance for protein. Children fed by their overcautious—and sometimes protein-fanatical—parents, get a whopping 209 percent. Surprisingly, vegetarians were getting only 15 percent less protein than their nonvegetarian counterparts, still 50 percent more than the Recommended Daily Allowance. Children had identical results in both categories. And in the two groups, women over age 65 consumed the least amount, yet still more than the recommended allotments.

Studies done in the mid-1960s concluded that both vegans (who eat no animal products) and lacto-ovo-vegetarians (who include dairy foods and eggs in their diet) both received protein in excess of the established requirements. The plant-eating vegan men ate an average of 128 percent of their requirements and the women 111 percent; the egg- and dairy-eating, lacto-ovo vegetarians all ate 150 percent; and the nonvegetarian men ate 192 percent. The nonvegetarian women consumed slightly less than 171 percent of their required protein requirements. It is not difficult to obtain your protein. One researcher at Harvard, whose studies showed that only one ounce, or 30 grams, of protein met daily amino acid requirements, has stated that "it is most unlikely that protein deficiencies will develop in healthy adults on a diet in which cereals and vegetables supply adequate calories."

When it comes to certain nutrients, the more the merrier. For example, research indicates that water-soluble vitamin C helps fortify our immune system, and in high doses it may even prevent or reverse certain forms of cancer. In the case of protein, however, more does not mean better. Depending on your age, sex, and the number of calories your require, the total amount of protein needed will average between 30 and 40 grams a day.

PROTEIN AND DIETING

It is estimated that nearly 80 million Americans in any given year are following some dietary program to lose weight. Regretably, many will be going on one version or another of a high-protein, low-carbohydrate diet, with the misconception that protein is low in calories. In fact, the protein foods, such as beef or pork, recommended on most of these diets, are very high in calories.

One gram of protein yields nine calories per gram. Filet mignon, for example, is nearly 40 to 50 percent fat; a single 10-ounce portion can contain up to 1,400 calories. But a certain nutritional sleight of hand makes those diets work for some people. Meats require six to eight hours to digest. You will probably not be very hungry during digestion. To really control overeating, exercise remains more important than limiting calorie intake, since exercise increases your metabolic efficiency. Like carbohydrates, proteins also contain four calories per gram. Four calories remain four calories.

Many diet doctors claim high-protein diets melt away fat. When we want to lose weight, they say, we should limit our diets to beef, hard-boiled eggs, chicken, and cottage cheese. But these foods contain substantial amounts of saturated fats and lack carbohydrates. Such low-carbohydrate, high-protein diets create an abnormal biochemical state within the body, resulting in weight loss.

But it is not a healthy weight loss. In effect, these diets prevent proteins from being stored as fat, leading to a buildup of high-calorie compounds called ketones in the blood stream or ketosis. Many dieters experience anorexia due to the toxic effects of ketones, eliminating large amounts of water and salt, which contributes to weight reduction. Under normal conditions, our bodies would not excrete this unburned high energy compound. Ketosis, therefore, can lead to dehydration, burning of essential body proteins, kidney infection, kidney stones, renal damage, and in several cases, it has lead to coma and death. These more dangerous conditions usually occur only during starvation or as a metabolic side effect of diabetes.

So before embarking on the new monthly best-seller's advice, consider the potential long-term health hazards. It is not uncommon for participants in fad diets to experience bleeding gums, depression, lowered resistance to infection, fatigue, weakness, irritability, and dizziness. A high-protein diet has been shown to encourage the onset of degenerative diseases such as arteriosclerosis (hardening of the arteries). Excesses of the amino acid methionine, can break down into the nonessential amino acid hymocycsteine, which can irritate the walls of the arteries, generating fat deposits in these vessels. And if we omit foods with carbohydrates or with fiber, like fruits, grains and vegetables, we may be inducing vitamin and mineral deficiencies and hurting our digestive system.

PROTEIN AND DISEASE

In the short run, your body can cope with an excess of protein by burning it for energy. This may be inefficient, since protein takes more energy than carbohydrates or fat to metabolize, but it is not harmful. However, over the long run, too much protein can hurt. Ammonium is released when protein is burned in the cell. The ammonium is turned into urea and excreted through the kidneys. Along with the excess of sodium that generally characterizes the animal protein diet, this stepped-up excretion process taxes the kidneys. Too much animal protein can also lead to localized edema and generalized dehydration, as people on high-protein diets require more water than others. To process a high-protein diet the body may require up to four times as much water as for a high-carbohydrate diet.

There are numerous other side effects of eating too much protein. Too much protein causes you to lose calcium through the urine, sometimes resulting in a deficiency in that important mineral. High-protein intake has even been linked to osteoporosis, a degenerative disease that causes the demineralization and loss of calcium from our bones by increasing urinary excretion of calcium. Older women suffer most from this condition.

High-protein diets can be dangerous. For example, eight ounces of beef supplies more than 500 calories, while it is only 22 percent protein. But it also contains lots of fat and water. High-protein diets provide too much saturated fats, cholesterol and sodium, all implicated in heart diseases.

If you eat more protein than you need, your body will have to dispose of extra urea, the nitrogen-containing waste product of protein metabolism. Urea is formed in the liver and excreted through the kidneys. This extra work for your liver and kidneys can be stressful, can make you tired or cause other problems if you don't drink lots of extra water to flush out the kidneys.

Older people and infants are specially vulnerable if they have to use too much water to flush out this excess urea. They can become dangerously dehydrated. Infants are particularly at risk for such conditions. Protein deficiency is very uncommon in the United States. If anything, as we've said before, we eat too much protein compared to our other food nutrients.

Statistics show that on average, individuals in the United States annually eat approximately 200 pounds of red meat, 50 pounds of chicken and turkey, 10 pounds of assorted fish, 300 eggs and 250 pounds of various dairy products.

In this country animal sources of protein often contain large amounts of synthetic hormones, saturated fats, antibiotics, pesticide residues, nitrates, and a host of other potentially harmful ingredients. Although we've heard warnings about the nasty ingredients in those plump "butterball" turkeys, about the carcinogenic (or cancer-causing) effects of charcoal broiling or frying fatty beef, the residues in milk and the mercury and toxic wastes in fish, we're still buying them.

Animal foods are much higher in saturated fats and cholesterol than vegetable protein foods. Especially when combined with the refined carbohydrates of the typical American diet, animal foods have been implicated in increasing our risk of heart disease and arteriosclerosis.

Studies indicate that animal sources contribute to arteriosclerosis much more than vegetable sources. The incidence of arteriosclerosis is substantially higher in those getting their protein from animals than with vegetarians whose protein comes primarily from plant sources.

PROTEIN AND ATHLETICS

One of the most enduring myths in the protein story is in the field of athletic prowess. Despite scientific evidence to the contrary, many athletes and trainers alike still equate protein with strength. This false notion is based upon the premise that protein, especially animal protein, is turned into muscle when ingested. But what is really needed during a strenuous workout or competition is a quality source of energy. For this, protein is actually a less efficient source than complex carbohydrates, since carbohydrates have more deliverable calories.

Depending on the athletic training schedule a person follows, some extra protein may be advisable. This can amount to about ten more grams of high-quality protein, which will be used to replace the nitrogen lost by perspiration and to provide the extra protein needed during periods of accelerated muscle growth. However, after the training period, the athlete only needs more calories than the average person, not more protein. Such misconceptions get many a hungry athlete into trouble each year.

Many trainers are well aware of the scientific void behind the "steak and egg" fortification diets, yet they continue high-protein diets because their athletes believe in them, a tradition that has a strong psychological hold and may, in fact, have an effect on their performance.

Yet these athletes are hurting themselves in many ways. As we work, play, or sleep, our systems are maintaining a biochemical balance of amino acids. If we make a habit of consuming more than we need, our bodies may start abnormally increasing the rate of amino acid replacement in our cells. This rapid turnover of cells is believed to accelerate the aging process. A high-protein diet, therefore, may be counterproductive to longevity. Athletes on high-protein diets also run the risk of dehydration. Protein does not give us that extra edge. Complex carbohydrates, if anything, may.

4 · VITAMINS

"People who have had surgery need more vitamin C; those with certain chronic infections or cancers require more folic acid; alcoholics require a full range of vitamin supplements because drinking results in poor absorption of all vitamins from foods; and heavy smokers need more vitamin C to repair cells damaged by the toxins in cigarette smoke and tars."

VITAMINS ARE ORGANIC COMPOUNDS necessary for life. They have no caloric value, but are important parts of enzymes, which help our bodies use food to supply energy. They also help regulate metabolism, assist in forming bones and tissue and build major body structures.

There are two categories of vitamins, the oil-soluble and the water soluble. *Oil-soluble vitamins* (A, D, E, and K) require oil to be absorbed and are stored in the body. When too much of an oil-soluble vitamin builds up in your tissues, it can be dangerous. The *water-soluble vitamins* (B complex, C, and the bioflavonoids) are not stored by the body and need to be replenished daily.

VITAMIN A

Vitamin A, an oil-soluble vitamin, is necessary for growth and repair of your body's tissues. It is essential in the maintenance of your body's immune response, which helps the body fight infections. It helps maintain healthy skin and protects the mucous membranes of the lungs, throat, mouth, and nose. It also helps the body secrete the gastric juices necessary for protein digestion, and it protects the linings of the digestive tract, kidneys, and bladder. Vitamin A is essential in the formation of blood, strong bones, and teeth and in the maintenance of good eyesight.

While abundant in carrots, especially in the form of fresh carrot juice, vitamin A is present in even higher concentrations in green leafy vegetables such as beet greens, spinach, and broccoli. Yellow or orange vegetables are also good sources. Eggs contain vitamin A, as do whole milk and milk products. And while animal livers are concentrated sources of vitamin A, livers also are waste-filtering organs, so one most take care when obtaining nutrients from them. Any hormone or chemical to which the animal was exposed will be concentrated in the liver. It is therefore a problematical food to eat.

One of the first symptoms of vitamin A deficiency is night blindness, an inability of the eyes to adjust to darkness. Other signs include fatigue, unhealthy skin, loss of appetite, loss of sense of smell, and diarrhea. The recommended daily intake of vitamin A, as established by the National Research Council, is 5,000 IU for adults. It is not difficult to obtain this amount from the foods mentioned above in moderate quantities. During times of disease, trauma, pregnancy, or lactation, supplements may be advisable, but should be administered under a physician's or nutritionist's direction, since megadoses of vitamin A can be harmful.

THE B VITAMIN COMPLEX

This family of water-soluble vitamins works together to unlock the nutrients in fats, carbohydrates, and protein, making them available as energy. When each component of the B vitamin group is present in the proper ratio, the entire complex will work harmoniously in every cell of the body. B vitamins are found in nutritional yeast, seed germs, eggs, liver, meat, and vegetables. Whenever muscular work increases, when you run or participate in other endurance sports, the need for B vitamin complex increases.

VITAMIN B_1 (THIAMINE)

Vitamin B_1 is essential to normal metabolism and normal nerve function. It converts carbohydrates into glucose, which is the sole source of energy for the brain and nervous system. B_1 helps your heart by keeping it firm and resilient. It is found in a variety of foods, including whole grains, legumes, poultry, and fish.

A deficiency of vitamin B_1 may result in the degeneration of the insulating protective sheath (myelin) that covers certain nerve fibers. Your nerves can then become hypersensitive, causing irritability, sluggishness, forgetfulness and apathy. If such nerve destruction continues, nerves in the legs may become weakened, and pain may develop in the legs and feet. Paralysis may result. A deficiency may also result in constipation, indigestion, anorexia, swelling, and heart trouble caused by increased blood circulation.

Adult males need a daily minimum of 1.4 mg. of vitamin B_1, and adult females need at least 1.0 mg. If you drink tea or coffee, perspire a great deal, or if you are under heavy stress, are taking antibiotics, or have a fever, your intake of vitamin B_1 should increase. Some nutritionists suggest that athletes should increase their intake to between 10 and 20 mg. daily. Such quantities are not easily obtained from food alone. Therefore, a low-potency, all-natural vitamin may be good insurance.

VITAMIN B_2 (RIBOFLAVIN)

Vitamin B_2 helps promote proper growth and repair of tissues, and enhances a cell's ability to exchange gases such as oxygen and carbon dioxide in the blood. It helps release energy from the foods you eat, and it also is essential for good digestion, steady nerves, assimilation of iron and normal vision. It is vital to the health of your entire glandular system, most particularly to the adrenal glands, those involved in stress control.

Dairy products, meat, poultry, fish, nutritional yeast, whole grains, leafy green vegetables, and the nutrient-rich soybean can provide ample supplies of vitamin B_2.

Lack of vitamin B_2 is one deficiency that can be seen readily. If your tongue is purplish red, inflamed, or shiny, you may need more B_2. Other symptoms are cracking at the corners of the lips; greasy skin; vision problems such as hypersensitivity to light, itchiness, bloodshot eyes, or blurred sight; headaches; depression; insomnia; or loss of mental alertness. A minimum of 1.6 mg. of vitamin B_2 daily for adult males and 1.2 mg. daily for females is recommended. Two servings of most grains will satisfy this requirement without difficulty.

VITAMIN B_3 (NIACIN)

Vitamin B_3 is essential to every cell in the body. It is the fundamental material of two enzyme systems and helps transform sugar and fat into energy.

Many vital functions in our body's food processing plant would stop without an adequate supply of vitamin B_3. Low levels of this vitamin have been linked to mental illness and pellagra, a disease that produces disorders of the skin and intestinal tract.

You can get a reasonable amount of vitamin B_3 from green leafy vegetables, wheat germ, brewer's yeast, beans, peas, dried figs, prunes, and dates. Organ meats, salmon, and tuna are also plentiful sources. Adult males need a minimum of 18 mg. of vitamin B_3 daily, and adult females need 13 mg. daily. Studies have shown that excessive amounts of B_3 can cause glycogen (a starch that helps the body utilize the energy of sugars like glucose) to be consumed hyperactively by the muscles, resulting in the early onset of fatigue. Again, a low-potency vitamin is a worthwhile investment to be sure you are getting sufficient amounts of niacin.

VITAMIN B_5 (PANTOTHENIC ACID)

Vitamin B_5 also works in all our cells. It converts carbohydrates, fats, and protein to energy, acts as an antistress agent, and manufactures antibodies that fight germs in the blood. B_5 is found in many foods including eggs, peanuts, whole grains, beans, and organ meats.

The signs of deficiency include high susceptibility to illness and infection; digestive malfunctions such as abdominal pains and vomiting; muscular and nerve disturbances like leg cramps; insomnia and mental depression. Although the requirement for pantothenic acid is not yet known, 5 to 10 mg. daily for adults is suggested. A low-potency vitamin supplement is suggested.

VITAMIN B$_6$ (PYRIDOXINE)

Vitamin B$_6$ nourishes the central nervous system, controls sodium/potassium levels in the blood, and assists in the production of red blood cells and hemoglobin. It helps protect against infection, and assists in manufacturing DNA and RNA, the acids that contain the genetic code for cell growth, repair and multiplication. It is valuable for those involved in endurance sports.

The best sources of B$_6$ are brewer's yeast, brown rice, bananas, and pears. It is also found in beef, pork liver, and fish such as salmon and herring. Deficiency signs are similar to those of vitamin B$_2$: irritability, nervousness, weakness, dermatitis and other skin changes and insomnia. The official recommended daily amount for adults is 2 mg. of vitamin B$_6$ per 100 grams of protein consumed. This amount is easily obtained from the food sources listed above.

VITAMIN B$_{12}$ (CYANOCOBALAMIN)

Vitamin B$_{12}$ is the most complex of the B vitamins. Every cell in the body depends on it to function properly. It is especially vital to cells in your bone marrow, gastrointestinal tract, and nervous system. It helps prevent fatty deposits from accumulating in your liver, and helps maintain normal weight. All B$_{12}$ in its natural state is manufactured by microorganisms, so it is not normally found in fruits and vegetables. Fermented soybean products such as tempeh, nonfat dry milk, poultry, and meat all contain B$_{12}$.

Common symptoms of B$_{12}$ deficiency are motor and mental abnormalities, rapid heartbeat or cardiac pain, facial swelling, jaundice, weakness and fatigue, loss of hair or weight, depression, and impaired memory. Adults need a daily minimum of 30 mcg. of vitamin B$_{12}$. If you are a vegetarian, you should include a low-potency vitamin supplement with your diet.

FOLIC ACID

Folic acid works mostly in the brain and nervous system. It is a vital component of spinal and extracellular fluid, is necessary for the manufacture of DNA and RNA, and helps covert amino acids.

Brewer's yeast, dark green leafy vegetables, wheat germ, oysters, salmon, and chicken all contain folic acid.

Your body needs comparatively miniscule amounts of folic acid; 400 micrograms daily are recommended. This is easily obtained from the food sources listed above. If you are pregnant, elderly, or suffer from any nervous disorder, you may benefit from additional amounts.

PARA-AMINOBENZOIC ACID (PABA)

Para-aminobenzoic acid is a component of folic acid, and acts as a coenzyme in the body's metabolism of proteins. It helps manufacture healthy blood cells and can help heal skin disorders. In addition, it protects your skin against sunburn by absorbing the portions of those ultraviolet rays of the sun known to cause burns and even skin cancer.

Eggs, brewer's yeast, molasses, wheat germ, and whole grains are good sources of PABA. Signs of deficiency include digestive trouble, nervous tension, emotional instability, and blotchy skin. No official daily requirements have been established for PABA.

CHOLINE

Choline is present in all your cellular membranes and works to remove fat. It also helps regulate your cholesterol levels and is vital to the liver's functions. It aids in building and maintaining a healthy nervous system.

If choline is not present in your system, your liver is unable to process any sort of fat. Fatty deposits in the liver interfere with its normal filtering function. A deficiency can also lead to muscle weakness and excessive muscle scarring. Choline is found in a variety of foods, including: wheat germ and bran, beans, egg yolks, brewer's yeast, whole grains, nuts, lecithin, meat, and fish.

Your body also produces its own supply of choline, using protein and other B vitamins. Daily requirements are not yet known, but the average daily intake has been estimated to be between 500 and 900 mg. In addition to the foods listed above, two tablespoons of lecithin granules may be taken as a supplement to help meet these requirements.

INOSITOL

Inositol carries the responsibility for breaking down fats, and thus plays an important role in preventing cholesterol buildup and normalizing fat metabolism. Studies indicate that inositol has an anxiety-reducing effect similar to some tranquilizers.

A good supply of inositol can be found in wheat germ, brewer's yeast, whole grains, oranges, nuts and molasses. Keeping your intestinal tract healthy may be the best way to make sure you are getting enough inositol. The bacteria or intestinal flora found there are indispensable for making inositol in the body. If you suffer from insomnia, hair loss, high cholesterol levels, or cirrhosis of the liver, you may have a deficiency of inositol. A minimum daily requirement for inositol has not yet been established.

BIOTIN

Biotin helps keep your hair, skin, bone marrow, and glands healthy and growing. It helps produce, and then change into energy, fatty acids, carbo-hydrates, and amino acids. It is vital to the production of glycogen. Your body manufactures biotin in the intestinal tract. You can also get it from eggs, cheese, nuts, and many other common foods.

Deficiencies are rare. However, when they occur, symptoms include fatigue, depression, skin disorders, slow healing of wounds, muscular pain, anorexia, sensitivity to cold temperatures and elevated blood choles-terol levels. Between 150 and 300 mcg. of biotin will meet your body's daily needs. This is best obtained from your low-potency vitamin supple-ment.

VITAMIN C

Vitamin C strengthens the immune system, keeps cholesterol levels down, combats stress, promotes fertility, protects against cardiovascular disease and various forms of cancer, maintains mental health, and ulti-mately may prolong life. Its presence is necessary to build collagen, the "cement" that holds together the connective tissue throughout the body. Athletes, for example, need more vitamin C for collagen synthesis and tissue repair. Vitamin C combats toxic substances in our food, air, and water, and is a natural laxative.

Whole oranges and other citrus fruits, sprouts, berries, tomatoes, sweet potatoes, and green leafy vegetables are important sources of vitamin C. Symptoms of vitamin C deficiency include bleeding gums, a tendency to bruise easily, shortness of breath, impaired digestion, nosebleeds, swollen or painful joints, anemia, lowered resistance to infection, and slow healing of fractures and wounds.

The daily recommended allowance of vitamin C is 45 mg., according to the Food and Nutrition Board. This amount is easily obtained from the fresh fruits and vegetables in your diet, including oranges, sweet peppers, and potatoes. Some nutritionists believe that much higher doses (up to 10 grams daily) can help heal serious illnesses and reduce the risk of cancer (see "The Megadose Controversy" below). Hence, supplements may be beneficial. Those with elevated needs for vitamin C are the elderly, dieters, smokers, heavy drinkers, users of certain medications including oral contraceptives, pregnant and nursing women, and those under any type of stress.

VITAMIN D

Vitamin D helps your body utilize calcium and phosphorus to help form strong bones and teeth and healthy skin. Its action also is vital to your nervous system and kidneys.

A prime source of vitamin D is sunshine, but it may be necessary to get this vitamin from food sources and supplements if sunlight is inaccessible, or if sunshine is to be avoided for other health reasons. Food sources include fortified milk and butter, egg yolks, fish liver oils, and seafood such as sardines, salmon, tuna, and herring.

The symptoms of deficiency include brittle and fragile bones, pale skin, some forms of arthritis, insomnia, sensitivity to pain, irregular hearbeat, soft bones and teeth, and injuries that take an abnormally long time to heal. At least 400 I. U. of vitamin D are needed daily. Greater amounts may be necessary to build strong resistance against bone disease. However, megadoses of this oil-soluble vitamin are not recommended. One-half hour of good sunlight per day is the best supplement.

VITAMIN E

Vitamin E is basically an antioxidant; that is, it protects your fatty acids from destruction and maintains the health and integrity of every cell. It is especially important for promoting the health of your muscles, cells, blood, and skin. It is a primary defense against respiratory infection and disease. Vitamin E also is an excellent first aid tonic for burns. It is believed that vitamin E's antioxidant effects make available larger amounts of fats for metabolism, providing the body with extra energy for muscle contractions, and so is useful in exercise as well.

Ideal sources of vitamin E are wheat germ and wheat germ oil. Leafy plant foods eaten with cold-pressed oils, whole grains, seeds, nuts, and fertile eggs are also good sources. Some common symptoms of low vitamin E levels are swelling of the face, ankles, or legs, poor skin condition, muscle cramps, abnormal heartbeat, and respiratory difficulties.

Nutritionists and doctors recommend a daily dosage for adults of between 30 and 400 I. U., unless a condition requiring higher amounts is present. It's best to supplement.

VITAMIN K

Vitamin K is an oil-soluble substance that helps your blood clot properly, and aids in proper bone development and function.

The microorganisms and bacteria that naturally live in your large intestine produce vitamin K. You can help them work by eating yogurt and other fermented dairy and soy products. Other good sources include green leaves of plants like kale and spinach, cauliflower, broccoli, and cabbage. A tendency to bruise easily is a symptom of vitamin K deficiency . It can be the symptom of other nutritional deficiencies as well. Little is known about the precise daily minimum need for humans, and supplements are not available over-the-counter.

BIOFLAVONOIDS

Bioflavonoids are a group of water-soluble substances that ensure the strength and proper function of your capillaries. Along with vitamin C, with which they are almost always found in food, the bioflavonoids help manufacture collagen. They also protect your cells against attack and invasion by viruses and bacteria.

Excellent sources of bioflavonoids are grapes, rose hips, prunes, oranges, lemon juice, cherries, black currants, plums, parsley, cabbage, apricots, peppers, papaya, cantaloupe, tomatoes, broccoli, and blackberries. The white pulp of the inside of a grapefruit is also an rich source.

Symptoms of bioflavonoid deficiency include bleeding gums and easily bruised skin. There is no established minimum daily requirement for bioflavonoids, but most nutritionists agree that 900 mgs. may be an optimum amount. This amount is obtainable from the foods listed above.

VITAMIN SUPPLEMENTS

Vitamin supplements may be necessary. The world has changed since our ancestors lived on diets without one-a-day vitamins with iron, special mixtures of stress vitamins, or supplemental vitamins for infants or children. For a variety of reasons, individuals often overlook foods that contain essential vitamins or nutrients. They may just be eating less regularly because of the hectic pace of their lives, they may be unable to eat certain foods for health reasons, or they may be dieting. For many of these people, supplements in controlled, recommended doses, could help.

Others who may benefit from vitamin supplements include:

• Infants—particularly those who are not breastfed and therefore may be getting uncertain amounts of various vitamins and minerals.

• Pregnant or lactating women—pregnant women often have reduced levels of a number of vitamins, even though their caloric intake is usually greater than normal, and therefore, they are getting more foods with more vitamins in them. Vitamin supplements are often prescribed. Iron, as a mineral supplement, is almost always prescribed as well.

• Women on oral contraceptives—studies indicate that birth control pills cause shortages of a number of water-soluble vitamins, including thiamin, riboflavin, B_6, B_{12}, folic acid and vitamin C. Diet changes may not be sufficient and supplements are often suggested.

• The elderly—older people tend to absorb less vitamin C and less of the B vitamins than the rest of the population. Also, many older people eat a limited choice of foods. Multivitamin supplements may be in order.

• Those with other special problems—people who have had surgery would need more vitamin C. Those with certain chronic infections or cancers require more folic acid. Alcoholics require a full range of vitamin supplements because drinking results in poor absorption of all vitamins from foods. Heavy smokers need more vitamin C to repair cells damaged by the toxins in cigarette smoke and tars.

THE MEGADOSE CONTROVERSY

Dr. Linus Pauling, the Nobel Prize winner, has engaged in an ongoing controversy in the media and the scientific press, and with other medical and biochemical researchers, about the possible values of megadoses of vitamin C to help fight the common cold and for use in a number of other health situations. While conflicting research studies support both positions, it would seem logical that Dr. Pauling has hit on something substantial. Vitamin C is known to increase the body's ability to ward off infection, to repair tissue damage, and in general to help the body's natural immune system to function properly.

Whether vitamin C is most effective in fighting the common cold or other more serious disorders is debatable. What is clear is that vitamin C plays a role in helping the body fend off diseases—common colds and others.

Vitamin C in large doses seems to have some efficacy in helping treat cancer of the colon, and while not curing the disease, it might slow its development. Research is still minimal in this area.

However, vitamins alone do not work miracles. Megadoses of vitamins should not be used in place of a balanced diet, or to replace days, weeks, or more of neglect of important natural vitamin sources in natural foods. It is important to remember that megadoses as well as vitamin supplements also cannot and should not replace a healthful regular regimen of exercise. Some research does indicate that megadoses of specific vitamins or nutrients can aid in certain specific conditions.

It is possible, for example, that depression can be relieved by taking typtophan (one of the eight essential amino acids) in elevated doses. However, more than one gram, should not be exceeded. Vitamin B_6 may also find some use in larger doses to help women taking the Pill fight depression, a possible side effect, and to help women relieve premenstrual syndrome (PMS) effects.

Megadoses of vitamin A for both acne and for deafness has received some experimental attention in recent years. However, large doses of vitamin A can be toxic to the system. Also women who are trying to conceive, or those already pregnant, should avoid taking any excessive doses of vitamin A, under any circumstances.

All in all, the case for megadoses of vitamins is yet to be made to the general population. Megadoses of, for example, vitamins A or D can be toxic to the body under certain circumstances. As for vitamin C, researchers are still studying effects of megadoses and the verdict is not yet in. However, there are indications that substantial healthful effects can sometimes be realized.

5 · MINERALS

"Your body needs between 55 and 440 mg. of sodium daily to perform its functions. Many of us consume between 7,000 and 20,000 mg. daily. Too much sodium can result in serious health problems, including hypertension, stress, liver damage, muscle weakness, and pancreas disease."

MINERALS SERVE AS BUILDING materials for bones, teeth, tissue, muscle, blood and nerve cells. They help spur many biologic reactions in the body and maintain the body's fragile balance of fluids.

You need minute amounts of minerals. They constitute only 4 or 5 percent of your total body weight. Although we will examine them individually here, understand that the actions of minerals within your body are interrelated. No one mineral can function in isolation.

CALCIUM

Calcium is the body's chief mineral. It is the principal component of your bones and teeth, and a vital component of the liquid that bathes your cells. Calcium is one of the raw materials used in the bloodstream. You need it to help you cope with stress. An active ingredient of some enzymes, calcium is also an enzyme stimulator, that is, it must be supplied before you can store the sugar (glucose) as glycogen in your muscles. Along with several other minerals, calcium also helps maintain the delicate acid/alkaline balance in your blood, protecting it against overacidity.

Without a steady supply of calcium, your bones and teeth would not remain hard and durable. Your brain would not function properly, nor would your muscles be able to store energy. Without enough calcium in your diet, the digestive, circulatory, and immune systems would suffer. Adequate amounts are necessary to avoid the many complications that can come from calcium deposits, which are caused by calcium that has been removed from the body's reserves and lodges in soft tissue. Warnings of calcium deficiency include nervousness, depression, headaches, and insomnia.

Milk is one of the best sources of calcium, as are other, more easily absorbed dairy products such as buttermilk, yogurt, acidophilus milk (a healthful bacteria-rich fermented milk product), and kefir (also a milk product). Most cheeses are good sources. Oatmeal, collard greens, and tempeh are also rich in calcium. Sesame seeds, torula yeast, carob flour, and sea vegetables all contain calcium in smaller quantities.

However, the body will not always properly absorb or utilize calcium. For example, if there aren't enough complete proteins in your diet, the necessary substances that allow calcium to be absorbed by your bones won't be available. Also, protein is needed for your body to make collagen. If you eat high protein foods, you will absorb 15–20 percent of the calcium in your food, as opposed to 5 percent if you don't. However, an excessively high protein diet will cause you to lose calcium thorough the urine. Sugar in the diet (except for lactose or milk sugar) will also antagonize the absorption of calcium.

For a healthy adult, 800 to 1,200 mg. of calcium daily is sufficient. This is usually obtainable from foods in the diet such as those listed above. For women who are pregnant or breast feeding, 1,200 mg. is required. As women age, calcium supplements, ideally in forms like amino acid chelate, might be necessary to fight the onset or severity of osteoporosis.

CHROMIUM

Chromium is important to your heart, liver, brain, and glucose metabolism system. It is vital to the production of protein and to white blood cells, where it helps fight bacteria, viruses, toxins, arthritis, cancer, and premature aging. To counteract stress, your adrenal glands must have an adequate supply of chromium.

The best food sources of chromium are whole wheat flour, brewer's yeast, nuts, black pepper, all whole grain cereals except rye and corn, fresh fruit juices, dairy products, root vegetables, legumes, leafy vegetables, and mushrooms.

Without chromium, insulin cannot transport glucose from your bloodstream to your cells, nor can your liver properly remove excess fats from your blood. A deficiency can result in rapid premature aging, since protein production will be seriously impaired. Symptoms of chromium deficiency include fatigue, dizziness, anxiety, insomnia, a craving for alcohol, blurred vision, depression, and panic.

No definitive guidelines have been established by the government on the amount of chromium necessary on a daily basis, but trace mineral experts suggest that 200 mcg. will provide an adequate daily supply. This is usually obtainable from the diet.

IODINE

Iodine is essential to the manufacture of thyroxin, the hormone that controls the speed at which your blood takes the food from your intestines to the cells, where it is used for energy. It is particularly important to your heart, your immune system and your system of protein synthesis.

Fresh seafood is a good source of iodine, as is garlic. You can enhance the iodine content of your diet by using sea vegetables such as hiziki, wakame, kelp, or dulse. Dried mushrooms, leafy greens, celery, tomatoes, radishes, carrots, and onions also supply iodine.

Without adequate amounts of iodine, the way your cells use energy would be seriously impaired. Proper growth in childhood could not take place, and maintenance of healthy adult tissue could not occur. An iodine deficiency can lower your resistance to infection and impair metabolism of fat in the bloodstream. Thyroid malfunctions are a direct result of iodine deficiency. Symptoms of inadequate iodine consumption include sluggishness, bad complexion, and unhealthy-looking hair, teeth, and nails. You need 150 mcg. of iodine. Some nutritionists believe that 3 mg. a day of this trace mineral is necessary to prevent serious thyroid disorders. Sufficient amounts of iodine are generally available in the foods we eat without supplements.

IRON

Without the oxygen-carrier iron, you could not live. The hemoglobin in your red blood cells, the myoglobin in your muscles, and the enzymes tied in with energy release, all depend on iron.

The most concentrated sources of iron are animal livers, but as we have mentioned, the liver is a waste-filtering organ, and any hormone or chemical—like pesticides or antibiotics fed to animals—to which the animal was exposed will be concentrated there. Egg yolks contain more iron than muscle meats. Other good sources include leafy green vegetables, dried beans, peaches, apricots, dates, prunes, cherries, figs, raisins, and blackstrap molasses.

A deficiency of iron can cause certain types of anemia. Deficiency symptoms include chronic fatigue, shortness of breath, headache, pale skin, and opaque or brittle nails. The daily requirements for iron are 10 mg. for adult males and 18 mg. for women. For pregnant women, 30–60 mg. are required. Starting the day with a hot cereal on which you've sprinkled two tablespoons of rice bran, torula yeast, or pumpkin seed meal will go a long way toward satisfying your iron needs. Daily iron supplements are also recommended.

MAGNESIUM

Magnesium is a versatile, tireless worker in your body's protein production process. In addition, it is one of your body's most important coenzymes. It works with calcium to turn it into something the body can use. It is necessary for the production of hormones, and it works in your muscles, cells, nervous system, digestive system, reproductive system, blood, and immune system.

Green leafy vegetables are one of the best sources for magnesium. Nuts, seeds, avocados, and turnips also contain significant amounts. Whole grains, legumes, organic eggs, and raw milk are excellent sources. Many fruits and natural sweets such as carob, honey, and blackstrap molasses also contain magnesium.

Magnesium deficiency can result in lowered immunity, improper muscle function, and impaired digestion. Without adequate magnesium, your nerves can become ragged and supersensitive to pain. Your bones would be too soft to support you, and production of new protein would be impaired. Without it you would be unable to store energy, synthesize sex hormones, or prevent your blood from clotting. Signs of magnesium deficiency are an irregular heartbeat, hair loss, and easily broken nails.

The recommended daily intake of magnesium is 350 mg., but 450–650 mg. may be a more realistic figure for maintaining optimal health. Sufficient amounts of magnesium can be obtained in the diet from some of the foods listed above.

MANGANESE

Manganese is a trace mineral that is active in protein production and essential to the correct structure of your bones, teeth, cartilage, and tendons. Vital in the formation of new blood cells in your bone marrow, it is also necessary for transmitting nerve impulses in your brain. Manganese plays an important role in the metabolism of blood sugar and fats, and is necessary for the production of sex hormones.

Nuts, seeds, and whole grains are excellent sources of manganese. Green leafy vegetables, if grown organically in mineral-rich soil, can supply you with manganese. So can rhubarb, broccoli, carrots, potatoes, peas, and beans. Pineapples, blueberries and raisins, cloves and ginger are also good sources.

Without manganese, a slow deterioration of muscle health—myasthenia gravis—can develop. Protein production and carbohydrate/fat metabolism would be inhibited. Manganese deficiencies can be related to blood sugar disorders and sexual dysfunction There is no official recommended daily requirement for manganese, but trace mineral experts suggest up to 7 mg. daily. It is worthwhile to supplement here.

PHOSPHOROUS

Phosphorous works in your bones, teeth, collagen, nerves, muscles, metabolic and cellular systems, brain, liver, digestive and circulatory systems, and eyes. It is an important part of your genetic materials, RNA and DNA, and helps maintain your body fluids in the right balance. It is indispensible to the runner since it plays a vital role in supplying energy to muscles by burning carbohydrates.

Phosphorus is available in nearly every food you eat. Eat a lot of refined foods, though, and you are in danger of getting too much. Protein foods like meat, poultry, fish, eggs, dairy products, whole grains, nuts, and seeds supply phosphorus in abundance. Vegetables that contain phosphorus include legumes, whole grains, celery, cabbage, carrots, cauliflower, string beans, cucumber, chard, and pumpkin. Fruits also contain a healthy supply. Too little phosphorus, although rarely seen, is responsible for certain anemias. It might also affect your white blood cells, and immunity to bacteria and viruses would be hampered. The recommended daily intake of phosphorus is 800 mg. for adults. Pregnant or lactating women need 1,200 mg. A well-balanced meal plan should provide you with all of this requirement.

POTASSIUM

Potassium, in conjunction with sodium, helps form an electrical pump that speeds nutrients into every cell of your body, while speeding wastes out. It is vital to the function of all cells, helping maintain the proper acid/ alkaline balance of your body fluids. Potassium is particularly vital to the workings of your digestive and endocrine systems, your muscles, brain, and nerves.

In general, vegetables, fruits, and other plant foods are far richer sources of potassium than animal foods. Green leafy vegetables are an excellent source. High potassium fruits include bananas, cantaloupes, avocados, dates, prunes, dried apricots, and raisins. Whole grains, beans, legumes, nuts, and seeds are also good sources.

If you find that injuries take a long time to heal, or your skin and other tissues seem "worn out," you may be suffering from a potassium deficiency. Lethargy and insomnia typically are other early signs of deficiency, along with intestinal spasms, severe constipation, swelling of tissues, thinning of hair, and malfunctioning muscles.

If you eat correctly, you needn't worry about your potassium intake, although studies show that runners can lose extraordinary amounts of potassium through sweating. You can easily consume the 2 to 4 grams needed each day to replace the amount normally lost in your urine. A variety of grains and legumes will meet this requirement easily. Runners can eat extra amounts of potassium-rich foods during times of heavy training. I suggest four medium soy pancakes or two potato fritters as a potassium-rich treat.

Those on certain medications, like diuretics to combat hypertension, also require extra amounts of potassium to replace the mineral that is lost by the diuretic's actions. However, potassium supplements should not be taken without a doctor's advice.

SELENIUM

Selenium's primary function in your body is as an antioxidant, protecting your cells from being destroyed. It plays a vital role in your enzyme system, and is necessary for the manufacture of prostaglandins, which control blood pressure and clotting. Selenium is needed to protect your eyes against cataracts, contributes to protein production, and protects the artery walls from plaque.

Animal foods tend to have more selenium than plants. Whole grains, mushrooms, asparagus, broccoli, onions, and tomatoes are the best vegetable sources. Eggs are excellent sources of selenium; they also contain sulphur, which helps your body absorb and utilize selenium.

Signs of selenium deficiency include lack of energy, accelerated angina, and the development of degenerative diseases. Deficiencies have been implicated in blood sugar disorders, liver necrosis, arthritis, anemia, heavy metal poisoning, muscular dystrophy, and cancer. There are no official recommended daily amounts for selenium, but the Food and Nutrition Board suggests an intake of 150 mcg. daily. It is best to supplement with a 50 mcg. vitamin and mineral tablet.

SODIUM (SALT)

Sodium, along with potassium, pumps nutrients into cells and waste products out. It also regulates fluid pressure in the cells, thus affecting your blood pressure. With other nutrients, it helps control the acid/alkaline blood levels in the body. Sodium is vital to the ability of nerves to transmit impulses to muscles and to the muscles' ability to contract. It also helps pump glucose into the bloodstream, produces hydrochloric acid for digestion, and keeps calcium suspended in the bloodstream ready for use. Sodium is available in almost every food we eat, including water. Refined foods contain enormous quantities of sodium.

Sodium deficiency is uncommon. But, when it occurs, it is usually caused by stressful situations such as exposure to toxic chemicals, infections, digestive difficulties, allergies, and injuries. Symptoms of deficiency include wrinkles, sunken eyes, flatulence, diarrhea, nausea, vomiting, confusion, fatigue, low blood pressure, irritability, difficulty in breathing, and heightened allergies.

Your body needs between 55 and 440 mg. of sodium daily to perform its functions. Under normal conditions, obtaining sufficient quantities is not the problem. Many of us consume between 7,000 and 20,000 mg. daily. Too much sodium can result in serious health problems, including hypertension, stress, liver damage, muscle weakness, and pancreas disease.

ZINC

Zinc plays an important role in the body's production of growth and sex hormones, and in its utilization of insulin. As a coenzyme, zinc helps start many important activities and sparks energy sources. It is an important element in the body's ability to remain in a state of balance, keeping your blood at a proper acidity, producing necessary histamines, removing excess toxic metals, and helping your kidneys maintain a healthy equilibrium of minerals. Zinc works in the protein production system, in blood cells, the circulatory system, liver, kidneys, muscles, bones, joints, eyes, the immune system, and the nerves.

Eggs, poultry, and seafood contain sizeable amounts of zinc, as do organ meats. Excellent vegetable sources include peas, soybeans, mushrooms, whole grains, most nuts, and seeds, especially pumpkin.

Lack of taste or smell is a sign of zinc deficiency. Skin problems also may indicate zinc deficienices. Stretch marks are an indication that elastin, the fibers that make your skin springy and smooth, are not incorporating enough zinc to keep your skin healthy. Acne and psoriasis can result from zinc deficiency, as can an abnormal wearing away of tooth enamel. Other signs of zinc deficiency include opaque fingernails, brittle hair, and bleeding gums The daily zinc requirement for adults is 20 to 25 mg. By including sesame, sunflower, and pumpkin seeds, we can supply a good portion of this daily.

6 · WATER, AIR, ENZYMES, AND ANTIOXIDANTS

"The urban or suburban dweller faced with these challenges should stock up on vitamin E."

THE ENVIRONMENT FROM WHICH we gain sustenance can also have an adverse effect on us. Consider these life-giving and life-supporting elements and aspects of the world around us. Although it comprises 50 to 70 percent of our body weight, water is too often overlooked or taken for granted when we consider amounts of water needed and proper balance of nutrients necessary for good health. Similarly, we too often pay little attention to the quality of air we breathe and the very activity of breathing itself. By not taking seriously the impact of our environment on the enzymes and antioxidants in our bodies, we place our health in danger. We must be as aware of the air we breathe and the water we drink as we are of the food we eat.

WATER

You can go 60 days without food, but only about 18 days without water, the sixth of the major nutrients. Water is second only to oxygen in importance, of all the components necessary for life. It is present in all tissues, including teeth, fat, bone, and muscle. It is the medium of all body fluids, such as blood, digestive juices, lymph, urine, and perspiration. It is a lubricant for the saliva, the mucous membranes, and the fluid that bathes the joints. And it regulates body temperature. Water also prevents dehydration, flushes out toxins and wastes, supplies the body with oxygen and nutrients, and aids muscle cells in producing energy.

The average body contains 40 to 50 quarts of water, with 40 percent of that water inside your cells. Lean persons have a higher percentage of body water than fat persons; men have a higher percentage than women, and children have a higher percentage than adults. Water is your life's blood. Indeed, 83 percent of your blood is water. With a loss of 5 percent of your body water, your skin shrinks and muscles become weak. The loss of less than a fifth of your body water is fatal.

How Much Water Do You Need?

Although water occurs naturally in most foods, it must be consciously included in our daily diets. Include 8 glasses, 8 to 10 ounces each ,every day. To rehydrate after exercise, drink one glass of water every 20 minutes for the first hour, then one glass for several hours afterward. Your body will determine how much it needs; it will absorb water at a particular rate and eliminate whatever is excess.

Eating a high-protein diet results in the body eliminating water. If you are not a vegetarian, it's especially crucial for you to keep careful track of water consumption to replenish the water lost in the excretion of animal protein wastes. If you are concerned or uncertain about pollutants in your tap water, buy pure spring water, not distilled water. Be sure to read the label, even on spring water jugs.

Despite popular theories and practices to the contrary, fruit juice, soda pop, and Gatorade-type drinks—ones that mix sugar and water—will not aid in athletic performance. A Rube Goldberg-type series of reactions occur instead. The sugar in these drinks triggers insulin to be released into the blood. The insulin inhibits epinephrine, which is needed to release free fatty acids, substances you will need for fuel. The insulin also lowers blood sugar levels, which causes glycogen stored in the muscles to leave the muscles and enter the blood. This reduces the store of energy you need to exercise. Drinking such sugar drinks 30 to 60 minutes before exercise, therefore, has a negative effect on athletic performance. Also, concentrations of too much sugar force the body to tap water from other cells to help dilute and digest the sugar. This activity will lead toward dehydration.

It's best to avoid beer, wine, and other alcoholic beverages, although some recent studies support extremely moderate amounts (one glass per day) for cardiovascular health. In general, though, they cause fatigue and dehydration through their diuretic actions. Avoid caffeine drinks like coffee and iced tea. They also act as diuretics, resulting in dehydration.

Drinking during meals, in a sense, can "drown" your enzymes, reducing their strength. When foods are dry, it is better to allow extra salivation prior to swallowing, to moisten them, rather than washing them down with liquids. Eating green and succulent vegetables with a meal also will help provide natural water to lubricate dry foods.

BREATHING

The first and last thing we do on this planet is breathe. But too often we go through life almost ignoring this vital process. Oxygen enters the body through the food we eat and the water we drink as well as the air we breathe. Our bodies have elaborately designed mechanisms for taking in, absorbing, distributing, and utilizing this oxygen.

Disciplined breathing exercises such as those performed in yoga are designed to control the vital energy represented by our breath. Some people believe you can tune into the larger energies of the universe by working on proper breathing techniques. Breath and thought are integrally related: calm one and you calm the other. It is known that deep breathing can reduce stress and tension and regularize body rhythms.

It is not within the scope of this book to provide a comprehensive discussion of proper breathing—a subject worthy of several volumes. But it is important to note here that attention should and must be paid to proper breathing in everyday life, even as we eat. This is an important key to success, as we try to relieve stress and relax.

ENZYMES

Enzymes are natural substances that stimulate some of the internal reactions necessary for life. Your body contains more than 700 types of enzymes, each one responsible for a different task. A shortage of even one type can dramatically affect health. Enzymes are found throughout the body, with the most vital ones in the salivary glands, pancreas, stomach walls, intestines, and liver.

Without enzymes, food could not be digested. Enzymes help transform food products into muscles, nerves, bones and glands. They assist in storing excess nutrients in the muscles and liver for future access, help create urea to be excreted in the urine, and facilitate the departure of carbon dioxide from the lungs. Enzymes also help stop bleeding and serve to decompose poisonous hydrogen peroxide to liberate needed oxygen. They help you breathe and attack poisons in the blood.

Enzymes are abundant in fresh, raw foods. However, they cannot survive at temperatures higher than 122°F., which means that they won't exist in cooked foods. The best sources of enzymes are fresh fruits and vegetables, which should be eaten in season and fresh. When cooking vegetables, use as little water as possible to conserve the enzyme content as well as the vitamin content. Cook vegetables only until tender, in a tightly covered pot. Do not soak most fresh foods; the water can destroy enzymes.

The enzyme that begins the entire digestive process is found in the saliva. Proper chewing is necessary to make that enzyme best perform its work. Food that is not chewed well enters the digestive canal only partially prepared; digestion is therefore less nutritious.

Mental strain or worry also has a deleterious effect on enzyme actions. It is better to avoid large meals during such times, since stressful situations tend to inhibit the flow of enzymes and interfere with the actions of the digestive tract.

In order to perform their life-sustaining tasks, enzymes must be continually replaced. Unnatural components of our environment, such as pollution, artificial additives in foods, and stress, all negatively affect the makeup of your cells and increase your need for health-promoting enzymes. To get enough of these fragile chemicals, it would be better to avoid processed, refined foods as much as possible, looking to natural foods for nourishment instead.

ANTIOXIDANTS

Antioxidants, which oppose oxidation or the burning of substances within the body, have been identified as important factors in helping make us live longer, helping fight heart disease and lung problems, and combating carcinogen formation. They accomplish these, in part, by battling the degenerative processes associated with *free radicals*.

Free radicals are substances released by your body when certain fats are broken down in specific ways. Radiation exposure—either accidental or intended—can cause the release of free radicals. They are also released by a variety of other inopportune circumstances—from the presence of chemical pollutants found in water, air, food, tobacco smoke, and in many cancer-causing agents.

Antioxidants can save us from these free radicals, trapping them and preventing the degenerative processes associated with their reactions with unsaturated fatty acids to form the molecules that ultimately cause harmful disruptions in our cells.

Free radicals also have been linked to certain symptoms of aging. It is with some degree of logic then that scientists believe antioxidants, which can slow down the destructive processes of free radicals, can also help reduce some of the effects of the aging process. Vitamin E is the most common antioxidant. It is known to have some effect, for example, on preventing or delaying the brown pigmentation of skin caused by the aging process—so-called liver spots. Vitamins A, C, and D are less powerful antioxidants, as are selenium and sulfur-containing amino acids.

Pollution can have a serious effect on a variety of body processes. Environmental pollution, for example, seems to defeat or otherwise interfere with the beneficial effects of antioxidants. It is therefore necessary to take nutrients that will contribute to their formation—in the face of such environmental obstacles.

Pollution poses a variety of challenges for those seeking healthful nutrition. Much of our fish comes from rivers, lakes, and waterways poisoned by sewage, chemicals, and a host of other pollutants. Shellfish, particularly, are prone to feed on this sewage and absorb them into their bodies. Fatty fish, as well, are more prone to absorb chemical pollutants and then pass them on to the humans who eat them.

In addition to all the obvious stresses environmental pollution causes, it also depletes our vitamin E supplies. Vitamin E, you'll recall, is a potent antioxidant, and therefore serves to help our bodies by blocking the actions of dangerous free radicals. A deficiency in vitamin E can put the urban or suburban dweller at even greater risk from pollution in the air we breathe, the water we drink, the food we eat. Vitamin E is our major hedge against environmental stress. It helps dilute the harmful effects of drinking water that may have lead in it, an excess of minerals like sodium in it, or an otherwise unbalanced mineral content. Vitamin E as an antioxidant protects us from many types of contaminants simply by impeding the formation of compounds that lead to cellular destruction.

The urban or suburban dweller faced with these challenges should stock up on vitamin E. Wheat germ and wheat germ oil are superior sources of vitamin E. All whole grains, unrefined cereals, whole grain baked goods, seeds, nuts, bran, and organic eggs are also excellent sources. Vegetable oils like safflower oil are likely to have vitamin E if they have been refined only minimally. The best source for such scarcely refined oils—so-called cold-pressed oils—are to be found in natural foods from health food stores.

The active chemical ingredient in vitamin E is pure alphatocopherol. If you're seeking a supplement, get natural vitamin E. There is some indication that the natural form is more active and therefore more useful than the synthetic variety.

Since environmental pollution and other factors seem to have a negative effect on antioxidants, it may be necessary to supplement your intake of nutrients to help you make more antioxidants for possible use.

For a more detailed discussion of the detrimental effects of our environment and suggestions on combating those effects, see Chapter 7, "Detoxification."

Part Two

Getting to
Ground Zero

7 · DETOXIFICATION

"Offer the body the right nutrients. Allow the body to open up the eliminative processes, in which the liver and digestive tract play key roles. Start to detoxify by getting used to natural juices, natural mineral sources, and other organic substances, sometimes supplemented by enemas or medically supervised short-duration fasts. The process may be a slow one at the start. When toxins have had so long to build up, their breakdown also will take time."

WE ARE SURROUNDED IN our world by toxic substances in the air, water, soil, and food. Food that is manufactured or processed is also usually treated with chemical preservatives, dyes, and food additives. A healthy body can usually eliminate these potentially toxic or harmful substances through the liver and other organs. But a diet that is too high in fats, processed proteins, sodium, refined sugars, and other refined foods, reduces this natural capacity to rid the body of these toxins. When that happens, the toxins in the body can accumulate.

THE PROBLEM

Toxins in food may not all be poisons in the classic sense. They often do their damage more insidiously, inhibiting the actions of enzymes in our bodies. Many things can go wrong if enzymes don't properly do their work. Since enzymes are important activators of almost every digestive or energy-producing activity in the body, our digestive systems can become sluggish and slow down if they are adversely affected by toxins, with the result that fat digestion can become difficult and protein digestion inefficient. Our kidneys and liver then become overloaded and fat may be deposited in arteries. Cardiovascular illness and other degenerative diseases can result.

Foods that are commercially fertilized may also be denuded of their proper mineral levels. Potassium, for example—our most important activator or catalyst of enzyme actions in the body—is one of the most vital minerals to be lost in this way. Without the right amounts of this mineral, the natural chemicals and enzymes that make our digestion efficient could not function. Yet potassium is reduced—and sodium added—in many of our processed foods and toxins will often deplete potassium supplies. This changes our basic metabolic balance, opening the door for a host of potential problems. The detoxification process will often depend on rebuilding potassium supplies in the body by including fresh fruits and vegetables in our daily diet.

Toxic substances may severely depress the immune system. It is only in the past half century, with the increase in environmental pollution and dependence on processed foods, that we have seen a rapid increase in diseases like cancer, heart disease, arthritis, Legionnaires disease—maladies, unknown not too long ago, that a healthy, normal immune system would be able to fight off.

While those who live in polluted urban or suburban areas may say they have little control over many toxic substances—like air pollution—there *are* things we all can do. People can stop smoking, drinking liquor, using drugs, and eating processed foods. These are all toxic substances. What we need to do instead is to start using fresh untreated foods, raw foods, and fresh juices, whose actual nutrients are more easily available to the body than packaged foods. They can help restore and reactivate our depressed immune systems and eliminate many toxins.

THE SOLUTION

Offer the body the right nutrients. Allow the body to open up the eliminative processes, in which the liver and digestive tract play key roles. Start to detoxify by getting used to natural juices, natural mineral sources, and other organic substances, sometimes supplemented by enemas or medically supervised, short-duration fasts. The process may be a slow one at the start. When toxins have had so long to build up, their breakdown also will take time.

FINDING OUT WHAT'S WRONG THROUGH PROPER TESTING

Once you have decided to make a change in your diet and life-style, you may want to undergo some simple inexpensive tests to ascertain whether there are specific aspects of your health that should be taken into consideration in your diet. According to Dr. Martin Feldman, a preventive medicine physician practicing in New York City, some of the most useful standard testing options include: the glucose tolerance test (also called the GTT or blood-sugar test), hair analysis, the SMA-24 blood test (Sequential Multiple Analyzer, a multiple blood-chemistry screening test), the complete blood count (CBC), and tests of the red blood cell sedimentation rate (also called the ESR or sed rate), and thyroid function. The tests are particularly appropriate if your decision is prompted by health problems or health complaints, such as generalized fatigue, that you already have. But very often a state of imbalance may be present long before symptoms appear. The best care is prevention, correcting the imbalance nutritionally before it has developed into a symptomatic disease state. In the last section of this book, there is a select listing of alternative health professionals, including physicians who recognize the importance of nutritive balance, preventative care, and responsible testing as integral parts of any program of detoxification.

Personal Medical History

Every individual is biologically unique. This should be reflected in the health profile. Testing should always be preceded by a proper medical history, taken by a physician. If you ever go to a medical facility and they don't take your medical history—thoroughly—then there is something wrong with that group of physicians. By taking a history, symptoms begin to stand out. Some of these symptoms are early warning signals of what later may become a toxic or imbalanced state.

Some types of symptoms that will appear during a personal history have not always been duly appreciated by physicians as indicators of an imbalanced or toxic state. For example, problems on the surface of the skin may signify underlying toxic states requiring attention and treatments. The skin, after all, is not just a covering on the body like a coat. It is a living, breathing part of our bodies. It is, in fact, our largest organ and has a great deal to do with our internal health. If the body is in a toxic state, one of the routes to eliminate poisons, besides the kidney, the liver, and the lungs, is the skin. Many early warnings of toxicities often appear as minor skin problems, even as simple blemishes on the face. Acne, for example, is a manifestation of an internal hormonal toxicity. Red, blotchy skin, may provide an early warning that the liver, kidneys, or lungs are malfunctioning by not eliminating toxins. Headaches also can provide clues. Many headaches are responses to stress or tension. But other headaches may instead signal a toxic condition. Generalized fatigue may also be caused by a toxic state. Premenstrual syndrome (PMS) in women may reflect a state of hormonal toxicity; cystic breasts may also reflect an imbalance; osteoarthritis may reflect a calcium imbalance associated with toxicity. These are a small sampling of conditions that may come up during the personal history taking. While many physicians will accept these conditions as being without a specific, treatable cause, these symptomatic states may in fact stem from correctable toxic states.

The Glucose Tolerance Test

The glucose tolerance test (also called the GTT, blood-sugar, or glucose test) measures the blood level of glucose, the most important sugar in the body. Glucose is usually maintained at a constant level by means of insulin and other hormones so that, for example, when a person fasts, the body produces glucose from its stores of fat and protein. Normally, blood glucose is obtained from the digestion of carbohydrates in the diet.

There are certain imbalanced states, however, where the glucose level is either too high or too low. Symptoms of lethargy, dizziness, or irritability may be caused by an abnormally low blood-sugar level, or hypoglycemia.

It can occur without a clearly identifiable cause, or as the result of excessive use of alcohol or strenuous exercise. At the other extreme, an abnormally high glucose level may cause frequent urination and chronic infections.

The glucose tolerance test requires that you eat adequate carbohydrates for several days prior to being tested, and then fast 12 hours immediately beforehand. Blood and urine samples are taken prior, during, and at the termination of the test, during which glucose is administered, either orally as a syrup or intravenously. The test should cost well under $50.

Other tests to measure glucose in the blood include the hemoglobin, A1C test, also called the glyco-sloated hemoglobin test. This measures the glucose in the red blood cells and may be performed during routine blood tests. It will measure average glucose levels over many weeks, rather than the minute-to-minute glucose levels measured by the glucose tolerance test.

Tests of pancreatic function, adrenal gland fuction, and liver function may also be used to measure the glucose levels since, ultimately, glucose is controlled by those three parts of the body. The pancreas, for example, is in charge of insulin production. If the pancreas does not create enough insulin, high glucose levels result. If insulin is excessive, low glucose levels appear. Chromium levels are also important in any glucose test since they control how cells actually absorb or use glucose. The chromium can be determined via hair analysis or blood analysis methods, which are inexpensive.

Hair Analysis

Hair analysis as a valid scientific measurement is often criticized and maligned. Yet, there is a specific advantage of hair analysis: When you examine just three inches of hair, you're observing growth over a period of three to four months. You therefore can obtain the average level of the body's status over a several-month period. As the hair grows each day, the mineral status of the body is reflected in the growth of the hair on that day. When examining hair, you're looking at a relatively stable part of the body—almost like examining a fossil—as opposed to the blood, which is constantly in flux.

In the case of exposure to mercury through a silver amalgam mercury filling that you received from your dentist, for example, the blood level of the mercury may rise for about 12 to 24 hours after you were exposed. After a day or so, the mercury leaves the blood stream. But hair analysis will show mercury's impact over days, weeks, or months. This is true of other minerals as well. Lead is another good example. In the case of exposure to lead in a work environment, blood levels rise during the exposure, but 12 to 24 hours afterward, the lead level in the blood will be nondetectable. Hair analysis will continue to show evidence of the change.

The cost of hair analysis is relatively modest compared to other tests (between $25 and $60). The most problematic aspect is in the proper interpretation of the results. Many labs overinterpret by overemphasizing data of minor importance. The hair has two major strengths in analysis. First, it is useful in showing when the body is not absorbing particular minerals efficiently and an imbalance has occurred due to this malabsorption, particularly of minerals like calcium, magnesium, zinc, manganese, and chromium. Second, the hair shows toxic metals very well, including lead, mercury, cadmium, arsenic, and aluminum.

The Classic Blood Test— SMA-24

The standard blood test gives us a lot of data, some of which can serve as an early warning, and some of which, unfortunately, is already a late warning. Commonly called the SMA-24, or the SMA-12 when abridged, the test is relatively complete, reasonably inexpensive, and provides a lot of data for the money. It should be performed as part of the six-month or yearly examination.

A patient should always be tested on an empty stomach, that is after not having eaten for six to eight hours. No food, no juice, no coffee, no tea. Water only. If you've eaten within four hours before the test, this makes it very difficult to interpret the glucose and triglyceride levels on the blood specimen that is drawn.

The first item on an SMA-24 is the *glucose level*. Glucose, if a body has been fasting, should be roughly between 75 and 100. A glucose below 75 is evidence of a possible hypoglycemic (low blood sugar) tendency.

Above 100 is too high. Does that mean you have diabetes? No. Does that mean that the body may get diabetes? The answer is maybe in time. A high glucose level serves as an early warning sign. The next step is to look into whether the cause is the glucose "thermostat" imbalance or a malfunctioning of the pancreas, the adrenal glands, or the liver. Chromium levels should be considered as a related aspect. A glucose imbalance may mean that something is going to go *more* wrong in the future and is deserving of more attention now.

Next on the SMA-24 are the *sodium levels*. Occasionally sodium is too low. An important aspect rarely appreciated by traditional physicians is that low sodium may indicate an adrenal malfunction. The adrenal gland may be sluggish, not making enough aldosterone, which is the sodium-retaining hormone.

Potassium is a potential problem if it is too low. This may happen when people take blood pressure medicines, and the body is asked to remove salt. One can remove too much potassium.

Carbon dioxide is usually tested on the SMA-24. An elevation of the carbon dioxide is a reflection of an alkaline state. The most comon cause of an excessively alkaline state is a diminished flow or amount of stomach acids.

Next is *blood urea/nitrogen*. If the urea/nitrogen levels are elevated, the body is experiencing urea toxicity. One should then look at whether the kidneys are working properly, or whether one is protein toxic. Too much protein can eventually lead to excessive urea.

Creatinine is a kidney-related enzyme. Its elevation is kidney related, so one has to go beyond the blood levels themselves.

Blood calcium may be normal and appear normal on the test, even if our true calcium status is not. Here's an example where one has to intelligently analyze the blood and not assume that the calcium overall is correcly balanced, just because the blood level is. In about one person in five with a severe calcium imbalance, the blood will show too low calcium levels. On the other hand, in four out of five people, the calcium may be off without the imbalance appearing on the blood test.

Phosphorous. When phosphorous is too high, it can adversely affect calcium levels.

Uric acid. Elevation of uric acid indicates a gout condition. Many people have gout early on. Even then, uric acid may not appear over the upper end of the range. But high uric acid can be a warning of gout that will develop later on, so one has to keep watching the uric acid. In such cases, the physician may also need to take a family history, since parents may have had gout.

Alkaline phosphatase is a complex part of the blood. If elevated, it may reflect a liver imbalance or bone problem.

The *total protein* in the blood may occasionally be low and may indicate a malabsorption of protein.

Albumin in the blood relates to its protein component as do *globulin* levels.

The measurement of *SGOT* and *SGPT* in most SMA-24's are measures of liver-related enzymes. Elevation of either may indicate that the liver is out of balance. If the liver is even slightly off balance, it can cause a variety of health problems. Such an imbalance should be dealt with nutritionally.

Bilirubin levels also are potentially liver related. Elevation of bilirubin may also have other meanings.

The *cholesterol* in the blood should be looked at. One also has to look at the *HDL* (high density lipoproteins, or "good" cholesterol) versus the total serum cholesterol levels. Ratios of four to one (of total cholesterol to HDL) or better are desirable.

In day-to-day practice almost all people with cholesterol levels above 225 provide some indication that the liver is sluggish or out of balance. This problem plays a major role in cholesterol elevation.

One should always also ask for a *triglyceride* level as part of the SMA-24 test results. Triglyceride levels are almost as important as cholesterol levels. An elevated level is usually due to malfunctioning of either the liver or the pancreas. Triglycerides are dangerous because they are blood fats and may play some part in clogging our arteries with harmful plaque.

These are the primary items of importance that can be tested with the SMA-24.

The CBC or
Complete Blood Count

In the CBC, we look both at the white blood cell components and the red blood cell components.

White Blood Cells. You could have a white blood count (WBC) as low as 4.8, or as high as 10.8 and still be within the normal range. It you fall below 4.8 WBC, it probably indicates that your immune system is not working properly. Even just slightly below the 4.8 level is an early warning sign that your immunity is not at 100 percent. The CBC is very inexpensive (roughly $10); at the same time it provides a lot of valuable information.

Occasionally the white blood count may be very high (counts in the range of 9, 10, or 11). This is usually indicative of an internal infection. The elevation of the white blood cells represents the body's attempt to deal with the invasion of a foreign substance or agent. The white blood cells are the soldiers that the body mobilizes to do battle. When the enemy has entered it, the body will, if it can, make many more white blood cells. The elevation that appears on the CBC is an indication that there is some kind of internal battle raging.

Conversely, when the body, even at rest, is not making enough white blood cells (in the case of a low WBC), it means there aren't enough soldiers around to do battle in case the need arises.

It is also important to go beyond the total number of the white cells, to look at the differential, or types, of white blood cells.

While all red blood cells are identical and do the same job, we have different types of white blood cells. The basic types of white blood cells are the neutrophils or the polymorphonuclear white blood cells, something called a segs, the lymphocytes, the monocytes, the eosinophils, and the basophils.

The neutrophils or polys tend to make up between 50 and 70 percent of the total white cells. We have more neutrophils or polys than any other type. That's normal. That's the way the body is set up. The lymphocytes comprise between 20 and 40 percent of our white blood cells. There are only a few eosinophils, monocytes, and basophils.

If there are more lymphocytes than neutrophils, an inversion of the usual ratio, most doctors would not even mention it to the patient. They may not even notice it, or if they notice, they don't mention it. But it should be examined. It's a potential early warning that the body's immune mechanism for making white blood cells is really not up to par. If there were a viral illness, either recently or at the time when the test is taken, that may explain the imbalance. During a viral illness, the body will make more lymphocytes because lymphocytes tend to be the main soldiers against viruses. In the absence of a viral problem or an infection, when lymphocytes still outnumber polys, the possibility of an immune imbalance should be examined further.

Red Blood Cells. There is basically one issue with red blood cells— anemia. Occasionally there's an excess of red blood cells, but that's a rare unusual state. Most of the time the question is are there too few, indicating anemia.

There are two types of anemia, depending on the size of the red blood cells. If the cells are too small, small-cell or iron deficiency anemia may be at cause. This condition is almost always related to an iron deficiency, where the body doesn't have enough iron or isn't properly handling the iron it does have. Since the body can't make enough cells without the necessary quantities of iron, it produces smaller cells and fewer cells.

In the second type of anemia, the cells are too large. The most common reason for this abnormality is a vitamin B_{12} deficient anemia. Treatment is different for each specific type of anemia.

Tests of Sedimentation Rates and Thyroid Function

People should also be tested on a routine basis to determine *sedimentation rates* and *thyroid function*. The sedimentation rate is a very inexpensive test. In women, if the sedimentation rate is above 20, there is an indication that some inflammatory process exists or is developing. If there is no cold, sore throat, or other obvious infection, one has to seek out other possible causes. In men, a sedimentation rate above 15 is considered an abnormal elevation.

Thyroid testing can involve special difficulties. For example, thyroxin is the hormone that allows the thyroid gland to carry out its function. You can have normal thyroxin levels and normal blood iodine levels at the same time as a food sensitivity to the thyroid gland is causing your metabolism to slow down, so that you gain weight at an abnormal rate. Chronic fatigue may also be caused by malfunctioning of the thyroid gland.

A standard blood test for thyroxin would not detect either the food sensitivity or the chronic fatigue.

An expenditure of $150 should cover most of the important tests for the average person to determine the state of their overall health.

DETOXIFICATION TECHNIQUES

There are a variety of detoxification techniques available. Several that can be used in combination to improve your well-being and increase your self-awareness are described below.

Maintaining Intestinal Fortitude

It is estimated that nearly half of all illness originates in the intestinal tract—the receptor of the foods we eat, the water we drink, and the air we breathe. Anything that passes through the intestines will impact, positively or negatively, on your health. Cleansing the intestines will help free the body of some hazardous toxic substances.

According to Heather Muir, an authority on the intestines and their role in maintaining good health, certain organisms proliferate in the colon, depending on what we eat and what foods go through it. One of those organisms is the *Candida albicans* organism, which causes candidiasis or yeast in the intestine. Another is the *E. coli* bacteria. Still other bacterial flora help maintain a healthy balance in the colon. If we eat the right types of food that can be digested quickly, transit time in the colon should also be fast. This helps keep bacteria in balance and diminishes harmful bacteria activity. However, if we eat animal proteins such as meat and hard cheeses, food transit time in the colon slows down. Everything begins to clog up, and the trouble begins.

Another concern in keeping the colon healthy is the sometimes deleterious effect of antibiotics on our digestive system. Most antibiotics destroy the friendly bacterial flora in the colon in a short time. This allows the proliferation of two harmful organisms, the *E. coli* and the *Candida albicans*.

We are exposed to antibiotics in many ways. We may take them as medication to cure infections, but we also get them in the meat we eat. The antibiotics, tranquilizers, and hormones that the animals have been fed before slaughter remain in the meat. Some believe that we also are being flooded by the animal's adrenalin, which it produces just prior to being killed.

In any case, there are a number of nutritional experts who urge people to consult with specialists on ways to cleanse the colon of these harmful substances—either by having a yearly colonic irrigation, where water is used to clean out the colon, or by using a variety of different types of enemas.

Yeast Infection Control

Successfully combating candida or common yeast infections may require changing the diet. But cleansing of the colon will also help. One reason these infections affect large numbers of people is that many of the foods we eat have molds in them. Mushrooms and wheat are prime examples.

To fight candida, people can go on a special diet. For their new diet, they should first go off wheat, breads and cereals, yeast, vinegar, cured or processed meats, and all sugars. They should include Kyolic garlic, vitamin C, Biotin, B$_6$, caprilic acid, beta carotene, paud arco, and acidopholis—all as daily supplements. Fresh vegetable juices and some fresh fruit juices also are important in any cleansing program because they provide needed vitamins and minerals, and they help specifically to cleanse the colon.

In particular, papaya and watermelon juices both have useful cleansing and therapeutic properties. Carrot juice, celery juice, and cucumber juice, mixed in a one to one ratio, are sometimes useful for intestinal cleansing.

Adding kelp to a carrot, celery, parsley, and spinach juice combination— quite rich in potassium—may be beneficial for the glandular system. The juice made from Jerusalem artichoke has alkaline mineral elements, particularly potassium and calcium. And small quantities of fresh garlic juice helps us to get rid of some intestinal parasites.

Detoxification with Herbs

Detoxification with herbs can be another key approach to renewed health. Two authorities in this area are Dr. Paul Lee, Director of the Platonic Academy in Santa Cruz, California, and one of America's leading spokespersons on the health properties of herbs, and Jeanne Rose, author of *Herbal Guides to Inner Health* and *The Herbal Body Book*.

Both experts point to specific herbs that are excellent detoxifiers, primarily because they stimulate macrophage activity. Macrophages are parts of our immune system that attack, engulf, and digest toxins and other substances that cause us to be ill.

Listed below are some of the substances that are characteristic of the herbal approach, along with brief descriptions of some of their properties.

Dandelion is an extremely useful medicinal herb that can be used as a tonic for the kidneys and the liver.

Arutheralcoctus senicosis is an herb that comes from Russia and China. It's called, for commercial purposes, *Siberian ginseng* because it's in the ginseng family, although it's not technically ginseng. It has an effect on the metals in our bodies and acts as an immune stimulant.

The *milk scissel (Silybun marianum)* a noxious weed to farmers, can be used as a liver tonic, helping the liver properly process toxins and poisons. It is available in tinctures. Milk scissel contains tyramine which stimulates secretions. In the winter, lungs may become congested. Milk scissel tea has been used to help stimulate the lungs to discharge these excess fluids and mucous.

Echinacea is probably the leading immune-enhancing herb, helping to cleanse our lymph system. With the first symptoms of a cold or flu, people should immediately take echinacea tincture. Frequently, they may ward off the illness because the herb immediately stimulates the immune system.

Jeanne Rose notes that during the cleansing activity of our bodies, fat is liquified and released over time into the bloodstream through our various excretory processes—sweating, urinating, and defecating. In this way, the body releases its toxins. Unfortunately, as these toxins are accumulated and released into the fat, we go through a process of intoxification. These toxins can make you feel sick.

Ms. Rose believes certain herbs can help overcome this. *Alfalfa herbs* in sprouts *(medicago satifa)* can be used as a tea or eaten whole. Alfalfa is rich in a variety of vitamins and minerals. It's also plentifully stocked with enzymes that can help in the digestive process. Cold alfalfa is an excellent diuretic and a mild stimulant for the bowels.

Another herbal remedy, *blackberry leaves*, acts as an astringent. It is considered an effective blood cleanser and may be useful for improving the circulation of the blood. Blackberry fruit is useful as a cleansing food to correct diarrhea. It can also be used as a gargle for throat inflammation or in douching to help with vaginal discharges.

Camomile is an herb that can be used as a tea or tincture. It has a slight alkalinizing effect on the blood. It also helps stimulate digestion and acts as a nerve tonic, hence its reputation as a calming herb. Therefore, it can be taken at night as a mild sedative. It also has antispasmodic qualities.

Celery has a cleansing diuretic affect, taken either as a tea or in a juice combination with other vegetables such as carrots, which contain a different kind of pectin than apples. Used to heal the digestive system, celery also has an alkaline affect.

Cherry stems are good because they affect the kidneys and the liver.

Comfrey is an ancient healing herb. It is an emollient and one of the few plant sources of vitamin B$_{12}$.

Seaweeds contain virtually all the vitamins and minerals needed in a diet. Algae and the sea plants such as Hijiki, kombu, wakame, nori, and arame combine with toxic elements of the body, enabling them to be more easily excreted. Seaweeds also contain above-average amounts of iodine, which helps stimulate the thyroid.

Rosemary is very important in any kind of cleansing diet. Its oils can be put in vaporizers and inhaled.

Remember, though, not all herbs are equal. How they are grown, harvested, stored, and prepared will affect their potency and their usefulness. Fresh and homegrown is always best, because you know the conditions under which the plants have been planted, monitored, fertilized, and cared for. When buying herbs from a store, especially in bulk, make sure you use your senses of smell and sight. The herb shouldn't have any strong aroma. If the herb looks brown instead of green, then it definitely will have reduced effectiveness. Consumers ought to insist on fresh herbs if they're buying bulk herbs in herbal stores.

There are various ways to prepare herbs. As many herbs as possible should be introduced into your daily diet. *Thyme* (*thumus bulgaris*), for instance, is a popular herb often used in French and Greek cooking. But there is more to it than its culinary properties. It is also a disinfectant and antigermicidal agent, actually helping cleanse the foods it's used with.

PRECAUTIONS

Even though herb use should be encouraged, certain precautions should be taken in their use. A city dweller should not pick herbs that are just growing on the streets. With people and animals circulating around them, such herbs can actually become quite toxic.

Also, some people may have allergic reactions or other problems with specific herbs. To test those sensitivities, use one at a time. Try them out, see what they're like, see which plants are for you, taste them, smell them. If one causes no problem, add another.

If you find that you have a reaction to many different plants, incorporate very simple wild plants into you life, one at a time. Generally, you can tolerate combinations of teas or herbs in moderate amounts, except for potent dried herbs available in powder or capsule form. The latter generally have *not* been tested for safety or efficacy and are all too often a rip off. Stay away from them. If you're going to incorporate herbs into your life, you should start with the whole plants. Make a cup of tea from the herb tea that you find in the store, rather than from the tincture. Make sure the plant has no eggs on it. After you become familiar with the plant, then you can go to a tincture, which is a liquified distillation or concentration of the plant.

If you are a novice in the world of herbs, go to a bookstore or library, look in their health and diet sections, read the books. Start small, perhaps with five herbs, like garlic, rosemary, cumfrey, echinecea, thyme. The best way to start to use them is in progressively increasing amounts in the foods you cook. Pour them in and just see how they taste. Also, start reading labels on the tea boxes in the stores. Pick out a tea you think would taste good. Or add an herbal to your shampoo, and use it on your hair, your body, in your bath tub. Within a short period of time, you will have incorporated a number of different herbs into your life. And you should start feeling better more naturally.

In addition to herbs, Dr. Lee believes that there is sufficient evidence at this time pointing to the utility of other substances that cleanse our systems. These include *rolled oats* and *pectin*. Rolled oats seem to reduce cholesterol and remove some heavy metals from our bodies. People should buy rolled oats and take them with apple juice, nuts, and raisins for breakfast. Apples are rich in pectin, a substance known to eliminate some of the toxic metals that may accumulate in the body. *Guar gum* also seems to lower cholesterol levels and should also be taken into the diet.

CAUTIONS

In recent years millions of Americans have been trying the herbal remedies commonly found in health food stores from different companies that very openly, and sometimes illegally, prescribe the remedies as cures for specific diseases. People take them with the expectation of being cured of their condition, often at great expense. I have contacted a number of the companies producing and marketing these herbal remedies and could not find one that had performed scientific tests to confirm the efficacy or safety of the cure as proclaimed on the labels. In my opinion, this is clearly an unethical policy.

As Dr. Lee notes, the problem of regulatory control is a burden to the herbal industry. Because herbs are neither food nor drugs, they are extremely difficult to define and hence hard to regulate. When the use is medicinal, they can be considered as drugs; when the use is culinary, they can be considered as spices; but it is not always easy to draw the line. The regulations of the Food and Drug Administration stipulate that a product that is being sold as a food or a nutritional supplement is limited as to the health benefits that can be claimed to result from its use. On the other hand, the cost of testing drugs, which tends to be in the millions or tens of millions of dollars, is prohibitive for herb companies, which tend to be relatively small as compared to the huge pharmaceutical conglomerates. This puts herb companies in a bind. Some, aware that the FDA usually takes several years before they will catch up with a company, choose to go ahead without scientific proof of the efficacy of their product.

If the mainstream health industry were to consider the health properties of herbs more seriously, there would not be this problem. Traditional Western medicine in this country has long been prejudiced against herbs. In no other country is this the case to such an extreme. In one recent case, for example, an internationally renowned scientist, Dr. Bruce Halstead, M.D., was sentenced to eight years in prison for prescribing an unapproved drug when he recommended herbal teas that enhance the immune system to his cancer patients. In less industrialized, less wealthy nations, there tends to be a greater acceptance of medicinal herbs. In part, this is due simply to economics. In many countries, if you are poor, your health care will depend largely on medicinal herbs because industrial medicine is only for those who can afford it. Recently, one of China's leading cancer researchers, Dr. Sun Yan, was invited to the University of Texas to perform a three-year study of two prominent Chinese herbs that enhance the immune system. Both are used in China to help bolster the immune systems of patients that have undergone chemotherapy and radiation therapy. Perhaps the willingness to test the herbs is a sign that the attitude in this country is changing. But there are few other signs. And it is all too characteristic that while America is one of the world's foremost producers of the renowned herb ginseng, 98 percent of the American crop is exported to the orient, and in this country its properties remain relatively unknown.

Were conventional health practitioners to include herbal medicine in their training and the delivery of health care, a significant improvement could occur almost immediately in the quality of medicine available to patients. In particular, the problem of iatrogenic (doctor-induced) illness, would be substantially reduced. The side effects of synthetic drugs are often substantial: The medicines we take frequently make us sicker. In many patient care situations, if medicinal herbs were used, there would be little or no side effects.

8 · FOOD ALLERGIES

"Environmental medicine experts say that one reason people are developing sensitivities to certain foods is their widespread occurrence in our diets in both the natural and processed forms. Just because you only rarely treat yourself to corn on the cob, for example, doesn't mean you're not eating corn every day. On a typical day you might eat corn flakes, a corn muffin, and processed food products containing both corn starch and corn syrup. Also, many of the daily vitamin C supplements are derived from corn."

IT IS A CLASSIC case of overreaction. Your body incorrectly senses that the food that has just been eaten is a foreign substance to be repelled. Cells begin to exhibit diseaselike symptoms as they react and overreact to the food.

Allergists conservatively estimate that up to 15 percent of the population suffers from a minimum of one allergy, frequently one that is serious enough to warrant medical attention.

Symptoms can range from a mild tension headache or irritablility to criminal actions and full-blown psychotic behavior. Most common are fatigue, headache, insomnia, rapid mood swings, confusion, depression, anxiety, hyperactivity, heart palpitations, muscle aches and joint pains, bed wetting, rhinitis (nasal inflammation), urticaria (hives), shortness of breath, diarrhea, and constipation. Reactions can be immediate following exposure to the allergen or delayed for many hours after contact.

Allergic symptoms are so diverse that the reactions can occur in virtually any organ in the body. Reactions in the brain or central nervous system may lead to behavioral changes and to paranoia or depression. A response in the gastrointestinal tract may translate into bloating, diarrhea, or constipation. Different food combinations can cause multiple reactions in the same person. If a person has an allergy to wheat that manifests itself in the brain, while their gastrointestinal tract is sensitive to milk, they may experience both fatigue and irritable bowel syndrome from a breakfast of whole wheat toast and milk.

Medical literature is filled with case studies in which children experience irritability, hyperactivity, insomnia, lack of concentration, poor memory, fatigue, and lethargy. After isolating and omitting all of the allergens from their diets, these sensitive children often improve. Not only do their physical symptoms clear up, but their behavioral imbalances also return to normal. With the control of the allergy, a normal personality is gradually established and maintained.

Read ingredient labels when buying food. All forms of a potentially offensive food can cause an allergic reaction, not just the whole form. Corn sugars and syrup, including dextrose and glucose, for example, will cause symptoms in many corn-sensitive patients. In many instances, researchers find, corn sugars will cause a more immediate reaction than will corn starch or corn as a vegetable.

Environmental medicine experts say that one reason people are developing sensitivities to certain foods is their widespread occurrence in our diets in both the natural and processed forms. Just because you only rarely treat yourself to corn on the cob, for example, doesn't mean you're not eating corn every day. On a typical day you might eat corn flakes, a corn muffin, and processed food products containing both corn starch and corn syrup. Also, many of the daily vitamin C supplements are derived from corn.

ALLERGIES AND HEREDITY, STRESS, AND PHYSICAL IMBALANCE

You can inherit allergic sensitivities. If both parents suffer from allergies, their children have at least a 75 percent chance of inheriting a predisposition to this hypersensitivity. When one parent is allergic, the chances of an inherited allergy remain as high as 50 percent. The child does not have to inherit the same allergic response. What is inherited is a genetic makeup that is more likely to have allegic reactions in general. For example, the mother may have chronic indigestion while the child's allergy manifests itself as acne. A mother may be sensitive to corn while her child is sensitive to yeast. Infants can develop allergies to the same foods as their mothers while still in the womb, through the placenta, or through breast milk after birth.

COMMON FOOD ALLERGENS AND TYPES OF FOOD ALLERGIES

The foods we eat most frequently are also the most common causes of allergies. These include milk, wheat, corn, eggs, beef, citrus fruits, potatoes, tomatoes, and coffee.

Food allergies fall into several categories.

- **The fixed food allergy**

    Each time you consume a specific food, you react. For example, whenever you eat beef, a reaction occurs.

- **The cyclic allergy**

    This is the most prevalent type of allergy. It occurs when you've had an abundance of a particular food. If exposure to the food can be reduced to no more than once every four days, little or no reaction occurs. The food, in other words, can be infrequently tolerated in small amounts. So, in a cyclic allergy, a person can remain symptom-free as long as he or she eats the offending food infrequently.

    Of course, other factors can influence the degree of this sensitivity. Infection, emotional stress, fatigue and overeating can increase susceptibility. The condition of the food (raw or cooked, fresh or packaged) may also be an important factor. Pollution, the presence of other environmental allergens, or marked environmental temperature change can also help trigger or subdue a reaction.

    A food eaten by itself may be tolerated. But if it is combined with other foods at the same meal, an allergic response may develop. The length and severity of the symptoms will depend in part on how long the allergens remain in your body after ingestion.

- **The addictive allergic reaction**

Here the person craves the foods they're allergic to. In essence, he or she becomes addicted to it. When the individual is made to go without the food, depression and other withdrawallike effects may appear. Moreover, eating the food may momentarily alleviate the symptoms, only to aggravate them later. Over time, the symptoms of the addictive allergy may grow increasingly complex.

This type of allergy often remains hidden or masked—even to the individual who is suffering from the problem. Because of its insidious nature, the person never suspects that the foods that seem to alleviate their symptoms might contain substances to which they're allergic, since they usually feel better right after eating them.

But allergies do not always fit neatly into one of the three categories. A fixed allergy in infancy can develop into an addictive allergic reaction later in life. Milk is a good example of such a food. When first introduced to a baby, it may cause an acute reaction in the form of hives or spitting up. However, if the parents don't recognize this as an allergic reaction and continue to keep milk in the diet, the symptoms may take on a more generalized and less obvious form.

What is first experienced by the body as an acute reaction will finally—in the body's attempt to adapt by assimilating the new foreign substance—lead to more chronic symptoms such as arthritis, fatigue, depression, or headaches.

For example, if you eat milk or milk products every day, symptoms of allergic reactions may blur with your natural personality traits and may become an accepted, even unnoticed part of your everyday life.

Eventually, you may develop a chronic condition, like arthritis, migraines, or depression. Your daily dose of milk would never be suspect at this stage. Your body has upped its tolerance levels in trying to adapt. At the same time, milk's harmful effects have been subtly registered. You keep on with a daily dose of milk, your own substance for abuse, to keep withdrawal symptoms at bay. Acute reactions are gone—except when the milk is withdrawn completely. Chronic reactions have replaced them.

Hidden or masked food allergies, no different from allergies generally, tend to be to the very foods we eat most frequently. In the United States, dairy products, including milk and eggs, are high on the list. Corn, wheat and potatoes are also common allergens, as is beef. Yeast, which occurs in many foods, is often at cause. Finally, many people have a hidden allergy to coffee. Considering that coffee is also an addictive substance and that Americans often drink it all day long (over 100 billion cups consumed annually), it is astounding to contemplate the overall adverse health effects of this one substance alone.

REDUCING THE ALLERGIC THRESHOLD

Most food allergies can be traced to an impaired digestive system. Proper digestion requires that the body secretes sufficient hydrochloric acid and pancreatic enzymes into the stomach to process foods. These substances break down large protein molecules into small molecules so they can be absorbed and utilized. When too few digestive juices or enzymes are secreted, the large protein molecules go directly into the bloodstream. The immune system reacts to these large molecules as if they were foreign invaders—the allergic response. To alleviate these allergies, we must set our nutritional house in order. Nutritional deficiencies and digestive imbalances must be corrected.

In addition, all the other stresses that can affect a person's "allergic threshold" should be reduced or eliminated as much as possible. These include environmental stresses such as air, water, and food pollution; inhalants such as perfume, aerosol hair spray, or room freshener; and emotional stress. The more healthful the physical and mental environment, the greater are our chances for achieving and maintaining a state of well-being.

In most cases, the more severe a person's food sensitivity becomes, the more numerous the allergens that induce it. One clinical study reported that the average person suffering from hay hever was allergic to five foods as well. A total picture of your allergen exposure, environment, habits, and history are vital for effective treatment.

The end result of repeated or prolonged sensitization of the body by recurrent allergic reactions is termed *breakdown*—the point at which diseaselike symptoms appear. They may be erroneously diagnosed as the onset of an illness. But the biochemical breakdown, although it manifests itself suddenly, was actually initiated years before by prolonged exposure to allergens.

ALLERGIES AND ENVIRONMENTAL POLLUTION

Environmental pollution may play a role in food allergies by pushing already hypersensitive individuals over their allergic thresholds. Over the past two centuries the barrage of chemicals introduced into our environment has disrupted the balance of our ecosystem. Residues of many toxic chemicals such as pesticides, herbicides, and insecticides are ingested into our bodies along with food additives and preservatives that are added during commercial food processing.

In many cases, the contamination of food is an irreversible result. Foods such as oranges, sweet potatoes, and butter can be dyed. Other processed and packaged goods like Jell-O, ice cream, sherbet, cookies, candy, and soda can contain large amounts of food additives.

Most of our commercially raised meats and poultry are riddled with residues of antibiotics, tranquilizers, and hormones. It is even common practice to dip certain fish in an antibiotic solution to retard their spoilage. A person allergic to these antibiotics and drugs may be unknowingly ingesting them continuously, provoking either long-term or short-term reactions or illnesses, the source of which might remain unidentified. It is estimated that more than 10 percent of all Americans are sensitive to food additives. But remember, even when a person eats only organically grown foods, they may still be food allergic.

THE MECHANISMS OF ALLERGY

Conventional allergists believe that the mechanism of food allergy is triggered by direct contact of the food antigens—the substances the body produces to fight the "foreign food invader"—with immune system antibodies in the gastrointestinal tract. The usually swift reaction that results is called an immune system-mediated response. This is the only kind of allergic reaction that conventional allergists recognize.

But there is a second mechanism recognized by clinical ecologists, through the absorption of the allergen from the gastrointestinal tract into the bloodstream. Circulating in the blood, allergens can react with elements other than antibodies. The resulting reaction can occur in the blood, in the nervous system, or the musculoskeletal system. Sometimes referred to as a sensitivity or intolerance, to distinguish it from a classic allergic reaction, this second mechanism can be extremely complex. However, tests to uncover these more subtle intolerances are available and are discussed in the next chapter, "Food Allergy Testing and Treatment."

Hypersensitivity to foods can come at any time of life and continue to any age, although the onset occurs most commonly in infancy and early childhood. This is largely because the gastrointestinal systems of the very young are less efficient than in the adult. One researcher refers to the progression of allergies from childhood to adulthood as the "allergic march." Symptoms can move from one organ system to another. A child may suffer from asthma as a result of drinking milk. During teen years the allergy may take the form of pimples. Unfortunately, many people erroneously believe that they have outgrown their allergy because they no longer suffer from the original symptom. They don't consider that their current problems may have the same underlying cause. Their allergic symptoms may continue to vary throughout their lives because of an underlying imbalance that remains constant. Hyperactivity as a child may be the result of ingested food additives. In later years, these same ingredients may cause migraines and fatigue.

FOOD ALLERGIES AND MENTAL HEALTH

If food and chemical sensitivities were routinely considered in each case of chronic disease, there would be a tremendous increase in well-being in this country.

An overly analytical medical system insists instead on classifying patients into narrowly defined disease states. Environmental aspects, including a patient's diet, are considered to be nonmedical. The person's whole experience—including diet, environment, life-style, emotional life, and work life—may also be considered to be outside the physician's domain, although few physicians would deny that the cause of almost any patient's illness will involve one or more of these factors to some degree.

It may be that up to 70 percent of symptoms diagnosed as psychosomatic are probably due to some undiagnosed reaction to foods, chemicals, or inhalants. Different allergic reactions occur. There are localized physical effects like gastrointestinal disorders, eczema, asthma and rhinitis (nasal inflammation). There are acute systemic effects like fatigue, migraine headaches, neuralgia, muscle aches, joint pains, and other generalized symptoms. And there are acute mental effects such as depression, rapid mood swings, hallucinations, delusions, and other behavioral abnormalities.

It has been estimated that over 90 percent of schizophrenics have food and chemical intolerances. More specifically, 64 percent are sensitive to wheat; 51 percent to corn; 51 percent to cow's milk; 75 percent to tobacco; and 30 percent to petrochemical hydrocarbons.

Researchers now believe that food allergies may directly affect the body's nervous system by causing a noninflammatory swelling of the brain, which can trigger aggression. Despite studies at various correctional centers showing clearly the connection between diet and behavior, little is being done to change the dietary standards of correctional facilities throughout the nation. Routine screening programs for food allergies and nutritional deficiencies in chronic offenders do not exist.

While many other factors—not food alone—mitigate criminal, antisocial behavior, or mental illness, a case can be made for testing for and evaluating food sensitivities in any overall treatment, prevention, or rehabilitation program.

FOOD ALLERGIES AND MIGRAINE HEADACHES

Migraines are an example of a condition in which recognition and elimination of food allergens can make a tremendous difference. The trick is to recognize the possibilities.

Right now, about 25 million people who consult their physicians each year complain about bad headaches. Although there are various types of headaches, about 50 percent of these people suffer from migraines.

Migraine sufferers usually experience pain on only one side of the head, lasting from several hours up to several days. (The word migraine means "half head.") Migraine sufferers average two headaches per month interspersed with symptom-free periods between attacks. While conventional medicine has very little to offer the migraine sufferer, clinical ecologists see migraine as a disorder frequently resulting from food allergies. The nontraditional medicine offered by the clinical ecologist may offer a unique opportunity to relieve the suffering.

Headaches due to food or chemical sensitivities often can be treated simply by eliminating the allergy, once it has been identified, with an elimination or rotary diet. (See Chapter 9, "Food Allergy Testing and Treatment.") Yet, as a rule, food sensitivities are not investigated in the diagnosis and treatment of headaches.

Today, the theory favored by environmental medicine specialists to explain how allergy-related migraines may occur describes an antigen-antibody reaction, initiated by an allergen, and starting as an immune reaction in the tissues where antibodies are localized. The allergic reaction induces the release of chemical mediators like histamine and noradrenalin. The excruciating pain associated with migraines occurs as a direct result of the allergic response: The antigen-antibody reaction affects the temporal arteries in the skull, causing the vessels to expand, with resultant thinning of the vessel walls and subsequent fluid leakage. As a result of the edema (fluid retention), the brain begins to swell, pressing against the inflexible skull structure. The intense pain is mainly due to the stretching of surrounding sensitive tissues in the area of the swelling.

While the pain may sometimes appear immediately after eating a particular food, it may also be delayed until hours afterwards. For this reason it is not unusual for a person to fail to identify the correlation between what they're eating and the onset of their headache. A food may even seem to relieve migraine symptoms temporarily—a classic example of an addictive allergic reaction.

Of course, allergic headaches typically occur as the result of combinations of factors, rather than from food allergies alone. Emotional stress, for example, may play a large role in triggering an episode. Thus, even when a food allergy is at cause, the specific food source may not produce the same symptoms on every occasion, depending on the array of associated circumstantial factors. In some individuals stress may be compounded when the allergic reaction triggers further emotional symptoms. A vicious cycle is created. Sudden changes in temperature or light may also affect one's susceptibility, as well as the presence of any other health problems.

Environmental medicine specialists have found that some of the foods that occur most frequently in the typical American diet are also the foods most commonly implicated in food allergy-related headaches. The list includes wheat, eggs, milk, chocolate, corn, pork, cinnamon, legumes (beans, peas, peanuts, and soybeans), and fish. Moreover, individuals with food allergies should avoid or limit their intake of fermented products like red wine, champagne, and aged cheese because of the presence in these foods of a substance called tyramine. Tyramine has been associated with migraine occurence in some cases.

Childhood Migraines

Children suffering from migraine tend to be sensitive, nervous, and temperamental, with various behavior disturbances as common predisposing factors. Preceding the actual attack, the child may be noticeably lethargic and may refuse to eat, possibly complaining of abdominal discomfort as well. Often, the child's temperature is elevated and may gradually rise to as high as 104°F. during an attack. This fever may draw attention away from the diagnosis of migraine in favor of a diagnosis of acute infection, especially when other symptoms are present, such as abdominal pain, nausea, and vomiting. Acute appendicitis may be erroneously suspected. The array of symptoms typical of migraines in children are often misdiagnosed, particularly as these differ substantially (especially with respect to the prodrome) from adult symptoms.

Migraine headaches, unfortuanetly, are not uncommon in childhood or even in infancy. And while migraine sufferers most can most often trace the onset of the headaches to the period of early adulthood, early symptoms occur during childhood in nearly one-third of cases.

Children five years of age and under often suffer from what are called "allergic syndromes," sometimes involving bronchial asthma with migraine symptoms as a secondary condition.

In the vast majority of childhood cases of migraine, hereditary factors seem to be present—with a close relative also having migraines.

In addition to food allergies, a variety of other factors may precipitate a migraine attack during childhood, including: sleeplessness, irregular meals, fatigue, extended exposure to bright sunlight and visual stimulation (e.g., movies or television).

In many cases a particular food or group of foods will be at cause. If so, the best way to identify that food will be by means of an elimination diet—and not by the standard skin tests. Among children, the most common sources of food allergies include chocolate, milk, wheat, eggs, and pork. In one recent study, over 90 percent of the children tested with severe frequent migraines recovered after following strict elimination diets. Moreover, the secondary symptoms from which the children also suffered, including asthma, eczema, abdominal discomfort, and behavioral disorders also improved.

Too often, conventional medical practitioners tend not to look toward nutritional solutions in cases involving allergies, including allergy-related migraines. In part, this is because the medical training they have received does not extend deeply into nutrition. And yet, a preponderance of evidence continues to point to the importance of nutritional solutions for an increasingly wide range of health problems.

FOOD ALLERGIES AND FATIGUE

Probably no allergic disorder is more puzzling and pervasive than "tension fatigue syndrome." Indeed, for many of us, varying daily levels of tension and fatigue are the norm; tranquility and energy, the rare exceptions. To compensate, we choose artificial solutions for moderating energy, from the first caffeinated gulps of coffee in the morning to the quick sugar, caffeine, or drug fix during the day, and the alcoholic "equalizer" in the evening. The result is that energy levels are either depressed or falsely elevated most of the time. In many cases, these quick pick-me-ups are responses to allergic disorders with their roots in food and nutrition.

Next to headaches, tension fatigue syndrome is the most common manifestation of cerebral and nervous system allergy. Yet, too often, this far-reaching malady is not even recognized by physicians or allergists.

Its symptoms are usually assigned a psychiatric origin and treated with drug therapy or some other conventional modality, when in fact, a simple elimination and rotation diet is the best medicine.

There are several reasons for this all too common oversight. First, there are similarities between tension fatigue syndrome and psychiatric disorders. And second, there is the failure of standard scratch tests to identify many food and chemical reactions. The scratch tests simply have not been shown to be effective in the diagnosis of food and chemical sensitivities. And yet they continue to be used by allergists.

Of course, tension, extreme nervousness, irritability, depression, and emotional instability may be symptoms of psychological disorders in some cases. But too often this is the only possibility that is considered by conventional practitioners. In too many cases, the end result is that a psychological origin is erroneously attributed while the actual physical cause remains unrecognized and the chronic allergic reactions persist.

The allergy may be due to any number of foods, and it is only through careful testing that a definitive diagnosis can be made. In all cases where such symptoms appear, food allergies should be ruled out first—before further traditional medical sleuthing occurs. This can save an awful lot of trouble and mistaken diagnoses.

Early research has suggested that an allergic syndrome may be responsible for certain nervous symptoms in adults and children by actually irritating the central nervous system. Thus, if certain allergies act directly on the nervous system, they can cause characteristic behaviorial and physical abnormalities.

Tension fatigue syndrome in a child is sometimes caused by an inhalant sensitivity; however, it is more often due to an unrecognized food intolerance. Reactions to food commonly occur along with other allergic disorders like migraine and asthma, or they can also occur alone.

The symptoms experienced in tension fatigue syndrome can include fatigue, weakness, lack of energy and ambition, drowsiness, mental sluggishness, inability to concentrate, bodily aches, poor memory, irritability, fever, chills and night sweats, nightmares, restlessness, insomnia, and emotional instability. Mental depression is another common symptom, ranging from mild to severe episodes of despondency and melancholia. Generalized muscle aches and pains, especially in the back of the neck or in the back and thigh muscles may also be present, as well as edema (fluid retention), particularly around the eye, and tachycardia (rapid heart beat). Gastrointestinal symptoms often associated with this syndrome are bloating, abdominal cramps or pain, constipation, diarrhea, and a coated tongue. Chills and perspiration are also frequently experienced in association with fatigue during food testing of symptomatic patients.

The disorder can begin at any age. It can last from several months to several decades. In some adults the extreme fatigue, bodily aches, depression, and mental aberrations that come from this continuing allergic state can be so severe that they interfere with work and domestic life.

As headache attacks or gastrointestinal upset caused by allergy increase in frequency, the fatigue is more likely to remain even between episodes. Fatigue soon becomes the allergic individual's major complaint. The allergic origin of the fatigue and weakness associated with migraines or gastrointestinal and respiratory disorders commonly remains a mystery.

It's not unusual for allergic individuals to sleep up to 15 or more hours for several successive nights to try to overcome their fatigue. Unfortunately, in most cases, these efforts prove futile. The fatigue experienced in allergic fatigue is quite different from the fatigue that naturally follows physical exertion. It cannot be relieved by normal or even excessive amounts of rest. It can only be relieved by eliminating its cause—the allergen.

Instead, the majority of these allergic individuals, many of whom have often sought a variety of medical avenues for relief, are eventually labeled neurotics.

What causes the syndrome? Before the diagnosis of allergic fatigue can be definite, a complete medical workup should be done to exclude both organic and functional origins. This should include a comprehensive case history, complete physical examination and diagnostic laboratory blood testing. Other causes for nervous fatigue include chronic infections and metabolic disorders, including diabetes, hypoglycemia, hypothyroidism, neurological disorders, heart disease, anemia, malignancy, and various nutrient deficiencies. Even if another disease is found, allergic fatigue can be still be a causal factor. In some cases, fatigue is caused both by an allergic reaction and an underlying chronic disease state.

The Monday Morning Blahs

It is common for people to binge over the weekend on foods to which they are sensitive. This destructive habit is all too often responsible for the Monday morning blahs. If you are feeling blue by coffee break on Monday, sit down and examine what you've eaten during the previous days. Clinical ecologists suggest that rotary diets may help pinpoint food allergies in patients complaining of fatigue when no other cause is obvious. Very often, patterns of stomach upset will disappear following a careful dietary change, and once the new diet has been maintained over a period of several weeks, fatigue and muscle weakness will be replaced by increased amounts of high energy.

FOOD ALLERGIES AND OBESITY

Many obese men and women believe that they are overweight due to heredity, or because they have a thyroid or metabolic problem, or because they simply eat too much. They may blame their lack of self-control or become convinced that they have psychological problems. And yet, some experts believe that roughly two out of every three obese individuals suffer from some form of allergy.

Of course, allergy may be only one of several factors affecting an obese person's weight. The presence of a thyroid condition or psychological problems can cause or aggravate a weight problem. Obesity is also related to many diseases including high blood pressure, heart disease, kidney problems, and diabetes. For obese individuals with allergies, the problems of each condition may adversely affect the other. Typically, someone who is obese will have allergic responses more often than his or her nonobese counterpart. The extra weight is a burden on the immune system, and the weaker the immune system, the more one may be affected by one's allergies. Obese individuals also may have increased difficulty breathing, with particularly severe implications for allergic persons with asthma. In many cases, problems will occur due to allergies in combination with other factors.

We store chemicals in the body in fat. Very often, allergies are triggered by a response to chemicals stored in this way. Because the obese person may naturally hold more chemicals in the body, he or she may tend to experience more frequent allergic responses. This also may explain why he or she feels worse, or has strong food cravings, at the beginning of a diet. Chemicals are stored in fat, and as the fat is burned, a large quantity of chemicals is passed into the blood stream, often causing such cravings.

The mechanism by which an allergy can trigger obesity may be that of the hidden addictive allergy, whereby a person is addicted to the very foods to which they are allergic. Often, these are high calorie foods, such as chocolate, cheese, or sugar. So, they may gain weight because they eat these high calorie foods too frequently.

Hunger itself can be an allergic response and compulsive eating and intense cravings for particular foods may also result from hidden allergies. In some cases, compulsive eating of the food one is allergic to may really be an attempt to stave off withdrawallike symptoms induced by going without the food for too long. Such withdrawal symptoms might include headaches, drowsiness, irritability, or depression.

Dr. Marshall Mandell, a physician who has written extensively on dietary problems, also notes that some individuals may experience specific food cravings because they know that particuar foods have a short-term positive effect on their mood, or provide them with a quick boost of energy. Such positive changes are only short-lived and are usually followed by a drop of energy, a feeling of fatigue, or some other negative mood change such as depression.

Allergies can cause weight problems if they interfere with the body's natural ability to regulate itself. As noted by Dr. Arthur Kaslow, physician and author, both humans and animals naturally attempt to maintain their bodies in a state of biochemical equilibrium known as homeostasis. Unless there is a flaw in their regulatory system, human beings will maintain their proper weight by eating the amounts and types of foods their bodies need to function properly. When the body needs food, it will send out a hunger signal. When it needs water, it sends out a thirst signal. If this mechanism breaks down, an individual may feel hungry when he or she does not really need food. It is possible that allergies can temporarily impair the cells responsible for sending out these signals.

As noted by several experts, including Drs. Marshall Mandell and Thomas Stone, another way that allergies can affect an individual's weight is by causing edema (fluid retention). The edema may be localized to specific parts of the body, such as the ankles, hands, abdomen, or face, or it can spread throughout the body. When it is evenly distributed through-out the body, the individual often doesn't realize it, and therefore, doesn't think that fluid retention has anything to do with the weight problem. Eating food to which one is allergic can cause water retention equal to 4 percent of total body weight.

Edema occurs when an allergen in a food to which the individual is allergic causes some of the body's capillary (small blood vessel) pores to enlarge. The fluid from the blood plasma may then seep into neighboring tissues. These tissues swell with this excess fluid. When the allergen leaves the body, the capillaries return to their proper size. But if the individual continually ingests the allergen, he or she will always have this excess fluid in the tissues, significantly affecting the weight problem.

A way to determine the possible role of edema in a person's weight problem is to try to have that person recall whether he or she ever lost more that $3^1/_2$ pounds on a reducing diet for a week. That is the largest amount you can burn up even if you were only drinking water. If a larger weight loss ever occured, edema may have been the cause.

Any initial weight loss on typical reducing diets occurs largely because the diet may eliminate food to which the individual is allergic. For exam-ple, if the individual is sensitive to sugar, and the diet restricts the intake of dessert foods, the individual will lose weight beyond that lost from calorie reductions. He or she would lose the extra water retained due to the sugar allergy as part of the edema. Allergic edema would also explain how some individuals can diet and still not lose much weight. This may happen because some food allergen is still in the diet—causing excessive fluid retention and leading to edema.

The orthodox treatment for weight loss is to go on a calorie restricted diet. But be forewarned! This diet may not work if allergic edema is playing a part in contributing to the weight problem. Even the depression many people experience on a standard reducing diet may be allergy re-lated.

An alternative dieting approach is to suggest that the individual initially follow a diet that is well balanced. Then a clinical ecologist can determine which foods or chemicals, if any, are causing any continued weight problems, and have them avoid those substances. A rotation diet may then be introduced to ensure that new sensitivities do not develop.

To help handle food craving in the short term, exercise is highly recommended. It can increase blood flow, bringing needed nutrients to the cells. It can also calm one's mood. Vitamin C as well as vitamin B_6 can also be useful in blocking allergic reactions.

FOOD ALLERGIES AND ARTHRITIS

Arthritis, or joint inflammation, affects over 50 million Americans and the disease is on the rise. While physicians have identified over 100 types of arthritis, two of the most common are rheumatoid arthritis and osteoarthritis.

Osteoarthritis alone affects over 16 million individuals. It is a condition that usually affects only a few joints in the body. The cartilage in the affected joints becomes rough-edged, and may begin to wear away. Grating sounds in the joint may even be heard.

Rheumatoid arthritis is usually considered a chronic condition. It mainly affects women between the ages of 20 and 40. While it may begin with only mild symptoms, it can become severe and even disabling. The most common joints affected are those in the hands, feet, arms, hips, and legs. Rheumatoid arthritis can also affect connective tissue throughout the body. Other conditions may occur in association with rheumatoid arthritis, including chronic fever, tiredness, poor appetite, weight loss, anemia, and enlarged glands and spleen.

The orthodox medical treatment of arthritis relies heavily on the use of drugs. Americans currently spend $2 billion per year on arthritis drugs. While these drugs may be useful, many also have serious accompanying side effects.

The Clinical Ecologist's Approach to Arthritis

Clinical ecologists take a different approach from that of conventional medicine. Some clinical ecologists estimate that from 80 to 90 percent of all cases of arthritis are either allergy induced or are allergylike reactions to some food the patient has eaten. The arthritis may also be related to an environmental factor to which the patient is sensitive, such as gas inhaled from constant proximity to a gas stove. Examining arthritics for both food and environmental allergies may help reduce current symptoms, prevent recurrences of symptoms and minimize the permanent damage that eventually results from joint inflammations.

Studies have shown that, in some cases, arthritic symptoms will lessen if a patient fasts. (Most food allergy symptoms will clear up during a four-day fast.) Studies also report that after arthritis patients fast, the symptoms may reappear if certain foods are eaten. The most frequent foods that caused the reactions were corn, wheat, and meat.

As is true with other food allergy problems, no one specific food causes arthritic symptoms in all patients. Some patients may be allergic to tomatoes while others are allergic to strawberries, wine, or grapefruits. Elimination of the food source from the diet can become an integral part of any treatment program.

For osteoarthritis, there are other factors to be considered. Usually, osteoarthritis is related to a calcium imbalance. Therefore, the imbalance must also be examined and taken into account. Because calcium is deposited in the joints in osteoarthritis, many people assume that the body has too much calcium, while actually the reverse is usually true. While the lack of calcium may be due to a dietary deficiency, it is also often due to a digestive problem. In such cases, the body is not properly handling the calcium it takes in. Therefore, the calcium is deposited in places where it does not belong. Such patients may need supplemental calcium. Vitamin D and vitamin C may also be suggested, since they can aid in calcium absorption by the body.

Dr. Marshall Mandell, a clinical ecologist in Bridgeport, Connecticut, has successfully treated hundreds of arthritis patients by putting them on a five-day distilled water fast and then allowing their usual foods, one at a time, back into their diet. If a food causes the arthritis symptoms, the symptoms will return when it is reintroduced into the diet and should be permanently eliminated.

This 5-day elimination diet can be adapted to allow individuals a way of self-testing specific foods: Keep a food out of your diet for five days, then reintroduce it. If it causes your problems to recur, eliminate it.

9 · FOOD ALLERGY TESTING AND TREATMENT

"Plan a diet in which you eat no individual food more often than once in four days. After five days, start a food and symptom diary. After reviewing correlations that may crop up through your record keeping, eat any suspected food the next time it comes up in the four-day rotation alone as one full meal. Note symptoms. Eliminate foods that stimulate adverse symptoms from your diet— permanently."

EVERY PERSON IS BIOCHEMICALLY and structurally complex and unique. Obviously, not all disorders have their roots in allergies. Therefore, a change in diet isn't always effective.

However, our environment—including the foods we eat—are responsible for more physical and emotional ill health than most health professionals and the general public realize. Approximately 30 million Americans are estimated to have food and chemical sensitivities.

So proper testing and treatment of these individuals could have an enormous impact on our individual well-being and on society overall. Some techniques for such testing have been around for some time. Other tests are just evolving. The same is true of treatments for those with food allergies.

Patient experience is most important in diagnosing allergies. Environmental medicine specialists now are highlighting the role the allergic individual can and must play in diagnosing and treating his or her own ailment. Articles written in the 1930s reporting the lack of attention paid to the patient regarding their condition could very well be republished in the 1980s. Unfortunately, very few physicians acknowledged this advice in the past, and few acknowledge it today.

TRADITIONAL TESTING

The most common test performed by the traditional allergist is one that really has very little use when seeking food allergies. Still, it is often used. Working well for dust, pollen, mold, animal hair, and insect stings, this is the classic scratch test. The doctor makes 10 to 20 scratches on a patient's arm, using a needle imbedded with the problematical substance being tested. If there is a reaction on the skin, it indicates a sensitivity. But this test picks up reactions only to allergens that stimulate a specific immune response in the body and detects only certain types of antibodies produced by the body with that defensive response.

Another test, developed in the1960s, relies on screening blood samples. Called the radio-allergo sorbant test, RAST for short, this test is much more expensive to perform than the scratch test and can have more false positives and false negatives.

NONTRADITIONAL TESTING

A comprehensive medical history might provide significant clues about your allergic profile. A trained clinical ecologist or environmental medicine specialist may find the needed information from such a medical history alone.

Clinical ecologists also use a skin test, evaluating different-sized doses of a questionable substance. The diluted substance is injected into the skin. After 20 minutes, the physician checks for redness and swelling, measuring the size of the skin raised by the suspected allergen. Progressively larger doses of the same suspected substance are administered in this way until the size of the skin reaction no longer increases. All the while, the patient writes down any other symptoms he or she may be experiencing, like headache, stuffy nose, or nausea.

Physicians can use this approach to determine the size of a particular dose of an allergen that might trigger a reaction, or counteract it. It is therefore useful in testing and in treatment.

While this approach has its advantages, it is time-consuming, expensive, somewhat painful, and can test only the part of the food that can be diluted in water. Other parts of the food (that are fat soluble, for instance) may be at cause that will not respond to the test.

A similar test takes another approach, putting extracts of food mixed with glycerin under the tongue, instead of into the skin by injection. While this test is not painful, it also can be time-consuming and expensive.

Another test, employing a technique called applied kinesiology, is based on the principle that there is a reflex response between a suspected allergen and the patient's body, in the patient's muscles. In this test, a doctor offers food to the patient and then measures or evaluates the energy or muscle function after the food is ingested. Here many foods can be tested in each session. However, the results may not be highly accurate, depending on the nature and experience of both the person administering the test and the person being tested.

Newer tests are being developed all the time. Some, like the cytotoxic test, mix blood samples with food extracts and measure how many white blood cells (cells involved in the body's natural defensive system) burst. In allergy smears, samples of different body fluids or secretions are evaluated in the laboratory to look for a specific type of white blood cell. The various immune system cells may also be evaluated. And in the Arest program, radioactive atoms are used to determine how antibodies respond to particular antigens.

There are also less technical tests, some of which can even be done at home. A fasting test, which should be done under medical supervision, begins by cleansing your system. Symptoms may still be present or, if your allergy is an addiction of some sort, may have worsened by the second or third day of the fast. Then foods are reintroduced one at a time to check for symptoms. This test should not be done for certain already ill patients, the elderly, the hypoglycemic, or young children.

Another test that can be performed at home is the Coca Pulse test. First find your normal pulse range, by taking it every two hours. Then take it again at specific, regular intervals after eating the suspected allergen. If your pulse rises more than 10 points, the food eaten last becomes suspect. The pulse is rising as a reaction to increased adrenalin in your system. The adrenalin, it is believed, usually is being released in reaction to an allergy.

Another home test involves keeping a food diary, and recording everything you eat for a week. Record symptoms and when they occur as well. After the week, look for a relationship between symptoms and food eaten.

Elimination testing is yet another approach. Eliminate the suspected allergen until symptoms clear up over a 12-day period. Reintroduce the food on an empty stomach. Usually symptoms, if they are to develop, will do so within an hour of testing.

A variation on that is the elimination of all common allergens—wheat, corn, dairy foods, citrus fruits, food colorings, sugar, and foods you may crave, over the course of a week. Then reintroduce the foods, one per day. If symptoms develop, the food may be an allergen. Don't eat it for five more days and then reintroduce it to double-check the result.

A final home test—perhaps among the most effective and sensible of all tests—also doubles as a treatment for food allergies. It is called the rotary diversified diet.

Plan a diet in which you eat no individual food more often than once in four days. After five days, start a food and symptom diary. After reviewing correlations that may crop up through your record keeping, eat any suspected food the next time it comes up in the four-day rotation alone as one full meal. Note symptoms. Eliminate foods that stimulate adverse symptoms from your diet—permanently.

The theory here is that food sensitivities become even more pronounced when a food is eliminated and then reintroduced into the diet. With this diet, your symptoms—and with them the responsible food—are clearly highlighted.

This approach is also useful as a maintenance diet, enabling food-allergy prone people to prevent the emergence of new allergies, since they never eat any food too frequently. And even then, if a new food allergy does develop, it is spotted and quickly eliminated.

TREATMENTS

Clinical ecologists offer an alternative to orthodox methods of treating disease. They test the whole person as they exist and react to their total environments.

Our understanding of allergies has been greatly expanded by the clinical ecologist. Because the traditional allergist only recognizes those allergies that are mediated by the immune system, he therefore can only treat a small portion of illnesses the clinical ecologist would classify as allergies. In addition, the traditional allergist has a limited number of alternatives to offer his patients. Other than avoidance of an allergic substance, the traditional allergist has only immunotherapy—"the allergy shot"—to rely on. With this, the physician administers guadually increasing increments of the substance to which the patient is allergic. It will usually take six months until the optimal dose, that is the dosage at which symptoms are blocked, is achieved. The theory is that the patient uses up his antigens on the allergy shot, and therefore has a higher threshold of response before he will respond badly to an allergen again.

The effectiveness of traditional immunotherapy may be limited only to those allergies directly related to the immune system response. Some experts believe this represents only 5 percent of all allergies. And even within this small group, there are some immune system-related allergies that do not respond to the treatment.

Traditional immunotherapy is not useful, for example, with food allergies or animal dander allergies. Nor is it always effective for dust allergies, for while the physician can desensitize the individual to specific particles that are components of dust, the patient may be allergic to other particles that were not in the allergy shot. And the treatment is a time-consuming process, with no results noticeable until the optimal dose is finally discovered.

THE ELIMINATION DIET

A technique that is used by many allergists that does seem to work on food allergies is the elimination diet. Employed for over 60 years, this plan removes the most commonly occurring food allergens from the diet along with any other foods suspected on the basis of case history or positive test results. In the process of eliminating foods, symptoms usually improve. After avoiding all suspected foods for five to seven days, one food at a time is reintroduced back into the diet. At this point, the patient and doctor observe any recurrence or worsening of symptoms. Some doctors introduce a new food at each meal, while others add only one food frequently for seven days before adding another. If an item causes a symptom, it is then avoided and once again introduced at a later date.

THE ROTARY DIVERSIFIED DIET

Clinical ecologists have improved upon the elimination diet by devising a combined diagnostic and preventive regimen called a rotary diversified diet. In it, certain foods may have to be totally avoided (if one has a fixed allergy), while some may be eaten every four to seven days without ill effects (if one suffers from a cyclic allergy). Rotation diets can be designed to deal with individual food sensitivities. But no food is eaten more frequently than every four days. Rotation diets also help to minimize the stress that preexisting allergens cause, at the same time preventing future sensitivities from developing. They are also valuable in diagnosing masked food allergies, since our bodies react acutely to allergens reintroduced after four to seven days of abstinence. Part Three of this book offers a unique rotary diet based on all these factors in combination with optimum nutrition and a gourmet palate.

Since most food allergies are cyclical rather than fixed allergies, that is they come and go in varying degrees of severity, a rotation diet is part of the treatment for many allergic patients. Foods to which the patient is sensitive are eliminated and the remaining foods are eaten no more frequently than once every four days. Foods you ate on Monday might be repeated on Friday or over the weekend, but not before. For some individuals who are highly sensitive, a 5-, 7- or even 12-day cycle may be necessary.

The rotation diet ensures against the development of new food sensitivities in a way that simply substituting one food for another does not. For example, if an individual was allergic to wheat, and eliminated it from his diet, but began to eat rice every day, he might develop a sensitivity to rice. Periodic retesting may be recommended several months after you've made the change to a rotation diet. By retesting your sensitivity to some of the eliminated foods, it may sometimes be possible to reintroduce them on a rotational basis.

A rotary diversified diet often also is recommended to check for obesity and edema (fluid retention) related allergies. Salt, sugar, and tap water is avoided. Then, for each week over a five-week period, the individual tests a common allergen such as dairy foods, wheat, corn, eggs, yeast, pork, soy products, chocolate, or apples. One would avoid each of these foods for four days. If, after five days, the individual has lost five or more pounds, which is then regained when the food is eaten, the test food should be considered an allergen and avoided for at least two months. Then, the food can be reintroduced on a rotational basis, checking to see that it is no longer causing problems. One can continue to test different foods throughout the five-week process.

When following a rotational diet, one should continue to weigh oneself daily, in order to check for edema. Once one has passed the withdrawal period, the avoidance of allergens and a rotation diet can help break food cravings and compulsive eating patterns.

NEUTRALIZING DOSE THERAPY

Another technique to treat allergies used by clinical ecologists is the neutralizing dose therapy. This method is especially useful in cases where avoidance of chemicals and medicinal inhalants is difficult, as during the pollen season, or when multiple food allergies are present. A neutralizing dose is determined for each allergen, and when it is injected or administered under the tongue, this dilution can bring about relief from the allergic symptoms.

These treatments are administered in a series during which the dose of the allergen is progressively increased, causing a desensitization to this substance. (They work on the same theory as allergy shots or vaccines. The only differences are in the dilution of the substance and the wide variety of the substances that can be tested in this way.) Eventually, the person can tolerate contact or ingestion of the allergen with only a mild reaction or no reaction at all.

With the neutralizing dose treatment, the allergist is first determining the amount of a particular allergen that causes a allergic reaction. The physician can work with many substances that the traditional allergist would be unable to treat, including foods, chemicals, perfumes, and cigarette smoke. The neutralizing dose approach seems to be effective in eight out of ten patients.

Like the traditional allergy shot, the neutralizing dose can be administered by injection. However, it can also be given as drops under the tongue. Instead of taking approximately six months to find the optimal dose, the physician can usually determine the correct dosage in one or two sessions using this technique. Another advantage of the neutralizing dose is that the patient can be given the drops to take at home. It not only works as a preventive measure, but also can block a reaction that has already started.

If a parent discovers that a child who is sensitive to wheat is acting hyperactively, and the parent finds out the child was given cookies at school, the parent can terminate the allergic response—the hyperactivity—by administering the drops. On the other hand, if a parent knows the child will be going to a birthday party and knows the child will most likely encounter an allergic food, the parent can administer the drops in advance to forestall an allergic reaction.

TOTAL ENVIRONMENTAL CONTROL

Elimination, rotation diets, and neutralizating dose therapy help in the diagnosis and treatment of many allergic disorders. However, for more serious problems that still resist such treatment, total environmental control in a hospital setting may be required.

This may be the case where the allergy is masked or the patient history reveals too little. A person's system can be cleared of all allergens in four to seven days. This is accomplished in the controlled hospital setting, by having patients fast on distilled water only for at least three days, then traditional tests are administered. The controlled environment also assures that they are not exposed to any environmental contaminants.

BOOSTING THE IMMUNE RESPONSE

Since allergies most often represent an immune system that has gone awry, another important aspect of treatment is finding ways to boost the patient's immune system.

Allergies occur when the immune system has been weakened. Therefore, any strengthening of the immune system should improve resistance to current allergies and reduce susceptibility to new ones. There are several ways in which the immune system may be strengthened. Making sure you are getting sufficient amounts of rest is essential, as is regular exercise. Keeping stress levels to a minimum will also help. You must also be receiving the right nutrients in the right amounts.

Many nutrients have been found to enhance the effectiveness of the immune system. These include vitamin C, beta carotene, vitamin E, selenium and glutathion. These are all antioxidants, which help to eliminate free radicals from the body.

Free radicals are highly reactive molecules created as a by-product during the process by which the body converts food into energy. They can easily latch on to cell membranes and DNA, causing cell damage. Free radicals also can develop from many sources, including X rays, heated vegetable oils and through exposure to ultraviolet light.

Garlic has been found to be an immune stimulant, having both antifungal and antibacterial qualities. Garlic is most effective when eaten raw. It may be either added to one's food or taken as a supplement in tablet or capsule form.

The essential fatty acids are also important to a proper immune response. Dr. Donald Rudin, along with other researchers, recognizes the importance of omega 3 fatty acids, which are found in such oils as linseed and walnut, and in many fatty fishes, like salmon, in warding off both diseases and allergies.

In addition to acting as immune stimulants, there may be other reasons why nutritional supplements may be useful for those with allergies. Dr.

Stuart Freyer has noted that 200 to 500 mg. of pantothenic acid plus 50 mg. of B complex vitamins can be useful for allergic individuals. Vitamin C, in addition to its importance as an antioxidant, also has an antihistamine effect, which may benefit those with allergies by reducing the swelling of tissue and cell membranes. One study found that asthmatics taking 1,000 mg. of Vitamin C daily had 25 percent fewer asthmatic attacks than those receiving a placebo. Another study found that asthmatic children benefited from magnesium supplementation.

STRESS MANAGEMENT

Since stress lowers the immune response, reducing stress should help in food allergy elimination. Stress management techniques are available, including progressive relaxation and biofeedback, to recondition the body to learn a new, more healthful way to respond to and deal with stress.

Many other techniques—from self-hypnosis and affirmations ("I have a healthy strong immune system") to visualizations (imagining immune system cells gobbling up invader allergens), meditation, yoga, and t'ai chi, may prove useful to promote physical and mental relaxation and reduce the stress in our lives.

Stress management techniques can serve to improve the digestion of allergy sufferers. Exercise, in particular, can be an excellent stress reducer. It can lower the levels of anxiety and boost the immune system by helping to eliminate water and toxins from the body and to speed the transfer of nutrients to the cells. It also normalizes blood sugar levels.

Aside from its many other negative affects on the body, sugar is an immune system weakener. One study found that it interferes with the white blood cells' ability to break down many harmful substances. A lack of dietary protein also can damage the immune system. Adequate protein is needed to provide the body with amino acids so that it can produce white blood cells.

PROPER DIGESTION

In addition to a weak immune system, some types of digestive imbalances usually have a role in the development of allergies. Since proper digestion requires the secretion of sufficient hydrochloric acid and pancreatic enzymes for easy absorption and utilization of the nurtrients in the food we eat, when there is too little of this secretion this process can be altered. One result may be that some portion of the nutrition in the food we eat is not made available to us. The large molecules of protein that should have been broken down by the digestive juices or enzymes go directly into the bloodstream. The immune system reacts to these large molecules as if they were foreign invaders, causing an allergic response to the particular food. To alleviate such allergies, it is vital to restore the digestive system to optimum functioning. Balancing the digestive enzymes may be a way to do this.

Thoroughly chewing one's food is essential to proper digestion since there are digestive enzymes in the saliva that break down starches. If food is bolted down, these enzymes do not have enough of a chance to work, and more will have to be done by the intestinal enzymes. The enzymes may then go out of balance.

A lack of stomach acid also may contribute to digestive disorders. Often, this is the case in allergic children. Also, with age, many adults suffer from a decrease in stomach acid. This can be corrected by taking hydrochloric acid tablets with meals. However, individuals should not attempt to self-medicate in this area. The problem may be either too much or too little stomach acid. Hence, if the individual takes antacid tablets when he or she has low stomach acid or takes hydrochloric acid when he or she is overly acidic, the result may be a worsening of the problem.

CREATING AN ALLERGY-FREE ENVIRONMENT

While we are primarily interested in food allergies in this section of *The Egg Project*, allergies and sensitivities to a host of other environmental stimuli are rampant. They range from reactions to the mercury fillings in your teeth to others: pollen, goose feathers and down, animal hair, dust, wool, car exhausts, or household chemicals.

All of these can increase your allergic threshold (the point at which your body starts overreacting) and make you prone to food or other allergies as well. They do this by increasing stress, encouraging free radical formation, weakening your immune system, or playing havoc with proper nutrition, digestion, and absorption.

A careful review of these potential sources of problems can uncover a number of areas of concern along with possible solutions. Your physician, allergist, or clinical ecologist can help inventory these allergy sources and suggest alternative approaches for dealing with or eliminating them.

Often, an allergy-sensitive individual may manifest sensitivities to a variety of environmental areas. The physician may use an adaptation of the rotary or elimination diet to pinpoint and correct environmental sensitivities.

10 · VEGETARIANISM

"When we sit down to a freshly mixed salad filled with dark green leafy vegetables, a variety of sprouts and carrots, millet with tahini-oat gravy and sautéed tempeh with garlic, we are receiving complex carbohydrates, essential fatty acids, complete protein, various B complex vitamins, calcium, iron, and a host of other nutrients....A nonflesh diet will, in the long run, lower your risk of developing many diseases and raise your chances of maintaining good health."

IS IT POSSIBLE TO eat without partaking of the poisoned fruits of technology? A natural food diet, which relies on unrefined grains, legumes, seeds, nuts, and fresh produce, and steers clear of unnatural additives (including sugar and salt), is a step in the right direction. A diet that cuts down or eliminates meat is even closer to an unadulterated, healthful ideal.

There is abundant scientific evidence that proves the adequacy and, in fact, the superiority of a vegetarian diet. The medical literature is filled with studies indicating the protective qualities plant foods possess against many common degenerative diseases currently sweeping the Western world. More importantly, modern medicine is discovering that many of these diseases are directly linked to animal products consumption.

Being a vegetarian offers a wide variety of benefits, but to fully understand this dietary option it is useful to understand that there are a number of diets included under the broad term "vegetarianism."

TYPES OF VEGETARIANS

Vegans, the strictest of the vegetarians, thrive solely on plant foods, specifically vegetables, fruits, nuts, seeds, grains, and legumes. This regimen omits all animal foods, including meat, poultry, fish, eggs, dairy products, and honey.

Lacto-vegetarians eat milk and milk products in addition to vegetable foods.

Lacto-ovo-vegetarians consume eggs along with milk products and vegetables. This basically is a nonflesh diet.

Pescovegetarians eat fish in addition to the plant sources. In Asia, hundreds of millions of people follow this type of diet, living on staples of rice and fish.

Pollovegetarians omit red meat from their diets, but eat poultry in conjunction with plant sources.

All these diets include an abundance of complex carbohydrates, naturally occurring vitamins and minerals, polyunsaturated fats, fiber, and easily digestible quantities of protein. A statistical analysis shows they closely resemble the diet recommended in the "Dietary Goals for the U.S." set by the Senate Select Committee on Nutrition and Human Needs.

MAN, THE HERBIVORE

Underlying any scientific evaluation of vegetarianism is evidence that humans are not biochemically suited to eat meat. Indeed, we possess all of the features of a strictly herbivorous animal. Our flat teeth are not sharp enough to tear through hide or bone. Our lengthy digestive tract resembles that of the classic herbivore. Most carnivores are anatomically constructed to quickly get rid of the meat they eat before it putrefies, and to eliminate the majority of their dietary cholesterol. We aren't. Our digestion begins in the mouth as the salivary glands secrete an enzyme designed to break down the complex plant cells. Carnivores don't have this enzyme. They secrete an enzyme called uricase that breaks down the uric acid in meat.

THE DANGERS OF MEAT

Although designed to subsist on vegetarian foods, man has perverted his dietary habits to accept the food of the carnivore, and thus has increased the risks of developing a number of disorders and diseases.

For instance, saturated fat and cholesterol, which are found in high amounts in many meats and other animal fats, increase the risk of hardening of the arteries and heart disease.

The leading cause of death in America, heart disease, is three times more likely to occur in meat eaters than vegetarians. Consuming meat doubles your chances for colon and rectal cancer, while tripling them for breast cancer. The high-protein intake of beef eaters places undue stress on the liver and kidneys, two important organs of detoxification. It may deplete your calcium supply, leading to osteoporosis, and the uric acid it contains can settle in the joints inducing painful gouty arthritis.

In addition, there are hidden poisons in meat and poultry that, when eaten, place undue stress on our digestive systems. These toxins burden our immune systems, our defense against disease. They include hormones, antibiotics, tranquilizers, additives, preservatives, and pesticides that are added to the meat in breeding and processing the animals. Such long-term bodily pollution creates a vast overall negative effect on our health, making us susceptible to a host of pathological abnormalities. Health benefits commonly noticed by vegetarians include improved digestion and decreased gastrointestinal disturbances, including less gas and constipation.

If meat is so bad for our health, how has it become the principle staple of the American diet? Alex Hershaft, president and founder of the Vegetarian Information Service, was asked that question at a Senate Subcommittee on Health and Scientific Research. He replied: "The answer goes to the very heart of what's wrong with the decision-making machinery of the federal government, where issues are decided less on the basis of their scientific merit than of their economic and political consequences. Few politicians are willing to face up to the $35 billion meat industry and to the several million farmers who make their living from raising animals for food."

Time after time, the public is warned against the nutritional deficiencies of "ill-planned vegetarian diets," or we read that "most nutritionists agree that vegetarian diets can be adequate, if sufficient care is taken in planning them."

The fact is that *any* ill-planned diet should be avoided, no matter what foods are eaten. Sufficient care should be taken in the planning and preparation of all meals—vegetarian and nonvegetarian alike.

The misguided meat eater reading the warnings that surround vegetarianism by rivals of that diet, such as the American Dairy Association, will incorrectly assume that as long as they are healthy, they don't have to give up anything in their diets—even pork, fat, or sugar. We have blindly assumed for too long that so-called "healthy" foods cannot hurt us and that meat is magical. These, quite simply, are myths that have been fabricated and propagated by the meat and dairy industries.

No one food is indispensible or magical. Animal flesh, for instance, is nearly void of carbohydrates, has little or no fiber, and is a poor source of calcium and vitamin C. It is naturally high in saturated fats and cholesterol. Meat eaters derive their complex carbohydrates, dietary fiber, and other nutrients from the same source as vegetarians—vegetables. When meat is omitted, you sacrifice all the harmful ingredients it has while still being able to acquire needed protein from plant sources. Lacto-vegetarians, for example, eat dairy products as sources of calcium and B_{12}. While one cup of whole milk contains 288 mg. of calcium, thiamin, iron, and trace minerals, nuts and other seeds contribute fat, protein, B vitamins and iron. Dark green leafy vegetables are sources of calcium, riboflavin, and carotene and should be eaten in generous amounts.

Depending not on variety but on meat instead for one's nutritional requirements can lead to a variety of health problems. We maintain a false sense of security because meat provides an adequate amount of high-quality protein. But amino acids, the component parts of protein, are only one of the things that make us thrive.

Vegetarians can dispense with animal products because a varied diet of whole grains, nuts, seeds, vegetables, and fruits will automatically provide all nine essential amino acids (the eight essential amino acids plus one, histamine, which is essential for children) in a quality and quantity equal to or sometimes surpassing the "incredible edible egg," nature's most complete protein food.

THE VEGETARIAN SPECTRUM

When we sit down to a freshly mixed salad filled with dark green leafy vegetables, a variety of sprouts and carrots, millet with tahini-oat gravy, and sautéed tempeh with garlic, we are receiving complex carbohydrates, essential fatty acids, complete protein, various B complex vitamins, calcium, iron, and a host of other nutrients. A variety of colorful, wholesome, unprocessed foods encompassing a flavorful spectrum provides the greatest nutritional package.

Americans have a number of misguided ideas about vegetarianism and how it might affect their health. Some, for instance, fear that a vegetarian diet is fattening. This would, of course, be true if one exceeded one's proper caloric needs, no matter what foods are eaten. People think of certain vegetarian foods as especially fattening, and they're often wrong. The biggest victim of this misconception is the potato. A medium-sized plain potato has only about 70 calories, and is packed with essential amino acids and Vitamin C. Excess calories come only from the garnishes that usually accompany the potato, from globs of butter, sour cream or oil, to chili, cheddar cheese, and bacon.

A nonflesh diet will, in the long run, lower your risk of developing many diseases and raise your chances of maintaining good health. Vegetarian diets are especially health promoting during periods of physiological or physical stress in which more nutrients are needed than at other times. These include pregnancy, lactation, periods of rapid growth as during childhood and adolescence, and times of illness and convalescence. Everyone from the very young to the very old can probably benefit from such a diet.

REASONS FOR CHOOSING VEGETARIANISM

Although health improvement is the primary reason why an increasing number of people are giving up meat, there are a number of other reasons for adopting a vegetarian diet.

Economics. The rising cost of living in general and of meat in particular has forced many people to adopt a vegetarian meal plan. Ounce for ounce, plant foods are more economical than other foods. They supply more fiber and a wider variety of vitamins and minerals. The same amount of protein costs one-fifth as much when obtained from plant sources as from animal sources.

In addition, agribusiness—huge agricultural companies—has dominated the animal food industry; its high technology and centralization have created unemployment and forced many small farmers out of business. Many people choose not to support these companies by not buying meat. The switch to a no- or low-meat vegetarian diet can benefit the individual without disrupting the overall economic structure by tending to support small farmers rather than giant agribusiness conglomerates.

Natural resources. The production and processing of animal products demands an enormous amount of land, water, energy, and raw materials. The rapid depletion of these precious, finite resources is of great concern. The grim reality of the fragility of our ecosystem encourages responsible vegetarian life-styles, which do not involve wasting more resources than they use, as does the meat industry.

Food resources. The idea of eating simply so that everyone may eat is supported by the animal-free diet. Our land is capable of supplying food for nearly 14 times as many people when it is used for human food crops as when it is being used to feed livestock, as animals are a grossly inefficient source of nutrition. They need to consume approximately 16 pounds of grain in order to yield one pound of flesh. It has been estimated that our current supply of plant foods could nourish more than double the world population if we managed it better. This substantial waste of protein, calories, and other essential nutrients contributes to global imbalances and starvation. Ultimately, our demand for meat must be drastically curtailed if we are to positively affect the worldwide hunger problem.

Reverence for life. Many people are now refusing a dietary style that supports the cruel treatment and wanton slaughter of million of animals. Since every person who consumes animal products perpetuates the unnecessary and agonizing existence and brutal death of these innocent creatures, these vegetarians actively defy the harsh reality of this inhumane treatment by adhering to plant food diets.

Religious belief. There are various contemporary and ancient faiths that advocate abstinence from meat. Some favor spiritual awareness and reincarnation, others emphasize ethical considerations and health benefits. In the East, these faiths include the Hindus and Buddhists; in the West, they include the Seventh Day Adventists.

Personal Taste. Meat consumption is an acquired habit, not an organic necessity. It starts in childhood for most people, backed by the encouragement of generations of misinformed parents. Our natural taste is actually for the full-flavored, wholesome taste of vegetarian cuisine. This is shown by the fact that most people lose their taste for flesh once it is omitted from their diet. Innumerable culinary delights can be concocted from a wide variety of plant foods, including herbs and spices, and these delicious dishes prove that the only limitations that exist are man-made.

There are numerous reasons why more people than ever before are adopting the vegetarian diet. Such a simple change in our individual style of eating not only enhances our health and well-being, but also strongly influences our economic, political and environmental systems. The dietary regimen we follow is an important aspect of our existence, making a statement for each of us that either supports or attacks the earthly sphere and natural order in which we dwell. The choice is ours.

11 · A GUIDE TO VEGETARIAN FOODS

"Rice, from a nutritional point of view, means brown rice—whole grain rice which, unlike white rice, has not had its bran, and with it much of its nutrition, removed. But be careful about your source of brown rice. Commercially produced rice is among the most heavily chemically treated food crops."

BEING A VEGETARIAN MEANS more than subsisting on lettuce. A variety of wholesome food combinations are possible within this dietary option. Creative preparation can yield an infinite array of culinary delights.

WHOLE GRAINS

To the vegetarian, grains are a particularly important food staple. Use a variety of them; each has a rich flavor to impart. But to enjoy these grains' true taste, choose those grown free of chemical fertilizers and sprays. Also, the less whole grains are processed, the greater their nutritional value.

Whole grains contain everything needed to nurture themselves, from germ stage to sprout to mature plant. Plant a whole kernel of any grain and, given the right combination of earth, water, and air, it will naturally sprout and grow to maturity. Not so with *refined* grains. Bury a milled kernel and cultivate it as much as you like; nothing will grow because the kernel is already dead.

Milling the root of whole grains only refines away a wide range of trace minerals and vitamins in the outer layers, resulting in grains that are bulkier and less healthy. Refined grains, robbed of the minerals and vitamins found in the discarded outer layers, strain the body's delicate mechanism of digestion. Nearly all of the B vitamins, vitamin E, unsaturated fatty acids, and quality proteins are found in whole grains, but refining removes most of these nutrients. Even in so-called enriched foods, only a few B vitamins and iron are replaced; the remaining B vitamins, as well as a rich variety of minerals and proteins, are "refined" out.

There are three ways to prepare whole grains for eating: sprouting, soaking, and cooking until tender. All grains can be sprouted in two to three days, or until the sprout reaches the same length as the original seeds. You can reconstitute some semi-processed grains such as bulgar wheat by soaking them overnight or pouring boiling water over them and allowing them to fluff up.

When you cook grains, first rinse them in a colander or strainer, then pour the grain into a pot of water, and swirl it with your hands, removing the hulls and bits of dirt that may float to the surface. Drain the grain through a strainer, dry pan-fry it in a heavy skillet, and add two parts boiling water. Cover the skillet, reduce the heat, and let the grain simmer for about a half hour (time varies with the grain).

Preparing grains in a pressure cooker, the proportion of water to grain is roughly $2^1/_2$ parts water for each part of grain. Add grain and water to the cooker and bring them rapidly up to full pressure. When the regulator on the lid makes a jiggling sound, the cooker has reached full pressure; reduce the heat to simmer and maintain the same pressure throughout the cooking. Allow the pressure to return to normal before loosening the lid, then open the pot and gently stir the grains, mixing the kernels toward the bottom with those at the top. Let them sit for a few minutes, then mix again.

Most grains at least double in size from their dry to cooked states. This means that 1 cup of cooked grain can feed two or three enthusiastic grain eaters or three to four people eating grain along with other foods. To achieve a sweeter flavor and crunchier texture, try dry-toasting the grain or sautéing it before cooking. To dry-toast, start with a cold skillet, preferably cast iron. To sauté, you must first heat the skillet and then quickly, evenly, coat it with oil. (If the oil smokes, it's too hot.) Whether dry-toasting or sautéing, stir the grain until a few kernels pop and a delicious aroma begins to rise.

Barley has much to offer as a solo grain dish. Some of the best barley in the world—consistently high in protein and minerals—comes from the rich soil of the Red River Valley of North Dakota and Minnesota.

Since unhulled barley is almost impossible to cook, practically all barley available in food stores has been "pearled" so as to remove its tenacious hull. The factor to consider here is just how much pearling has taken place; too much results in a whiter product robbed of the nutrients in its outer layer. Look for the darker barley available in most natural food stores.

Allow 30 to 35 minutes to cook simmered barley using $2^{1}/_{3}$ parts liquid (water, stock, etc.) to 1 part grain. The barley can also be browned before adding it to the boiling liquid. Pressure cooking (2 parts water to 1 part grain) takes approximately 20 minutes. If the resulting grain seems too chewy, simply add $^{1}/_{4}$ cup more water, cover, and simmer until soft. You might also try cooking barley with other grains, such as brown rice and wheat berries.

Barley can be sprouted, but first it has to be dehulled (try seed houses and grain suppliers). Harvest the sprout when it's about the same size as the grain. Barley flour can be obtained already milled or ground fresh from the pearled grain. It is often pan-roasted before being used in breads, muffins, and cakes. Recently, researchers have found that barley, eaten daily, was successful in lowering cholesterol levels by 25 percent.

Buckwheat is actually not a true grain but a grass seed related to rhubarb. When raised commercially as a grain crop, buckwheat is unlikely to have been fertilized or sprayed. Fertilization encourages too much leaf growth; spraying stops the bees from pollinating. The best buy is whole, hulled, unroasted (white) buckwheat grains, known as groats. Roasted (brown) and cut groats are less nutritious, and the roasting can easily be done just before cooking without disturbing the flavor or the B vitamins.

Buckwheat cooks quickly, so it is rarely pressure cooked. Simmer for 15 to 20 minutes in the same saucepan or skillet you first roasted it in, using 2 parts water to 1 part buckwheat. If you prefer a porridgelike consistency, use 3 parts water. Cooked buckwheat can serve as a stuffing for everything from cabbage leaves and collard greens to knishes. Buckwheat flour combined variously with whole wheat, unbleached white, and soy flours is a delight to pancake lovers. Whole grain buckwheat flour is always dark; light-colored buckwheat flour is made from sifted flour rather than from unroasted groats. A Japanese pasta called soba (containing anywhere from 30 to 100 percent buckwheat flour) is now readily available in natural food stores and in Oriental markets. Its subtle flavor and light effect on the stomach should encourage pasta enthusiasts to give it a try. It needs no heavy sauces; try a simple garlic or onion and oil topping.

You can prepare a buckwheat cream for morning cereal from buckwheat flour sauteed in oil in a heavy skillet. Allow it to cool and then return it to the heat, gradually adding water and bringing it to a boil. This mixture is then stirred and simmered about 10 minutes or until it reaches the desired consistency.

Sprout buckwheat from the unhulled groats in half an inch of soil or on wet paper toweling and allow it to reach a height of three to four inches. The sprouts or young grass, called buckwheat lettuce, can then be juiced or chewed. The bioflavinoid rutin, which is reported to speed the coagulation of blood, helping stop bleeding, is very high in sprouted buckwheat.

Corn, a staple food for thousands of years, has changed from a small shrub with only a few kernels to today's hybrid varieties with six-foot stalks bearing several ears that contain over a hundred kernels apiece. Both white and yellow varieties of dried corn are readily available, but in the American Southwest the blue and varicolored older types of corn are still grown. "Sweet" corn is normally boiled or steamed in water; field corn is likely to be ground into meals and flours. Field corn is allowed to dry out completely, which changes the simple sugars of the grain into starches.

Yellow cornmeal contains about 10 percent protein and is higher in vitamin A than the white variety. The only difference between a meal and a flour from yellow corn is its degree of coarseness. The germ of cornmeal starts deteriorating in a matter of hours, so you should grind your own meal or flour as you use it for cornbreads, muffins, Southern spoon bread, johnnycakes or whatever. You can fry it in a pan and then cook it with a 5 to 6 parts water as a hearty "mush." Adding cornmeal to whole wheat flour in a tempura batter gives it a delicious crunchiness.

Another favorite form of this versatile grain is creamed corn. You can make creamed corn by cutting off the kernals just far enough down to allow the milky, sugary liquid to flow. Pour in enough water or milk to cover, a dash of salt, and cook the mixture gently for a few minutes. Corn flour can also be used in small amounts in whole grain pastas. A variety of Texas Deaf Smith County sweet corn can be sprouted successfully until the sprout is about a half-inch long.

The many virtues of *millet* are often overlooked because of its reputation as "the poor person's rice." Being the only grain that forms alkaline, millet is the most easily digestible. It is also an intestinal lubricant. Its amino acid structure is well balanced, providing a low-gluten protein, and it is high in calcium, riboflavin, and lecithin.

Millet is cooked the same way as most grains, with 2 parts water or stock to 1 part grain. Pre-roasting releases a lovely aroma and adds texture to the cooked grain. Leftover cooked millet is a highly versatile stuffing for anything from hollowed-out zucchini tubes to mushroom caps.

Millet meal and millet flour are quality protein additions to any bread recipe. Millet meal also makes a good hot cereal. Sprouted millet makes an excellent base for morning cereal; just harvest the sprout when the shoot is the same size as the grain.

Oats must be hulled before they can be eaten; after hulling they are cracked or rolled into the familiar cereal forms. Rolled oats are shot with steam for a number of seconds and then passed through rollers; thus some nutrients are lost. Rolled oats will cook faster than whole oat groats, but whole oat groats are the most beneficial. Known variously as Irish oatmeal, Scotch oats, or steel-cut oats, whole oat groats are soaked overnight before being cooked as porridge. (None of these or any other cereals or porridges should ever be prepared in a pressure cooker; they tend to clog the vent on the lid of the cooker.) Whole oats are wonderful in soups. You can add both rolled and whole groats to all sorts of breads and patties.

Oat flour, available at most natural food stores, can be used in equal proportions with whole wheat flour to bake up a tasty batch of muffins. Oat sprouts can be used in soups, salads, and baked goods; just harvest the sprout when it is as long as the groat.

Rice, from a nutritional point of view, means brown rice—whole grain rice which, unlike white rice, has not had its bran, and with it much of its nutrition, removed. Brown rice is available in short, medium, and long grain varieties, the difference being largely esthetic. The shorter the grain, the more gluten, which means that short grain rice cooks up stickier and long grain comes out fluffier. There's even a sweet rice grain, the most glutinous of all. Excellent quality long and medium grain brown rice comes from southeast Texas and Louisiana; this rice is hulled by a special process that protects the bran layers.

Rice is traditionally simmered, the proportions of water to grain being as follows: short grain—$2^1/_2$ to 1; medium grain—2 to 1; and long grain—$1^1/_2$ to 1. All three varieties take from 25 to 35 minutes to cook fully. Stir regularly to prevent the grains that are on the bottom from scorching.

For pressure cooking, the proportion of water to grain is different: short grain—2 to 1; medium grain—1$^1/_2$ to 1; long grain—1$^1/_4$ to 1. When the rice is cooked, allow the pressure to return slowly to normal. Some of the cooling steam will add moisture to the grain.

Brown rice is a versatile grain aside from its variety of lengths. Rice cream is made commercially by a dry-roasting method, after which the grain is stone ground to a consistency somewhat coarser than rice flour. You can prepare it as a porridge from the whole grain itself, or from prepacked rice-cream powder. Combine the rice with 4 cups of lightly salted boiling water and stir constantly over a low heat to prevent lumping. Rice flour is used extensively in baking, especially by those on gluten-resticted diets. Rice flakes make quick additions to soups or casserole bases when no other leftovers are available.

The flaking process for grains and beans was originally developed to improve animal nutrition. The grains are cooked for 15 to 20 seconds under dry radiant heat and then are dropped onto rollers and flattened into whole grain flakes. Since no wet methods of processing are used, there is only very minimal leaching and modifying of nutrients. And flaked grains and beans cook in half the usual time. You can add them to breads and casseroles for protein, texture, or taste. In chili, wheat flakes serve to complete the protein of the bean.

A rice-based grain milk called *kokoh* is available prepacked at natural food outlets. This mixture of roasted and ground rice, sweet rice, soybeans, sesame seeds and oatmeal is good as a morning cereal or tea.

But be careful about your source of brown rice. Commercially produced rice is among the most heavily chemically treated food crops.

Rye is mostly known in its flour form, used in bread loaves often flavored with caraway seeds. Especially in its sprouted form, rye is rich in vitamin E, phosphorus, magnesium, and silicon. Like wheat sprouts, rye sprouts sweeten as they lengthen because the natural starches turn to sugar. For salad purposes, use the rye sprout when it's the same size as the grain; allow it to lengthen up to one inch for a sweeter intestinal cleansing sprout and for cooking. Rye can also be harvested as a grass and chewed for its juice.

The whole rye berry is a good grain, adding chewiness and nutritious value, to combine with rice (use about 1 part rye to 2 parts rice). Rye flakes can be added to soups and stews, or used as a cereal if soaked overnight. Rye flakes, like wheat and oat flakes, make good homemade granolas. For cream of rye, somewhat coarser in texture than rye flour, add 4 parts water to 1 part grain and simmer it over a low heat for about 15 minutes.

Triticale, a highly nutritious grain with a relatively high protein content (approximately 17 percent) and a good balance of amino acids, can be cooked whole in combination with other grains, especially rice (2 parts water to 1 part triticale). Sprouted, it can be used in salads or breads; flaked, in granolas and casseroles. Triticale flour has become a favorite of vegetarians because of its unusually nutty sweetness and high protein content. As a flour it must be mixed with other flours containing higher gluten contents, since its own protein has a low gluten content.

Today, *whole wheat* holds a preeminent position among grains because of its versatility and high nutritive qualities. Containing anywhere from 6 to 20 percent protein, wheat is also a source of vitamin E and large amounts of nitrates. These nutrients are distributed throughout the three main parts of the wheat kernel or berry. The outer layers of the kernel are known collectively as the bran; there is relatively little protein here, but it is of high quality and rich in the amino acid lysine. The dietary fiber of wheat bran is also the site of about half of the 11 B vitamins found in wheat, as well as the greater portion of the trace minerals zinc, copper, and iodine. Next comes the endosperm, the white starchy central mass of wheat kernel, which contains some 70 percent of the kernel's total protein, as well as its calorie-providing starch. Finally, there is the small germ found at the base of the kernel, which, in addition to containing the same B vitamins and trace minerals as the bran, is the home of vitamin E and the unsaturated fatty acids.

If you use the wheat berry in conjunction with other grains such as rice, you get the entire nutritive value of the grain. Try pan-roasting $1/3$ cup of wheat berries with $2/3$ cup rice and then simmering them with 2 cups water for 25 to 30 minutes until both grains are tender. You can also eat whole wheat as wheat flakes, cracked wheat, bulgur, couscous, sprouts and flours (both hard and pastry). The flaking process preserves most of the nutrients of the original form.

Wheat flakes lend themselves especially well to chili dishes, where their addition to the beans provides a completed protein. If added dry to the vegetarian chili about 20 minutes before serving, they will break down into tiny pieces to satisfy the appetites of even the most ardent chili con carne aficionados. Cracked wheat (simple coarse-ground wheat) is most often used as a morning cereal cooked with about 3 cups salted water to 1 cup wheat; it is often added cooked or uncooked to breads and muffins.

Bulgur is a variety of whole grain wheat that is parboiled, dried (often in the sun), and then coarsely cracked. This Near and Middle Eastern staple has found its way to America in a distinctive salad called taboulie. Bulgur does not require cooking but is simply reconstituted by spreading the grain an inch deep in a shallow pan and pouring enough boiling water over it to leave about half an inch of standing water; once the water is absorbed, stir the grain several times with a fork until it's cool. It can then be chilled, combined with greens such as parsley, fresh mint, and watercress, and marinated in a dressing of sesame oil, lemon juice, and tamari.

Couscous is a form of soft, refined durum wheat flour ("semolina") that has been steamed, cracked and dried. It can be prepared for eating by adding 1 cup of couscous to 2 cups of boiling salted water with a teaspoon of butter or margarine if desired, reducing the heat and stirring constantly until most of the moisture is gone. Remove the couscous from the heat and let it stand covered about 15 minutes, fluffing it up several times with a fork.

Wheat also makes an excellent sprout, containing substantially larger amounts of all the vitamins and minerals found in the dormant kernel. The sprout, which sweetens as it lengthens, can be used in desserts.

Whole wheat flour can be made from hard (high protein, high gluten) or soft (lower protein and gluten, high starch) wheat or from spring or winter wheats. Hard wheats are excellent for making bread. The spring wheat contains a higher gluten content than the winter wheat. Soft wheat, either spring or winter, is known as pastry wheat because it yields a fine, starchy flour. Wheat flours are available at natural food stores in many pasta forms—from alphabets to ziti—often combined with other flours such as buckwheat, corn, rice, soy, and Jerusalem artichoke.

Standard white flour is purely endosperm, with most of the bran and germ removed, which means a loss of up to 70 percent of the essential nutrients of wheat. In addition, white flour may be bleached by chlorine dioxide, which completely destroys the vitamin E. "Enriched" flours are actually attempts at making up for these losses; but only four nutrients—compounds of thiamine, niacin, riboflavin (vitamin B_2), and iron—are replaced. Most unbleached white flour has had much of its bran removed, but at least it has not been bleached. Soft wheat pastry flour, which can be substituted for unbleached white flour in any recipe, is a nutritionally superior, whole, refined flour.

Whole grain flours can become rancid. Rancidity occurs when the unsaturated fats in the flour are exposed to the oxygen in the air. The vitamin E in the whole wheat flour acts as a natural preservative, but within three months it is exhausted. This problem can best be handled by storing the flour in a cool dry place immediately after milling. There are a number of small natural food companies that mill and distribute their fresh-ground flour. Home grinding machines are now available at many natural food stores.

Wheat gluten (*kofu*, in Japanese cookery) has long been a popular vegetarian source of protein in many places around the world. It is prepared by mixing whole wheat flour and water in a 2½ to 1 ratio and kneading it into a stiff dough. This dough is then covered with cold water and kneaded underwater; as the water clouds up with starch sediment, it is replaced and the procedure is repeated about five or six times until the water remains clear. Then the remaining gluten dough is steamed or cooked in a double boiler for 30 minutes. Kofu may be eaten as is, flavored with soy sauce, or baked in casserole loaves combined with other grains, such as rice and beans.

Amaranth and Quinoa are two grains new to the American diet that have recently come on the market.

Amaranth is a native grain. It has been cultivated in the American southwest for hundreds of years. The plant yeilds a tiny seed that should be prepared similarly to rice. When cooked, it has a very soft, nutlike consistency.

Quinoa, a staple of the Inca Indians, is a delicate, light-textured, high-protein grain that resembles tiny granules of tabouli or couscous. Known as "the mother grain," it is high in complete protein, cooks in 10 to 15 minutes, and approximately triples its volume when cooked, somewhat mitigating its current high price (up to $4 a pound) in health food stores.

BEANS (LEGUMES)

The members of the bean family are important, inexpensive sources of protein, minerals and vitamins. Legumes can be cooked whole, flaked like grains, sprouted, ground into flours, even transformed into a variety of "dairy" products.

As a general rule, 1 cup of dry beans will make about 2½ cups of cooked beans, enough for 4 servings. Some beans should be soaked, preferably overnight; these include adzuki beans, black beans, chick peas (garbanzos) and soybeans. As an alternative to overnight soaking, you can bring the beans (1 cup) and water (3 to 4 cups) to a boil, remove the pot from the stove and cover, let the beans sit for an hour, then cook the beans by simmering after first bringing them to a boil, or by putting them in a pressure cooker.

When using beans for a soup dish, allow five times as much water as beans at the beginning of the cooking process. Don't salt the water until the beans are soft (or after the pressure in the cooker has come down), because the salt will draw the moisture out of the beans.

Adzuki are small red beans that have a special place in Japanese cuisine as well as in traditional Japanese medicine, where they are used as a remedy for kidney ailments (when combined with a small pumpkin called *hokkaido*). Very high in B vitamins and trace minerals, adzukis should never be pressure-cooked because it turns them bitter.

After overnight soaking, simmer adzukis with a strip of kombu (a kind of kelp) for about 1 to 1½ hours until tender, with 4 to 5 cups water to each cup of beans. One favorite preparation: add 1 cup each of sautéed onions and celery to the tender beans and then puree them together in a blender. The resulting thick, creamy soup can be thinned with water or bean juice and flavored with a dash of lime juice, tamari, and mild curry.

Black beans and their close relative, *turtle beans*, have served as major food sources in the Carribbean, Mexico, and the American Southwest for many years. These beans should not be prepared in a pressure cooker since their skins fall off easily and may clog the valve. A smooth, rich black bean soup, a specialty of Cuba, is made by cooking the soaked beans until tender, adding sauteed garlic, onions, and celery, and then pressing the mixture through a colander (or, more easily, quickly blending it in an electric blender). A small amount of lime juice may be added to lighten the taste.

Black-eyed peas, a Southern favorite, provides a delicious complete protein-balanced meal. Among the quickest-cooking beans, they become tender in 45 minutes to an hour. Eating this bean on New Year's Day is said to bring good luck throughout the year.

Chick-peas, or *garbanzos*, are so versatile that they have been the subject of entire cookbooks. High in protein, they are also good souces of calcium, iron, potassium, and B vitamins. They can be roasted, like peanuts, or boiled. After a very thorough roasting, chick-peas can even be ground and used as a coffee substitute. *Hummus* is a thick paste that combines mashed chick-peas, hulled sesame-seed tahini, garlic, and lemon juice. Bean patés using chick-peas as a base offer many creative opportunities for creating complete proteins, by combining different beans. Cooked grains, ground seeds and nuts, raw vegetables, herbs, and miso may all be combined with the cooked beans to produce a sophisticated and appealing paté or paste.

Great northern beans and their small counterpart, *navy beans*, cook in less than an hour and require no presoaking. They are often used for hearty soups. Cook the beans with 5 to 6 parts water or stock to 1 part dry beans. Firmer vegetables, such as carrots, rutabagas or turnips should be added ½ hour before the soup is finished; other vegetables, such as onions, celery and peppers, should be added 15 minutes later, either sauted or raw.

Kidney beans, standard in all sorts of chilis, will cook in about an hour, after having been soaked overnight. The fragrant brown bean juice produced in cooking the beans makes the addition of tomato virtually unnecessary. Once the beans are tender, try dicing onions, garlic, and red and green peppers; saut them lightly in sesame oil until the onions are translucent, then add them to the beans. Season them to taste. Rich Mexican chili powder seems to lend more flavor to the beans than does a scorching Indian one. Tamari, a dash of blackstrap molasses or fresh-grated ginger root can further enhance the beans. For a perfect final texture, add dry wheat flakes to the chili about 20 minutes before serving; this allows time for the flakes to cook and disintegrate, thickening the dish while complementing the protein of the beans.

Lentils come in a rainbow of colors, but generally only the green, brown, and red varieties are available in the United States. All are inexpensive and nutritious sources of iron, cellulose, and B vitamins. Lentils require no presoaking and disintegrate when cooked, leaving a smooth base to which you can add fresh or sautéed vegetables (including carrots, turnips, onions, and peppers). They sprout well in combination with other seeds and produce large quantities. The flavor of the uncooked sprout is similar to that of fresh ground pepper on salad; when cooked it has a more nutlike taste. The sprouts should be harvested when the shoot is as long as the seed.

Mung beans are probably best known in their sprout form, eaten raw or lightly sautéed with other vegetables. They can be cooked as a dry bean, using three times as much water as beans, and then pureed in an electric blender into a smooth soup. The result is rather bland and benefits from the addition of tamari and fresh or dried basil. But as sprouts, mung beans really come into their own. Mung sprouts are rich in vitamins A and C and contain high amounts of calcium, phosphorus, and iron. Th hulls are easily digestible and rich in minerals. Mung sprouts can be harvested any time from the second day, when the shoot has just appeared, to the third or fourth day when the shoot is about four inches long. Mung beans make a good first choice for beginning sprouters.

Peanuts, though commonly grouped with seeds and nuts, are actually members of the legume family. Their high protein content is well known. In the United States eating peanut butter is virtually a national pastime. Peanut butter can—and should—contain 100 percent peanuts; sugars, colorings, stabilizers, and preservatives are neither necessary nor desirable. A single grinding under pressure extracts enough oil from the nut meal to give the peanuts a creamy texture.

Pinto beans are popular in American Southwest dishes and lend themselves especially well to baking. Naturally sweet in flavor, they adapt to many types of seasonings, and once cooked tender, they can be used in casseroles. Pinto flakes cook quickly and reconstitute themselves into tender round beans in about 40 minutes (2 parts water to 1 part dry flakes). Cumin blends nicely with these beans, if used sparingly.

Soybeans, unquestionably the most nutritious of all the beans, have been the major source of protein in Oriental diets for centuries. They are increasingly being viewed as the most realistic source of high-quality, low-cost protein available today on a large enough scale to meet worldwide needs. In addition to high-quality protein, soybeans contain large amounts of B vitamins, minerals, and unsaturated fatty acids in the form of lecithin that help the body emulsify cholesterol.

Thanks to their bland flavor after cooking and their high concentration of nutrients, soybeans can be made into an amazingly diverse array of foods. Western technology in recent years has focused on creating a wide range of synthetic soybean foods. There are protein concentrates in the form of soy powder containing from 70 to 90 percent moisture-free protein, isolates (defatted flakes and flours used to make simulated dairy products and frozen deserts), spun protein fibers (isolates dissolved in alkali solutions for use in simulated meat products), and textured vegetable proteins (made from soy flour and used in simulated meat products and infant foods). Most Western cooks also have come across soybeans in the form of full-fat soy flour, soy granules, and defatted soy flour and grits— all of which are available in natural food stores. Full-fat soy flour, which contains about 40 percent protein and 20 percent naturally occurring oils, makes a fine addition to many forms of baked goods. Soy granules contain about 50 percent protein, as do defatted soy flour and soy grits, which are basically by-products of the extraction of soy oil. Both are used in breakfast cereals, simulated meats, and desserts. Soybeans are also processed into flakes which, unlike raw soybeans, require no presoaking and only about 1½ hours of cooking.

In striking contrast to these highly refined products of the West are the traditional East Asian soy products, tamari soy sauce, miso (fermented soy paste), and tofu. The first two fermented products will be discussed later in this chapter. *Tofu* (soy curd or soy cheese) is a remarkable food. It is very inexpensive when purchased at Oriental markets or natural food shops and even more so if made at home.

You can make your own tofu by grinding soaked soybeans, cooking them with water, pouring the resulting mixture into a pressing sack, and collecting the soy "milk" underneath by squeezing as much liquid as possible from the sack, leaving the bean fiber behind. The soy milk is then simmered and curdled in a solution containing sea-water brine (called *nigari*), lemon juice, or vinegar. Any of these three solidifiers will work well, although commercial nigari is most often used for this coagulation process.

After the white soy curds curdle and float in a yellowish whey liquid, they are ladeled into a settling box, covered and weighted, and allowed to press into a solid cake, which is then ready for immediate use as is—or for further transformation into a virtually unlimited variety of tofu products. Tofu is high in quality protein and is excellent for creating complete protein, especially when combined with grains. Tofu contains an abundance of lysine, an essential amino acid in which many grains are deficient; on the other hand, grains such as rice are high in the sulfur that contains methionine and cystine, amino acids which are absent in soybeans. These soy and grain proteins complement each other naturally.

Tofu is easy to digest, low in calories, saturated fats, and cholesterol. When solidified with calcium chloride or calcium sulfate—as in most commercial American tofu—tofu contains more calcium by weight than dairy milk; it's also a good source of other minerals such as iron, phosphorus, and potassium.

Since it's made from soybeans, tofu is free of chemical toxins. Soybeans are an important feed crop for the beef and dairy industries and the spraying is therefore carefully monitored by the Food and Drug Administration.

In addition to tofu, the soybean can be enjoyed in many other ways. It can be served as a fresh green summer vegetable, simmered or steamed in the pod. Roasted soybeans are now available in many varieties: dry-roasted, oil-roasted, salted, unsalted, and with garlic or barbecue flavors. They contain up to 47 percent protein and can either be eaten as a snack or added to casseroles for texture.

When cooking whole dry soybeans, a pressure cooker can save a great deal of time. Use $2^{1}/_{2}$ to 3 cups of water over a low flame for each cup of dry soybeans. Once the right pressure has been reached, cook until tender—about 90 minutes. Before cooking soybeans by the ordinary simmering method, soak them overnight in 4 cups of water. Bring them to a boil in 4 more cups of liquid and simmer about 3 hours, adding more water whenever necessary.

An interesting soybean preparation called *tempeh* is made from cooked dehulled soybean halves, to which a *Rhizopus mold* is introduced. The inoculated bean cakes are then fermented overnight, during which time the white mycellium mold partially digests the beans and effectively deactivates the trypsin enzyme, which could inhibit digestion. The soybeans have, by this time, become fragrant cakes bound together by the mold; you can then either deep-fry or bake them into a dish that tastes remarkably like veal or chicken. Tempeh is rich in protein (from 18 to 48 percent) and highly digestible. In addition, like the other fermented soy products and sea vegetables, it is one of the few nonmeat sources of vitamin B_{12}. Tempeh can be made easily in any kitchen. The tempeh starter (*Rhizopus oligosporus*, mold spores) is available from the Department of Agriculture, complete with an enthusiastic brochure on its use.

A further use of this "queen of the beans" is as a sprout. Significant amounts of vitamin C, not found in the dried bean, are released in the sprouts, which are also rich in vitamins A, E, and the B complex, as well as minerals. The yellow soybean does well for sprouting, and the black variety can also sprout prolifically. Rinse the sprouts two to three times a day and harvest them when the shoot is from $1/4$ to $1^1/2$ inches long. As a matter of taste, you may or may not prefer to remove the outer husk before using the sprout. Steaming or boiling the soybean sprouts lightly before eating will destroy the urease and antitrypsin enzymes that interfere with digestion. The sprouts can be ground and used in sandwiches and salad dressings, and they make a fine addition to any sauté of crisp Chinese-style vegetables.

Split peas, both green and yellow, make a simple soup filled with protein and minerals. They do not require soaking. Start with 1 part dry peas and 5 to 6 cups water and cook quickly in about 45 minutes. Once the peas are cooked, the soup will continue to thicken; this leftover paste can be diluted several times in the following days for a quick hot soup. Sautéed onions, tamari, and $1/2$ stick of soy margarine complete the soup.

NUTS AND SEEDS

Nuts and seeds are fine sources of protein, minerals (especially magnesium), some B vitamins, and unsaturated fatty acids. They can be eaten as snack foods or used with other foods to add interesting flavors, textures, and nutritional values.

A general sprouting procedure for seeds and nuts: soak the dried seeds for about 8 hours (approximately 4 parts water to 1 part seed). Don't throw away the soaking water; use it as a cooking liquid, or water your houseplants with it. Rinse the seeds with cool water and place them in a sprouter.

Keys to successful sprouting include keeping the sprouts moist but never soaked, keeping them moderately warm, rinsing them as often as possible, and giving them enough room so that air can freely circulate around them. Actually, only about five minutes a day is needed for growing a successful sprout garden. Use the sprouts as soon as possible. They have a refrigerator life of seven to ten days. Sprouts can also be dried easily for use in beverages, nut butter, and spreads. Place the sprouts on cookie sheets for a few hours in a warm room, or keep them in a warm oven until they're dry.

Then grind them in a blender and store this nutritious food concentrate in a jar and refrigerate.

Many people think of *alfalfa* as a barnyard grass, which it is. Because its roots penetrate deep underground to seek out the elements it craves, alfalfa is one of the best possible fodders. But the fresh, mineral-laden leaves of this plant are especially nutritious for humans when juiced. Alfalfa seeds purchased at a natural food store may seem expensive, but a few of them go a long way—1/2 teaspoon of dry seeds yields an entire trayful of sprouts. The sprouts have a light sweet taste and are particularly rich in vitamin C, as well as in chlorophyll (when allowed to develop in light). They also have high mineral values, containing phosphorus, chlorine, silicon, aluminum, calcium, magnesium, sulfur, sodium, and potassium. Alfalfa seeds sprout well in combination with other seeds and have a high germination rate. They can also be used when dried.

Almonds will sprout only from the fresh unhulled nut after soaking overnight; they must be kept very moist until their sprouts reach a length of about one inch (four days). They can then be used to make almond milk: a combination of 1 cup of almond sprouts (or merely almonds soaked overnight) blended with 4 times as much water or apple juice. Almonds, which have an exceptionally high mineral content, are delicious raw or roasted with tamari. The raw nut can be sliced, slivered, or chopped, and even can be ground into almond butter.

Brazil nuts, like other seeds and nuts, have a high fat content. But because they are also high in protein, they are actually not much higher in calories per gram of usable protein than are whole grains. They also offer unusually high amounts of the sulfur-containing amino acids. For this reason, you can serve them to good advantage as a chopped garnish for fresh vegetables, such as brussel sprouts, cauliflower, green peas, and lima beans. These vegetables are all deficient in the sulfur-containing amino acids but high in the amino acid isoleucine lacking in Brazil nuts.

Cashews are also popular nuts that can be added to many dishes. Use them as a layer in a casserole, or simply roast them lightly and toss them in a bowl of steamed snow peas. Cashew butter, from both raw and roasted nuts, is fast growing in popularity and is well suited for use in sauces, where it can be diluted with water and miso paste. You can mix it yourself in a nutritious soy "milkshake." Blend 2 cups of plain or sweetened soy milk with 1/2 cup of cashew butter; add 2 tablespoons of carob powder, a pinch of salt, and a dash of vanilla extract and nutmeg.

Chia seeds, now available in natural food stores, have long been a staple in Mexican and American Indian diets, where they were traditionally used to increase endurance on long hunts and migrations. Although a member of the mint family, chia seeds have a mild flaxlike taste. They can be chewed raw or sprinkled into hot or cold cereals. Since they are in a class of seeds called mucilaginous, which become sticky when soaked in water, their sprouting procedure is slightly different. Sprinkle the seeds over a saucer filled with water and allow to stand overnight. By morning, the seeds, having absorbed all the water, will stick to the saucer. Gently rinse and drain them, using a sieve if possible. Then, as with other seeds, rinse twice daily. Also try sprouting the seeds in a flat covered container lined with damp paper towels. Harvest the chia seeds when the shoot is one inch long.

The red variety of *clover*, makes a delicious sprout similar in taste to alfalfa. In its sprout form, this forage plant can be an excellent source of chlorophyll; when the primary leaves are about one inch in length, spread them out in a nonmetallic tray and dampen them. They should be covered with clear plastic to hold in moisture and placed in a sunny spot for one to two hours.

Cress seeds are tiny members of the mustard family. They add a zesty taste to salads when used in their sprout form. They are also mucilaginous seeds and so are sprouted in the same way as chia seeds. Harvest the sprouts at about one inch long and use them in sandwiches instead of lettuce.

Fenugreek seeds were first used to brew tea by the ancient Greeks. This strong tea is an excellent mouthwash, as well as a tasty and nutritious addition to soy or nut milk. The ground dry seed is one of the components of curry powder. When sprouted, fenugreek can be added to soups, salads, and grain dishes. The sprout should be harvested once it is one-fourth inch long, for it will become very bitter soon afterward.

Filberts or *hazelnuts* are tasty nuts that, once chopped, make a delicious garnish for both greens and creamy tofu pudding. These nuts, however, contain an excess amount of calories for the amount of protein they provide.

Flax, also known as *linseed*, is a versatile plant. The fiber of the mature plant is used to make linen and pressed to extract its oil. As a sprout, flax has been used for centuries; it is recorded that at Greek and Roman banquets, flax sprouts were served between courses for their mild laxative effect. Though flax is sprouted as a mucilaginous seed, its sprouts work well in conjunction with wheat and rye kernels. Harvest when the shoots are about an inch long and serve as a breakfast salad. Taken on an empty stomach, this sprout mixture cleanses and lubricates the colon.

The small seeds of the common black *mustard* plant will sprout quite readily and are usually available at herb and spice stores. Small amounts of these sprouts add a spicy flavor to salads and sandwiches. Harvest when shoots are about an inch long.

Pecans are nuts that are cultivated organically in Texas and New Mexico. Though high in potassium and B vitamins, pecans are not good sources of protein; like filberts, they contain too many calories for the amount of protein they offer. Pecans are delicious as tamari-roasted nuts: dry-roast in a heavy skillet and, when they begin to emit a pleasing fragrance, remove to a plate and sprinkle lightly with tamari.

Pignolias, or pine nuts, have an unusual flavor, but are a poor source of protein. Pignolias, found in the cones of the small piñon pine, which grows in the American Southwest, have been used by many Indian tribes as a food staple. Most of the pignolias consumed in the United States, however, come from Portugal. Pan-roasted pine nuts are delicious with green vegetables like peas and beans, and are also tasty in bread stuffings.

Pistachio nuts are familiar to many as an Italian ice cream flavor. For snacking purposes, use the naturally grown pistachio rather than the dyed varieties. Like other nuts, pistachios should be consumed only in small quantities, since they are high in calories.

Pumpkin seeds, *pepitas* and *squash seeds* are delicious seeds rich in minerals that can be eaten as snacks or ground into a meal for use in baking and cooking. Eastern Europeans, who eat many more pumpkin seeds than do Americans, use them to help prevent prostate disorders. Save the seeds from a pumpkin or squash and sprout them. Harvest when the shoot is just beginning to show (after three or four days); if allowed to lengthen any further, the sprouts will taste bitter.

Radish seeds, both black and red, make wonderfully tangy sprouts. They sprout easily and work well when combined with alfalfa and clover seeds. They're relatively expensive compared to most sprouting seeds, but you don't need many of these peppery-tasting sprouts to perk up a salad. Harvest these shoots when they're about an inch long.

Sesame seeds, or *benne*, are popular around the world because of their taste and high nutritive content. Most sesame seeds available in the United States are grown in southern Mexico, where few sprays are used, and they are available hulled or unhulled. The unhulled variety is nutritionally superior since most of the mineral value is found in the hull.

The seeds are an excellent source of protein, unsaturated fatty acids, calcium, magnesium, niacin, and vitamins A and E. The protein in sesame seeds effectively complements the protein of legumes, because both contain high amounts of each other's deficient amino acids. Therefore, an especially good addition to a soy-milk shake is *tahini*, or sesame butter.

Used extensively as the whole seed in breads and other baked foods, in grain dishes, and on vegetables, the unhulled seeds can also be toasted and ground into sesame butter, which has a stronger taste and higher mineral content than sesame tahini. Tahini, made from toasted and hulled seeds, is a mild sweet butter. Tahini is used extensively in the Middle East, where the oil that separates from the butter is used as a cooking oil. Tahini is an excellent base for salad dressing and acts as a perfect thickener for all sorts of sauces.

The unhulled seed must be used when sprouting. The sprouts can be used, like the whole seed, in cooked foods or blended into beverages. Harvest when the shoot reaches one-sixteenth inch in length (usually within two days). At this stage the sprouts are sweet, but become bitter with further growth.

Sunflower seeds are sun-energized, nutritional powerhouses rich in protein (about 30 percent), unsaturated fatty acids, phosphorus, calcium, iron, fluorine, iodine, potassium, magnesium, zinc, several B vitamins, vitamin E, and vitamin D (one of the few vegetable sources of this vitamin). Its high mineral content is the result of the sunflower's extensive root system, which penetrates deep into the subsoil seeking nutrients; its vitamin D content is partially due to the flower's tendency to follow and face the sun as it moves across the sky.

Sunflowers were cultivated extensively by American Indians as a food crop. In their raw state, sunflower seeds can be enjoyed as snacks or included in everything from breads to salads. The seeds are also available in a toasted, salted nut butter.

Sprouted sunflower seeds should be eaten when barely budded or they will taste very bitter. However, it usually takes four to five days for the shoot to appear. Unhulled seeds, or special hulled sprouting seeds, are used when sprouting, but the husk should be removed before eating.

Walnuts are a good source of protein and iron. Black walnuts contain about 40 percent more protein than English walnuts (also known as California walnuts in the United States). Walnuts will keep fresh much longer when purchased in the shell. This is true of all nuts. It also brings down the price considerably.

SEAWEEDS

Seaweeds rank high as sources for the basic essential minerals, as do green vegetables such as dandelions and watercress. They all contain calcium, magnesium, phosphorus, potassium, iron, iodine, and sodium. Most Westerners dislike the idea of eating seaweed. If they were to sample what they're missing, though, they'd find a new world of taste and high-quality nutrients—especially trace minerals—in the six varieties of sea vegetables available in most natural food stores and food co-ops.

Agar, or *agar-agar* (called *kantan* in Japanese, and also know as *Ceylonese moss*) is a translucent, almost weightless seaweed product found in stick, flake, or powdered form. You can use it like gelatin to thicken fruit juices or purees. Agar also can be used to make aspics and clear molds of fruit juices, fruits, or vegetables. If you tear 1 to 1¹/₂ sticks into small pieces and dissolve them in 1 quart of liquid, you will produce a pudding-like consistency. More agar can be used to achieve a jellied texture. When used in stick form, agar should be simmered in liquid for 10 to 15 minutes, to ensure that all the pieces have dissolved. This simmering isn't necessary when using the flaked or powdered varieties.

Dulse is the only commercial sea vegetable that comes from the Atlantic Ocean (specifically, the Canadian Maritime Provinces). This ready-to-eat seaweed can be chewed in its tough dry state, but a short soaking to rinse it and to remove any small, clinging shells is worthwhile. Dulse can be added to miso soup.

Another Japanese seaweed is the jet-black *hijiki*, or *hiziki*. This stringy, hairlike seaweed contains 57 percent more calcium by weight than dry milk and has high levels of iron as well. Dried hiziki should be soaked in several cups of water for about 20 minutes, then strained in a colander and lightly pressed to squeeze out excess moisture. Once reconstituted, hiziki is best when sautéed together with other vegetables—especially onion and leeks—or cooked with beans and grains.

Kombu is the Japanese term for several species of brown algae. In English, these are usually referred to collectively as *kelp*. Kombu is especially rich in iodine, vitamin B_2 and calcium. When using the dried form of kombu, rinse it once and soak for 10 to 15 minutes.

Note that all dried seaweeds increase greatly in size when reconstituted. For example, ¹/₄ cup of dried hiziki would yield 1 cup when soaked. Save the water in which the seaweeds are soaked and use it as soup stock. Reconstituted kombu strips can be used whole in the cooking water for beans and grains, or can be cut into thin strips or diced for use in soups and salads.

Nori is the most popular Japanese seaweed, also known as dried purple *laver*. It is sold in the form of paper-thin purplish sheets, with eight to ten sheets per package. Laver has been used as a food by many peoples— including the American Pacific Coast Indians. The Japanese and Koreans are, however, the only people to cultivate these plants and dry and press the mature leaves into sheets.

The nori sheets are toasted over a flame until crisp, during which their color changes from black or purple to green. They are then crumbled or slivered and used as a condiment for noodles, grains, beans and soups. Remarkably rich in protein, nori is also high in vitamins A, B_2, B_{12}, D, and niacin.

Wakame is a long seaweed with symmetrical and fluted fronds growing from both sides of an edible midrib. Although generally used fresh in Japan, it is only available dried in the West. It is reconstituted in the same manner as kombu: rinsed once, soaked, and pressed of excess moisture. If the midrib is particularly tough, it can be removed. When used in soups, wakame should be cooked for no more than several minutes and should therefore be one of the last ingredients added to miso soup. This delicious vegetable is rich in protein and niacin, and contains, in its dried state, almost 50 percent more calcium than dry milk.

FERMENTED FOODS: MISO AND TAMARI

Miso and tamari, derived from soybeans and grain, deserve special consideration in any sensible vegetarian diet.

The fermentation process in the healthy human intestine isn't that different from what occurs in the production of fermented soy foods. For example, in our digestive tract, maltose and glucose are broken down to form lactic acid, ethyl alcohol, and organic acids. The microorganic cultures responsible for these syntheses enter our own bodies when we digest them in fermented foods and help us to assimilate the nutrients we need.

Miso, a fermented soybean paste, has long been a staple seasoning in the Oriental kitchen. It is produced by combining cooked soybeans, salt and various grains. Barley miso is made with barley and soybeans. Rice miso is made with both hulled and unhulled rice plus soybeans, and soybeans alone are used to make matcho miso. These cooked and slated combinations are dusted with a fungus mold, *koji*, which produces the enzymes that start to digest the bean-and-grain mixture.

Tamari is naturally fermented soy sauce. Originally considered excess liquid, it was drained off miso that had finished fermenting. Today it is a product in its own right and is made from a natural fermentation process of whole soybeans, natural sea salt, well water, roasted cracked wheat and koji spores, all aged for 12 to 18 months. Tamari, like miso, has a range of colors, textures, and aromas as wide and varied as that of wines and cheeses.

Miso and tamari contain between 9 and 18 percent complete protein; the higher the soybean content, the higher the protein. The protein in these products is "predigested": it is already broken down into 17 amino acids, which makes for easy digestion. Also, the digestion-inhibiting enzyme present in raw or poorly cooked soybeans is destroyed by their fermentations. During the microorganic synthesis of miso and tamari, the amounts of B vitamins, riboflavin, and niacin increase. In addition, miso and tamari are among the few vegetable sources of vitamin B_{12}, which is actually manufactured by fungi and bacteria in the fermenting mixtures just as it is synthesized in the human intestine.

Miso and tamari are useful in all cuisines, but because of their high salt content—11 percent for the saltiest of hatcho miso and 18 percent for tamari—they should be used sparingly. Miso diluted with water can be used as a base for a sauce made with tahini; a dash of tamari brings out new flavors in familiar grains. Miso also makes a wonderful soup base to which tofu, mushrooms, seaweeds, and many fresh or cooked vegetables can be added.

All of the natural miso and tamari available in the United States today comes from Japan. If a package of miso you purchase has started to expand, you can be assured its contents have not been pasturized and that the microorganisms are still alive and producing carbon dioxide gas. Get rid of it.

In the future, the United States may begin producing its own fermented soybean foods. A lively market now exists and many people are acquiring the necessary technical know-how. Organic farmers are already producing soybeans, wheat, barley, and rice; the koji starter and engineering skills are always available from the Orient. As fermented soy foods play a larger role in American diets, we may start to develop and adapt our own distinctive varieties.

SALT: SOME ALTERNATIVE SOURCES

A controversy continues about the virtues and dangers of salt. Some people consume large quantites of salt. Many others attempt to get their salt from the juices of celery, spinach, beets, or carrots; very little sodium, however, is derived from these supposedly sodium-rich foods. Still other people decide upon, or are prescribed, low-sodium or even "salt-free" diets. People on low-sodium diets have often been suffering from hypertension or kidney problems. Overconsumption of salt will lead to hypertension: The salt draws water out of blood cells and vessels, which in turn causes dehydration of the tissues and forces the heart to pump much too strenuously. Overconsumption of salt also clogs the kidneys and creates an excess of water that cannot be properly eliminated from the body.

On the other hand, moderate and intelligent consumption of salt helps the body retain heat by slightly contracting the blood vessels, which is why we tend to consume more salt in cold months. Sodium also helps maintain intestinal muscle tone. You should evaluate your own salt needs according to your physical activity, climate, water intake, and—above all—diet. People in meat-eating cultures seldom need extra salt per se, because they get all they need from the blood and flesh of the animals they eat; vegetarian or agricultural peoples, however, tend to have a high regard for salt and use it to cook, pickle, and preserve foods.

If you want to eat salt, you should use the natural sun- or kiln-dried variety, which still contains important trace minerals. Refined "table" salt is made fine by high heats and flash-cooling, and then combined with such additives as sodium silico aluminate to keep it "free-flowing." Kosher salt is an exception; it has larger crystals due to its milder processing, and nothing is added to the better brands. Natural salt—rock salt or sea salt—is not free-flowing, but some brands add calcium carbonate, a natural compound, to prevent caking. All salt is or once was sea salt, so differences between salt obtained from inland rock deposits or from the sea are minor and unimportant.

No natural salt contains iodine, which is far too volatile a substance to remain stable for long without numerous additives. But there is an excellent source of iodine from the ocean: sea vegetables, the most common being kelp. These contain a natural, sugar-stabilized iodine—as well as about 4 to 8 percent salt. They are harvested, roasted, ground up, and marketed as salt alternatives.

Another healthful way of adding salt to your diet is to use *sesame salt*, sold as *gomasio*. This versatile condiment can be used in place of ordinary salt on cooked greens, grains and raw salads. Gomasio can be purchased in most natural food stores, but the serious cook should grind his or her own.

The ridged ceramic grinding bowl called a suribachi is needed to make sesame salt. A proportion of 15 parts sesame seeds (unhulled) to 1 part salt is recommended by Lima Ohsawa in her cookbook, *The Art of Just Cooking*. She suggests that this formula should be adjusted to fit the individual taste and climate and advises a milder salt content for children. Start with 1 cup of sesame seeds, wash them in a fine strainer, and set aside to drain. Roast 1 level teaspoon of salt in a heavy skillet until the strong odor of chlorine is no longer released. Then transfer the salt to the suribachi and pulverize it with the wooden pestle.

Roast the drained sesame seeds in the skillet over moderate heat, constantly stirring until they are light brown in color and they begin to release their characteristic aroma. Transfer these browned seeds to the suribachi and grind lightly with salt until about 80 percent of the seeds are crushed.

Store the mixture until needed in an airtight container. Making gomasio becomes a beautiful ritual well worth the effort.

Another alternative is *salted umeboshi plums*. These small Japanese plums are known for the high quality and quantity of citric acid they contain. The citric acid in plums allegedly helps neutralize and eliminate some of the excess lactic acid in the body, helping to restore a natural balance. An excess of lactic acid in the body is caused by excessive consumption of sugar; if not converted to body energy, the sugar turns into lactic acid and combines with protein to contribute to ailments like headaches, fatigue, and high blood pressure.

In Japan, these organically grown plums are available in a variety of preservative-free forms—from concentrates to salted plums. In most American natural food stores, only the salted plums are available. These are potent alkaline sources, excellent to aid indigestion, colds, and fatigue. Umeboshi also have many culinary uses. Use them to salt the water in which grains will be cooked or use several in tofu salad dressings instead of tamari or sea salt.

SWEETENERS

Carbohydrate sugar is unquestionably essential to life, but try to get it in as unadulterated a form as possible. Common table sugar has been processed to 99.9 percent sucrose, devoid of the vitamins and minerals found in sugar cane or sugar beets. This refined sucrose taxes the body's digestive system and depletes its core of minerals and enzymes as the sugar is metabolized. For this reason and others, white sugar has earned a bad reputation and the label, "empty food."

Carbohydrates include many sugars. The best known is *sucrose*, or white table sugar, which breaks down in the body into simpler sugars— glucose and fructose. There are also starches in whole cereals (together with their own component enzymes, vitamins, minerals, and proteins) that break down uniformly in the body into simple glucose molecules once they have been cooked, chewed, and digested. Compared with these refined starches, refined sugars tend to overstrain the body's digestive system. So, it would seem wiser to get the sugars you need from abundant natural stores in cereals, vegetables, and fruits. Eaten in moderate amounts, starches are not fattening, contrary to public opinion. In fact, according to Dr. Alfred Meiss, "the body's adaptation to starch is nearly perfect" since starch is the "biochemically most efficient" carbohydrate, while "sucrose makes it harder for the body to produce energy over the long run."

When cooking with natural foods, you should simply replace refined sugars with the richer flavors of naturally occurring sugars. *Maple syrup*, for example, or honey or fruit juice can substitute for sugar in almost any home recipe. Maple sugar is expensive and very sweet, so use it in moderation. Use 1/2 cup of maple syrup instead of 1 cup of sugar and either reduce the other liquids in the recipe or increase the dry ingredients accordingly. Maple syrup is believed by some to be a source of the trace mineral zinc. But be sure that the maple syrup you buy has not been extracted with formaldehyde.

All *honeys* are basically the fruit sugar fructose, which consists of varying amounts of dextrose, levulose, maltose, and other simple sugars. The flavor of honey depends on the source of the bees' nectar. All honey you use should be unheated and unfiltered so that its natural enzymes and vitamins are still intact. When cooking with honey in a recipe originally calling for refined sugar, divide the amount of sugar called for in half and adjust the recipe with less liquid or more dry ingredients.

In fact, not too much sugar of *any* kind should be used in cooking or baking, because heat can be destructive to protein in the presence of sugar. This is especially true when using honey or a refined glucose such as corn syrup. Try using fruit juices or purees made from soaked dried fruits to sweeten dishes; a little of these natural sugars will go a long way.

Granulated date sugar, available in many natural food stores, is indispensable when your recipe specifically calls for a granulated dry sugar. This sugar has the distinctive flavor of whole dry dates. Another dry sweetner is *carob*, or *St.-John's bread*. This powder comes from the dried pods of the carob tree and can be purchased roasted or unroasted. Use the unroasted variety and toast it yourself for a fresher taste. In addition to its natural sugars, carob is rich in trace minerals and low in fats. Not much of this strong sweetner is necessary; either mix with the dry ingredients or dissolve in a little water or soy milk before adding to the other liquids. Carob is also available as a syrup. If you are using carob as a substitute for cocoa or chocolate, the equivalent of 1 square of chocolate is 3 tablespoons of carob plus 2 tablespoons of water or soy milk.

From the starches, two grain sweeteners are available: *barley malt* (also made from other grains and containing the sugar maltose) and a rice syrup called *ame* in Japanese. These grain syrups are produced by combining the cooked grains—rice in this instance with fresh sprouts from whole oats, barley, or wheat. This combination is allowed to stand for several hours until it has reached the sweet stage, when the liquid is squeezed off through cheesecloth, lightly salted, and cooked to the desired consistency. This thick, pale-amber syrup works well in pastries and sauces. Its semisolid state can be softened by beating to the consistency of thick honey. It is also sold in health food stores in the West as a chewy taffy.

For those who use dairy products, *noninstant dry milk powder* is a versatile natural sweetener containing the milk sugar lactose.

So-called *raw sugar*, or *turbinado*, is available in many stores, but is only slightly more nutritious than white sugar. It is 96 percent sucrose, compared with the 99.9 percent sucrose in white sugar. The only refining step to which it has not been subjected is a final acid bath that whitens the sugar and removes the final calcium and magnesium salts. This "pure" sugar was, as a juice from either sugar beets or sugar cane, only 15 percent sucrose; in its final form, all natural goodness has been lost.

Several sweeteners produced in the intermediate stages of sugar refining can be used somewhat more nutritionally than white table sugar. Once the cane or beet juice has been extracted, clarified to a syrup form, and crystallized, it is then spun in a centrifuge where more crystals are separated from the liquid. This remaining liquid is *molasses*, which is then repeatedly treated and centrifuged to extract more and more crystal until the final "blackstrap" form contains about 35 percent sucrose. Blackstrap molasses also contains iron, calcium, and B vitamins. Another variety of molasses is known as *barbados*. This milder, dark-brown syrup is extracted from the processes described earlier, resulting in a lighter-tasting product with a higher sucrose content. *Sorghum molasses* is produced by a similar process, but uses as raw material the cane from the sorghum plant. It has a distinctive, rather cloying, taste and is best used in baking, especially cookies.

UNREFINED OILS

For a healthful diet, you should obtain necessary unsaturated fatty acids primarily from unrefined vegetable oils. Like other unrefined foods, these oils still contain all the nutrients present in the grains, beans, or seeds from which they were derived.

Nearly all cooking oils are made by first heating the grains, beans, or seeds; then, to produce "unrefined" oils, they are pressed with a centrifuge and expelled without the use of chemicals or solvents. No further processing occurs, but some firms do filter their "unrefined" oils to remove the remaining particles of the germ. It is better, of course, to purchase unfiltered, unrefined oils with some sediment left in the bottle; too much filtering removes nutrients. Commercial processing also results in the loss of vitamin E, which is found naturally in the oil and is essential for the proper utilization of important unsaturated fatty acids. You therefore benefit very little from refined oils, since they are a poor source of unsaturated fatty acids.

Refined oils also lack the natural odors and flavors that are noticeable in all unrefined oils. The mildest of the unrefined oils are *safflower* and *sunflower*. Unrefined *sesame oil* imparts a unique nutty taste to sautéed foods, while unrefined *corn-germ* oil gives a buttery taste to baked goods. Everyone has appreciated the full-bodied flavor of unrefined *olive oil* in salad dressings. *Peanut* and *soybean oil* are stronger in flavor and can be better utilized in sautéing, which reduces the intensity of their taste. Unrefined *coconut* and *palm oil* are also available in natural food stores; these partially saturated oils are used extensively by Southern cultures for all types of cooking (and in many processed foods).

Another reason for using unrefined oils is that at high temperatures the chemical makeup of an oil is altered and possibly becomes detrimental to health. Many advertisements praise refined oils for their ability to be used at extremely high temperatures, but these high heats are neither necessary nor desirable. Unrefined safflower oil can be used for deep-frying at about 400 degrees, and can withstand higher temperatures than most other oils. Cooking temperatures above this simply aren't necessary. Overheating of unrefined, unfiltered oil causes the germ to scorch and most nutrients to be lost. When substituting unrefined oils for solid fats in recipes, reduce the amounts of other liquids slightly or increase the dry ingredients.

OTHER USEFUL FOODS

Bancha tea is high in calcium. It is a coarse green undyed tea. The leaves, which must have remained on the bush for three years, should be roasted in the oven until browned. *Bancha twig tea*, known as *kukicha*, consists of the twigs of the tea bush and is generally available. One spare teaspoon of kukicha should be used for each cup of tea, which is prepared by simmering the twigs for about 15 to 20 minutes.

Baking powders are used to make "quick breads" that can usually be put together and baked in less than half an hour and that rise by virtue of the baking powder included. It's best not to use too many quick breads, but they occasionally do lend themselves well to the use of concentrated nutrients such as seeds and nuts, and they can contain a mixture of flours such as whole wheat with fresh ground corn, millet, triticale, and soy flour. Never use sodium bicarbonate in making quick breads; its action is not only unnecessary but potentially unhealthy, destroying vitamin C and some B vitamins. Instead, the baking powder you choose should be low-sodium and aluminum-free; aluminum is known to be toxic. Potassium bicarbonate does not destroy vitamin D in the body. Most natural food stores carry this type of low-sodium baking powder, but you can make your own by using 1 part potassium bicarbonate, 2 parts cream of tartar (potassium bitartrate) and 2 parts arrowroot powder. It may be necessary to obtain potassium bicarbonate through a chemical company because it is not generally available at pharmacies.

Nutritional yeast is a natural treasurehouse of proteins, vitamins, and minerals that can be used as a dietary supplement when added to juices or included in cooked dishes. Often called *brewer's yeast* because at one time it was a by-product of the brewing industry, nutritional yeast is the tiniest of cultivated plants. The miniscule plants are grown on herbaceous grains and hops under carefully controlled temperature conditions. The yeast plant grows at an astoundingly fast rate. Once it has multiplied many times and matured, it is harvested and dried in a way that preserves all its nutrients. These yeast "flakes" are one of the most economical sources of the B vitamin complexes—B_1, B_2, B_6, niacin, B_{12}, folic acid, pantothenic acid, and biotin. In addition to these vitamins, yeast flakes contain minerals such as calcium, phosphorus, iron, sodium, potassium, and 16 of the amino acids, all working in conjunction with the B vitamins. Many people take several tablespoons of yeast daily. If yeast is to be used in a beverage such as a vegetable juice, the flakes should first be mixed with a small amount of the liquid and stirred into a paste, then added to the rest of the liquid and thoroughly mixed again. A blender will simplify this method of preparation. Yeast flakes also may be added to baked foods such as breads and casseroles or mixed in small amounts with nut butter or bean paste sandwich spreads.

Thickeners for smooth soups and sauces are usually based on a finely ground starch or flour, the most widely used being whole wheat, rice, and whole wheat pastry. The thickness of a flour sauce is determined by the ratio of flour to liquid. One tablespoon of flour to 1 cup liquid yields a thin sauce; up to 3 tablespoons flour to 1 cup liquid, a thick sauce. *Cornstarch*, corn flour in its finest version, is used in the same way to thicken sauces. *Arrowroot powder*, or flour made from the arrowroot plant, produces a finer sauce than cornstarch. The arrowroot starch should be dissolved in cold water before being added to hot foods to prevent lumping. Once the arrowroot has been added, simmer the thickened sauce to allow all the flavors to merge. *Kudzu* is another high-quality but rather expensive thickening agent. The kudzu plant grows wild in the United States as well as in Japan, where it has long been used in folk medicine, often prescribed for diarrhea and head colds. The crumbly white chunks should first be dissolved in cold water before being added to hot sauces to prevent lumping.

If *vinegar* is called for in a recipe, never use the white distilled or wine varieties; use an apple cider vinegar made from whole, unsprayed apples, undiluted and naturally aged. Refined, distilled vinegar has few of the naturally occurring nutrients (such as potassium) and virtually none of the indefinable subtle flavors of slowly aged cider vinegar. Because of the predominance of acetic acid in white distilled and wine vinegars, use them sparingly. Apple cider vinegar, on the other hand, contains a predominance of malic acid, which when wisely used is a constructive acid, naturally involved in the digestive system. Besides its culinary uses for preparing salad dressings and preserving foods, vinegar has long been useful as an antiseptic and blood coagulant. Rice vinegar is also available at natural food stores and in Oriental markets. It has a distinctive aroma and taste; so use it with utmost discretion in pickling and salad dressings. Thanks to its natural fermentation, it contains none of the problematical properties of commercial distilled vinegars.

Part Three

The Egg Project

MORE THAN A DOZEN years ago, I reviewed the available literature on protein requirements for human beings and found that there was an inconsistency between the prevalent beliefs of the scientific community as stated in the medical literature and the personal experience of many individuals. The people who should have been feeling healthy because they were getting more than adequate amounts of protein in their diet were frequently not receiving the healthful benefits from the protein in their diet. There was an escalating incidence of kidney disease in America that had no apparent cause. The prevaling myth stated that all of the protein from animal sources was complete, meaning that it contains all the essential amino acids, and furthermore, that all other amino acids, from plant foods, is incomplete—capable of sustaining life, but not of promoting optimum growth and maturation. Plant food diets were considered to be both faddist and dangerous. Clearly, this view had to be challenged.

I, along with Dr. Hillard Fitsky, who has a background in computer sciences, did a computer-assisted analysis of the 110 or so most commonly consumed vegetarian foods. We matched each one of the amino acids in the given food against the food source that is considered to contain the most complete protein, the chicken egg.

As the research progressed, it became clear that many of the assumptions concerning protein and our selection of foods were grossly in error. First, we found that not all animal protein is high quality and complete. Generally, only 40 percent is high quality. Second, we confirmed that not all vegetarian foods are incomplete. To the contrary, the vast majority of vegetarian foods are complete, containing all the essential amino acids. The bean or legume family in particular tended to have protein in large quantities and of a high quality. This made it easier to understand how the oriental and Indian cultures have been able to sustain themselves and demonstrate remarkable longevity on a limited vegetarian diet.

Taking this logic one step further, I reasoned that if single foods in the grain, legume, and sea vegetable families tended to have remarkably high-quality protein, what would be the result of combining two or three of these together? What I found was that the overall quality of the protein tended to increase tremendously. Not only did I find specific combinations that approximated the completeness of the egg, but some that actually exceeded the egg in terms of the amounts of complete, usable protein they provided.

Of the 5,000 combinations that I was able to compute over a five-year period, all offered protein of a quality nearer to the egg than the closest animal protein food source, milk. Other animal protein foods, including fish, hamburger, veal, chicken, and cheese all proved to offer far less complete and less usable protein than that available in the right combinations of vegetarian foods. Of course, the plant foods had far less calories, none of the cholesterol, the high saturated fat, the toxic growth-stimulating hormones, or the antibiotic residues such as penicillin that you would find in the animal products. They offered instead quality protein, abundant fiber, plentiful B vitamins, vitamin A, vitamin C, minerals, and the full spectrum of other nutrients. In other words, the concept of protein complementation allowed the acknowledged benefits of the vegetarian foods to be viewed alongside an appreciation of their demonstrable protein value even when compared to meat. In effect, it was time to virtually rewrite in a revolutionary way the whole notion of how we perceive protein. Even vegetarians, we found, are generally receiving between two and three times more protein than they require.

In the two chapters which follow, the principles of food combining and food rotation are observed. In both, a four-day rotational program is recommended.

Chapter 12 is specifically designed for individuals interested in managing their weight. It does not take for granted that you are already a vegetarian, and several types of fish are suggested as main courses.

Chapter 13 includes only vegetarian foods and features 50 of my favorite recipes. In preparing these recipes and adjusting your diet in favor of plant foods as protein sources, you will be applying many of the principles discussed in earlier chapters.

In both diets, you will be eating only 3 to 4 ounces of any given food at one time. Whether your goal be to lose weight, to increase the variety of your diet, or to discover the nutritiousness of vegetarian foods, you will find something here that will assist your search.

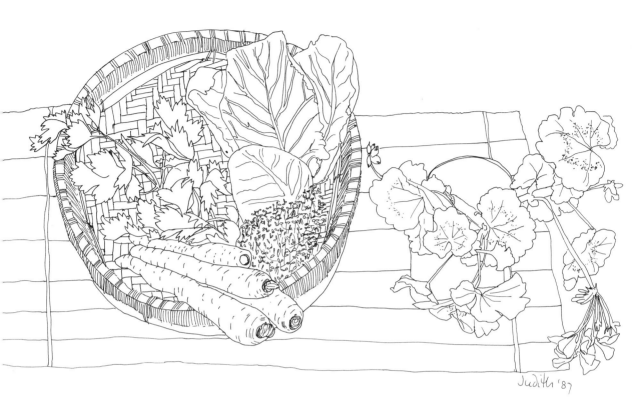

12 · A BEGINNER'S WEIGHT MANAGEMENT DIET

"*Another benefit of eating starchy, high-fiber foods is that, because they digest rather slowly, you benefit from the natural sugars they contain over a period of several hours. Unlike that quick jolt of energy that you get from sugar when you have a soft drink, or a dessert, that makes you very high and then very low very quickly, potatoes and other complex carbohydrates provide sustained energy.*"

HAVE YOU EVER WANTED to start a diet plan but kept finding reasons to put it off? Or perhaps you've tried quick weight-loss programs, only to gain back what you've lost and then some. You can lose that weight and keep it off.

This chapter will explore how you can break the cycle of overeating and crash dieting with a program that's appetizing, nutritionally sound, and designed to last a lifetime.

In this program, you'll learn how to detoxify your body—how to get rid of the poisons accumulated from years of poor eating habits. You will gain tips on how to determine your individual nutritional needs, and how to satisfy them. And you'll learn about food rotation: why it's important, what kinds of foods to eat, and when. This chapter will outline a 14-day plan for you, so you can rebuild your health, lose that weight, and never have to worry about gaining it back.

This chapter is organized around the experiences of a group of average, overweight Americans whom I gathered together so that their real diet experiences might serve to help others beginning on the road to improved health.

Joyce is 55 years old and wants to lose 20 pounds. She describes herself as having been "on every ridiculous diet that one can think of. At my age, or any other age," she says, "it's not healthy to be doing that. It worries me that I weigh so much. I am really serious about learning to diet right, and I am determined to lose the weight. But where do I start?"

BEGIN WITH DETOXIFICATION

There is no need to upset your whole system and your life in the process of losing weight.

In our society, most people don't really eat right for total health. Are you like most Americans? Do you tend to eat too much of foods that under-mine your health: animal proteins, saturated fats, fried foods, overly spicy foods, and foods made of refined carbohydrates, such as pizzas, french fries, and different types of confections? Do you indulge, all too often, in bagels, donuts, white bread products, and preserved, pickled or processed foods? These foods have been denatured. That is, much of their vitamins and minerals have been destroyed.

Once you have done all that to yourself, your body, in effect, has become a toxic waste dumpsite. Thousands of man-made chemicals end up in your lean muscle and fat tissues. They don't belong there. They can't be utilized for energy, for repair or growth of your body. On the contrary, they disrupt your normal biochemical processes.

One by-product of this disrupted biochemistry is a malfunctioning metabolism. Your metabolism—the way in which your body burns foods—is the process that allows you to have energy when operating normally, or lack energy when it is out of balance; to gain weight properly, or to gain it excessively. You may be overweight because your body's biochemistry is out of balance.

Yet you don't have to be a biochemist or an endocrinologist to understand the basic rules of proper eating. If you drink a lot of alcohol, you can't compensate by taking a vitamin B_1 tablet. Your body doesn't work that way.

The first step toward proper eating is to detoxify, and rebalance your body so you can start afresh. A Taj Mahal built on quicksand would soon sink. You don't have a strong foundation until you get rid of the debris that litters that foundation. You can't just repaint an old house whose wood is rotted and deteriorated. You first have to repair it; otherwise the decay continues hidden under that fresh coat of paint.

The single most important thing anyone who wants to change his or her diet can do is to detoxify by getting rid of the pollution in the body.

The rewards will be substantial. You will feel better, have more energy, feel lighter, and have an easier time maintaining a normal weight. You will find you have more endurance. Your body will no longer feel sluggish, and you will probably find you need less sleep.

Detoxifying need not be harsh upon either the mind or body. To begin, though, you have to know your relative state of health. Each of us is biologically unique; we all have particular needs and wants. Any diet doctor, who says everyone should have 5 mg. of B_2, and 10 mg. of B_6 is wrong, because no other person has the same biochemistry as you. Even two people who are the same age, the same sex, the same height, and the same weight—even identical twins, will have different biochemical needs.

That's why faddish popular diets, in general, don't work. Too often, they try to provide specific information for a general audience, as if everyone were the same. *We're not all the same.* There is no message I could share with you that would be more important, no specific counsel I could give you, no recipe I could offer, that would have the significance of this statement.

You will maximize your health, normalize your weight, lose weight, and feel good when you understand what you own nutritional requirements are. They have nothing to do with anyone else's.

Steve is 40 years old. He describes his weight problem in the following way: "For as long as I can remember I've been about 10 or 15 pounds overweight. Nothing I do seems to get rid of that excess weight. I can lose weight temporarily, but I've tried everything from grapefruit to horseradish, and nothing really seems to help me get my weight down and keep it down. How do I find out what my own nutritional requirements are?"

THE IMPORTANCE OF PROPER TESTING

The answer to Steve's concern begins with a basic blood chemistry test that evaluates the different components of your blood (the SMA-12, or SMA-24; see Chapter 7, "Detoxification"). It measures a variety of vitamin, triglycerid, cholesterol, and mineral levels. Steve should also have a hair analysis done to determine whether there are toxic levels of different minerals in his system—harmful metal like cadmium, mercury, and lead. An excess of lead or cadmium can come from smoking cigarettes. These metals will directly affect the mechanism in the brain that determines the appetite and satiety levels.

When you get your blood chemistry results back, you may find that your individual biochemical profile indicates a need for some nutritional support and detoxification. What other tests can help you determine your nutritional and health needs?

Everybody should also have a musculo-skeletal examination. An osteopath or a chiropractor can make this diagnosis for you, checking to see whether your muscular system is functioning properly. Frequently, the posture is so poor that there are blocked energy pathways. When you use certain muscle groups improperly, other muscle groups overreact in the body. For example, if you lean on one side while watching television, then the muscles on the opposite side of your body pull in the opposite direction. The result may be a sore back, sore arms and legs, hunched shoulders, or a hunched back.

We are a nation of people who sit, stand, and walk with poor posture. Posture can make an enormous difference in your energy levels and how you feel.

To summarize the way to begin: Step one is to cleanse out the old debris. It is necessary to eliminate the toxic metals, pesticides, herbicides, fungicides, and other synthetic substances from your system. Then you want to determine your own biological nature. What do you need—how much vitamin C, how much B_1? You don't want to put excessive amounts in your system, and yet you don't want to be deficient.

Numerous studies show that as a nation we are deficient in vitamin C, selenium, calcium, magnesium, and vitamin A. Those are easily obtainable from food in the diet. If you're eating what would be considered the average American diet, you're still almost certainly eating poorly.

Barbara is 25 years old. She says, "I've always been about 15 to 20 pounds overweight. A couple of times in my life I've gone on crash diets.

I've lost all the weight I wanted to and felt great for two weeks. But I also have these terrible junk food habits with midnight binges. I think I'm ready to change my entire way of looking at the way I eat food, because what I've been doing is obviously not helping me. I've taken the tests and I've gotten back the results. What do I do now?"

COMBINING DETOXIFICATION WITH REBUILDING HEALTH

A detoxification program will show you which foods and nutrients you can take into your system on a daily basis, to help take away some of the negative effects of eating a high sugar, high calorie, high fat, animal protein diet. You should then go on to a special 14-day eating program. First you detoxify, then rebuild health by losing weight, and then continue to eat right.

What are some good foods for building good health? At the top of the list is a group of foods called sprouts. Sprouts are the knockouts of nutrition. The sprout, quite simply, is one of the most nutrient-rich, powerful, health-building foods in nature. You just cannot find anything healthier. They will help cleanse and rebuild your entire system.

What kind of sprouts should you try? Don't stop with just common sprouts like alfalfa or mung beans. Expand your cuisine. Try high-protein buckwheat sprouts; the sweet sunflower sprout; the aromatic fenugreek sprout; clover sprout; and for a little bite and pinch, try a radish sprout. A mustard sprout will turn your tongue twice around your mouth. It tastes as good as mustard, and yet it has that nice salad feel to it.

Over 15 different seeds for sprouting are available commercially. They're inexpensive and versatile. You can make salads out of them, put them into pita bread, use them in casseroles and put them in soups.

Next, add miso to the list of detoxifying and rebuilding foods. For over 3,000 years, this nutritionally superior food has been helping people to better health. Miso is a fermented product. Like yogurt, its bacteria work well in your intestines. After all, the health of the intestine determines the health of your body. Remember that miso is to be used sparingly, however, because it does have a high sodium content.

Vegetable juices are a third health-giving detoxifier. Generally speaking, take no more than one glass of carrot juice per day. Beta carotine is a precursor of vitamin A in the body. If you drink too much carrot juice, you'll be overloading the liver with vitamin A and your skin may turn yellow. One glass a day is fine. You wil get the beneficial effects of vitamin A, which has been shown to be an anti-viral vitamin; it protects against viruses.

Add to carrot juice: celery, cabbage, parsley, sprouts, or cucumber for a variety of delicious juices. For people who've never really enjoyed vegetables, juices are another way to get good-tasting, high quality nutrition into your diet.

Grains are another group of foods that help the body cleanse itself and rebuild its strength. It is unfortunate that most Americans, unbelievably, never taste whole grain. They taste refined carbohydrates in white bread, or white rice, but never eat brown rice or whole grain bread. Yet these are inexpensive and readily available, even in supermarkets.

Whole grains are loaded with far more nutrition than their refined counterparts. The grain family includes rice, corn, buckwheat, rye, oats and millet, as well as less well-known, newly available grains like triticale, amaranth, and quinoa (pronounced keen-wa), a light, fast-cooking grain from South America now available in some health food stores.

The next group of foods to include as part of your health rebuilding program is the sea family of vegetables. These include hijiki, a form of seaweed that tastes salty like fish.

You can buy seaweed dry and store it for months. There are many types, including konbu, wakami, and nori. To cook them, place a small piece in cold water. After five minutes, replace the water with fresh water; after five more minutes, replace the water again. You now have rinsed the seaweed and it's ready for cooking. You can cut it into pieces, flake it, or put it into casseroles or soups. Include seaweed in your miso soup to increase its nutritional value.

You can add cold seaweed to salad, or serve it with vinegar or lemon juice as an appetizer.

You can wrap up seaweed like grape leaves.

Seaweed is so versatile that entire books are devoted to its use in cookery.

Seaweed is loaded with minerals. In fact, there is ten times more available calcium in hijiki, by dry weight, than in cow's milk.

At this point, we can answer a question raised by Joyce, who speaks for many when she says she's "been told for years that starchy vegetables such as potatoes and yams are fattening." She asks, "but are they?"

RETHINKING THE MYTHS

These foods are low in calories and rich in minerals and vitamins. It's what you put on them that makes them high in calories. A potato alone has only about 80 calories. But people often put about 150 calories' worth of butter or margarine on it. In fact, potatoes are an excellent source of vitamin C, in quantities comparable to that found in oranges.

Another benefit of eating starchy, high-fiber foods is that, because they digest rather slowly, you benefit from the natural sugars they contain over a period of several hours. Unlike that quick jolt of energy that you get from sugar when you have a soft drink, or a dessert, that makes you very high and then very low very quickly, potatoes and other complex carbohydrates provide sustained energy.

There's one last group of healthy, detoxifying foods although, too often, Americans deliberately stay away from them. These are the beans, or legumes.

Why do people leave the room when Aunt Gertrude helps herself to beans? We have kept ourselves away from one of nature's most important sources of vitamins, minerals, and fiber, because we have never really understood how to cook them. Most people, and most restaurants, do not soak beans overnight. Because beans are not soaked overnight, when our body finally digests them, gas is formed in the colon, causing indigestion and flatulence. That uncomfortable feeling needn't be. All you have to do is soak beans overnight and then boil them for one to two hours. That usually takes care of most gas-producing properties. Then be sure to combine them with the right foods: Don't eat fruit or sugary foods with a bean meal.

Beans have more protein than grains or seeds. They are an excellent source of protein, as good in protein quality as animal proteins, yet also high in fiber.

Try adding legumes to your diet. Legumes include black-eyed peas, red beans, kidney beans, great northern beans, lentils, garbanzo beans, alfalfa, lima beans, and split peas, among others. There are over 60 different legumes.

Beans are a great way to help your body. They are low in calories, and high in protein, minerals, and complex carbohydrates.

If you eat this way, you're not going to have a problem with weight. You will be able to lose the extra weight that you are carrying, while you cleanse your body. You won't be taking toxic materials into your body and will meet the body's nutritional needs for proteins, vitamins, essential fatty acids, and minerals. And you will spend less on food. A detoxifying diet is exciting eating. And it's the basis of good health. The foundation is where we start.

Now let's look at what we can do to incorporate all this into a 14-day eating program. Keep in mind that the 14 days could be 1,400 days, 14 years, or the rest of your life. But here is a menu for two weeks to help get you started. Let's begin on Monday. We're going to take this on a four-day rotational basis. I'll explain why later in the chapter.

THE FOUR-DAY ROTATION

Day 1

BREAKFAST Monday morning, start your day with hot cereal breakfast. Today the hot cereal can be oatmeal.

SNACK For a midmorning snack you can have a fruit if you are not hypoglycemic or severely diabetic. If you are, you may want to have a food such as cottage cheese or yogurt.

Take only small quantities of each food. On this eating program, you won't be eating until you're full, but only approximately 3 to 4 ounces of a given food. Thus, you may have as many as 12 to 14 ounces of total food in a given meal. The idea is to space your food over the day rather than eat a lot at one time.

By spacing your food, you will provide your body with energy, protein, carbohydrates, vitamins, and minerals throughout the day. After all, your body needs them 24 hours a day. People who skip breakfast, skimp on lunch, and then have the entire kitchen sink for dinner are only—after all is said and done—utilizing about 12 ounces of the food they eat. They're only able to use a small percentage of the protein they're taking in; the rest becomes fat. When you eat small amounts of food, several times throughout the day, very little becomes fat because your body is using it for energy throughout the day. This is a very important lesson if you want to lose weight and stay healthy.

LUNCH For Monday lunch, help yourself to a sardine salad, an egg salad or a tofu salad. Or, you can have a regular salad with a side order of any vegetables you like. You can choose steamed or stir-fried vegetables, and eat them with a grain, such as brown rice. If you are eating a salad, you might want to try serving your rice cold, the way the Japanese sometimes do. But remember—brown rice is preferable to white.

SNACK For your midafternoon break, let's say between two and four o'clock, you can have a juice, a fruit, or perhaps some marinated vegetable sticks. If you marinate them the night before in a vinaigrette sauce, you will find that your vegetables have a nice tangy quality to them.

DINNER For dinner, you can start off with a soup. Try, for example, split pea soup with an appetizer of seaweed. There are many recipes for either cold or warm seaweed.

As a main entree, have a soy food over rice. In this way you combine a grain in rice form with a legume, soy beans in this case, in the form of either tofu or tempeh. By the way, if you like the taste of chicken and want to give it up, tempeh is a great alternative. It contains no cholesterol and is made from soy beans. It tastes like chicken, has as much protein, is low in calories and high in calcium. It is, in fact, one of the best foods, nutritionally.

Finally, you can enjoy a salad at dinner. It should be a sprout salad on Monday. Make yourself a dressing, one without oil. There are many recipes for oilless dressings. There are also already prepared mixes to which you need only add water, vinegar, or lemon juice.

BEFORE BEDTIME If you feel hungry before bed, drink some carbonated water with a pinch of lime or lemon in it.

Let's take a look at what Monday's foods will do for you. You will have eaten foods that are low on the food chain, meaning they contain lower concentrations of pesticides and other chemicals than animal protein. You've eaten plenty of fiber. Not only are high-fiber foods low in calories, they will also improve your digestion. You have eaten plenty of calcium and moderate amounts of protein. You've consumed no refined sugar or starch. You've eaten modest amounts of foods that are easily digested, therefore ones that don't overtax your digestive systems, taking away the oxygen and blood that you need in your brain. You've eaten foods from which nutrients are readily and easily available for absorption. Also, because so much chewing is necessary with these foods, you've been helping your jaws and lowering your appetite. The more you chew, the more quickly your appetite is satisfied. Chewing each bite well prevents you from gorging. A short list of foods for the day—Oats, rice, tofu, split peas, sprouts, seaweeds, and, if you wish, sardines or eggs—have accomplished so much to help detoxify and rebuild your health!

Day 2

Hopefully, you are starting off your day with exercise. (See Chapter 15, "Nutrition and Exercise.") Fifteen minutes of aerobic exercise will improve your metabolism and stimulate the cells to burn more fatty acids, reducing overall body fat content and improving muscle tone as well as your overall sense of well-being.

BREAKFAST For breakfast, begin with a glass of fruit juice. Fresh fruit juice is preferable to frozen or canned juices. Try making yourself fresh-squeezed grape juice. If you do, dilute it with some water, because grape juice is sweet.

Then, enjoy a different hot cereal. Today, try an alkalinizing cereal, millet. With the millet, you can puree in a banana, adding a sprinkle of cinnamon or nutmeg. Add just a little soy milk, fruit juice, or regular milk.

SNACK   For a midmorning snack, I generally carry a little extra millet with me in a plastic container, and eat 4 or 5 tablespoons when I get hungry. If I tell myself I'm going to have 5 tablespoons and no more, I count them out, and that's all I have, as a way of controlling the urge to overeat.

LUNCH   For lunch today, try a three-bean salad of black beans, kidney beans, and lentils. These beans supply protein, fiber, vitamins, and minerals galore. Also, try a salad of vegetables different than those eaten on Monday. For instance, if on Monday, you ate watercress, rugala and spinach, then on Tuesday, take chickory, romaine, or Boston lettuce. You might have a soup as well. This would be a good opportunity for a black bean soup with a slice of whole grain bread. No butter, no margarine. Just moist, chewy whole grain bread.

SNACK   For midafternoon, have a piece of fruit, perhaps with another piece of whole grain bread. Whole grain bread only has around 100 calories and plenty of fiber in it. Therefore, it will be easily and quickly digested.

DINNER   For dinner on Tuesday, you might have hot millet, stir fried. Again, I like to make extra millet in the morning and have it all day long. Cooking it is just a matter of heating it up. Add a salad, and a different soup: kidney bean soup or a great northern bean soup.

For your main dish, eat fish. Salmon is a good choice. Fish not only gives you quality protein, but also essential fatty acids that your body needs. Omega 3 fatty acids—the kind found in many fish—have been shown to help the heart by lowering cholesterol levels.

SNACK   Later on, you can have your dessert. Never eat your dessert right after your meal: That's improper food combining. You do not want to combine a protein food, such as fish, which may take four or five hours to digest, with a simple sugar food that might have honey or fruit in it that might take only a half hour to digest. Combining sugary foods with protein or fat in the same meal leads to acid indigestion.

Wait till later in the evening and then have a banana. Try freezing it and then putting it into a blender or food processor. Whip it up, and it tastes like banana custard. For a special treat, take frozen cherries and frozen bananas and whip them together in a blender. You will be rewarded with a delicious, nutritious, and tasty dessert, low in calories, and high in complex carbohydrates, vitamins, and minerals. It is also very filling.

Thanks to your banana dessert late in the evening, and your fish, salad, soup and millet earlier, you will feel full without having consumed too many calories. That's eating right for total health.

Day 3

BREAKFAST   On Wednesday, begin your day with a hot rye cereal. Add to the rye cereal a fruit of your choice. Make it a fruit you have not eaten on either Monday or Tuesday. Take your cereal with some juice, milk, or soy milk.

SNACK   Later in the morning, eat a bit more of the morning cereal cold.

LUNCH   For lunch, enjoy a salad. Make it with different vegetables or different sprouts than Monday's or Tuesday's. Toss a handful of garbanzo beans into the salad today. Garbanzo beans are loaded with protein and are very nutritious. Mix some black-eyed peas or great northern beans in with the garbanzo beans to enhance the protein value of the beans.

Then, enjoy a soup made from any legume you didn't already eat on Monday or Tuesday. For example, you might want an aduki bean soup for lunch.

SNACK   Later in the day, have some fruit or a vegetable if you still feel you need a snack.

DINNER   For dinner, start with miso soup. Then, try a guacamole, or avacado salad, made with mashed avacado, tomatoes, and lemon. Avacado is the fattiest fruit, so use only a quarter of an avacado for your quacamole. If you don't want guacamole, try another nutritious appetizer, babaganoush. This is a dish made from eggplant, garlic, and lemon juice. Anyone who's enjoyed Middle Eastern foods knows the joy of babaganoush.

For your main course, turn again to fish, this time filet of sole. You can also have a side dish of vegetables, such as peas and corn. In the salad, try such vegetables as marinated asparagus tips, broccoli, and cauliflower. That gives you a lot to eat, and you'll feel full, but not filled out, having kept your calories low but nutrients high.

Day 4

BREAKFAST   Start off your day with a juice as before—a different fruit juice than the other days this week. For example, if one day you drank orange juice, you shouldn't repeat orange juice for another four days. Instead, you should have apple juice, prune juice, or grapefruit juice.

Then, enjoy a steaming bowl of wheatena or cream of wheat. These cereals are available everywhere. They are loaded with nutrition and high in fiber. But, to get more fiber into your system, to help cleanse your system, eat a bran muffin as well and be sure it's unsweetened.

SNACK   For a midmorning snack, have another bran muffin, since it contains only 70 calories. The muffin will help fill you up, but will also pass easily through your system.

LUNCH   For lunch, start off with some navy bean soup. Have salad, this time a marinated salad, like a cold salad or a seaweed salad. For your main entree have eggs, sardines, or tuna, whichever you didn't have on Monday.

SNACK   For later in the day, enjoy any type of fruit or vegetable, one that you haven't eaten yet on other days.

DINNER   For dinner, begin with a vegetable soup. Then, enjoy a tabouli salad, made with wheat and chopped parsley. As your main entree, we try either sea bass or blue fish, served with hot seaweed. For your vegetable, have some red potatoes. This meal supplies complex carbohydrates, complete proteins, and plenty of fiber, along with chllorophyl, vitamins and minerals.

SNACK   Later at night, you could have a frozen fruit or juice, if you feel the need.

THE REWARDS OF ROTATION

What was just described is an eating program for the first four days of your diet. This will form the pattern for the subsequent ten days and thereafter. The basic concept is a four-day rotational diet.

Why a rotational diet? Because, very often, people's headaches, mood swings (going from a pleasant to an angry disposition), fatigue, musculoskeletal aches and pains, indigestion, post-nasal drip, puffy eyes, and many other symptoms of not-quite-perfect health are exacerbated or caused by food sensitivities. We can become sensitive or allergic to any food we eat too frequently, including wheat, dairy, beef, chicken, corn, citrus fruits, peanuts, chocolate, soy, or any other food.

If you generally eat one or all these foods every day, you are likely to be food sensitive. This list includes the foods that clinical ecologists and allergists have found most likely to cause allergic reactions, as they predominate in the typical American diet.

Most people are familiar with the kind of allergies in which a person gets a skin rash immediately after eating, for example, strawberries. But there are other kinds of allergies that can be at cause when a child can't pay attention in class, or when an adult feels so tired after eating that he or she just wants to lay down and sleep. The allergies that cause these symptoms are very often caused by food sensitivities and can also lead to unnecessary pounds.

Studies have shown that when we are allergic to a food, we frequently have a faulty metabolism and gain weight above normal.

One of the fastest ways, then, to lose weight healthfully is to go on a four-day rotational diet and eliminate those foods to which we are allergic, or rotate them so that we don't have any one of them more frequently than every fourth day.

For example, if on Monday we ate oats, rice, split peas, the seaweed hijiki, and soy foods such as tofu or miso, we wouldn't have them again until Friday.

On Tuesday, if we ate millet, black-eyed peas, lentils, and kidney beans, we wouldn't have those again until Saturday. On Wednesday, if we ate rye, garbanzo beans, adzuki beans, sole, broccoli, asparagus and cauliflower, we wouldn't eat those foods again until Sunday. If on Thursday, we ate cream of wheat, navy beans, blue fish or sea bass, and red potatoes, we wouldn't consume those foods again until Monday.

Thus, we are creating a four-day rotational diet plan. Virtually all of the environmental medicine experts (they are known as clinical ecologists; *see* Resource Guide Listings at the back of the book) believe that our bodies need four days to recuperate after exposure to a food to which we are sensitive.

By now it should be clear how to turn a four-day rotation into a 14-day eating program. You simply continue the same eating plan for 14 days. In other words, every fourth day you would start from the beginning. You can change your recipes, adding any vegetables or fish you haven't eaten for at least four days or longer. Give yourself two weeks to see the effects of combining exercise (see Chapter 15, "Nutrition and Exercise") with a rotational eating plan, 14 days of eating wholesome, nourishing foods. If you've been allergic to foods, weaning yourself of them will frequently assist weight loss. You will also feel much better, and this will help inspire you to eat right from then on. The four-day rotational diet can be used as the basis for a maintenance dietary program. It's easy, it's inexpensive, and the rewards of eating right for a lifetime will pay off a thousandfold.

This program doesn't just address the problem of weight loss. Excess weight is a symptom of a larger problem, one that can't be solved by going on a crash diet, even if you do lose ten pounds in one week. This program is not an instant solution, but it offers you the chance to revitalize yourself in many areas of health. Weight loss is only one benefit. If you follow these guidelines, you'll feel more energetic and less stressed, and you'll probably live longer. In short, the quality of your life will improve.

If this diet seems to work for you after two weeks, try moving on to the vegetarian food diet contained in the next chapter. Begin by extending your original 14-day program into a 21-day program, using only vegetarian foods during the final week. Then try staying on the vegetarian diet alone. Use the recipes and the three different four-day rotations contained in Chapter 13 to get you started.

Judith '87

13 · A VEGETARIAN ROTATION DIET AND RECIPES

"Generally, you should eat no more than 3 to 4 ounces of a given food at any one meal. In these quantities, you may eat the same food several times during the day, however. This approach will reduce your overall caloric intake and keep your body functioning with optimal energy."

THE RECIPES IN THIS chapter have benefited from years of research and exper-
imentation. They have been designed to fit easily into a four-day roata-
tional diet plan in which specific foods such as brown rice, soy beans, or
wheat are eaten only once every four days. On any one day, a food may be
eaten several times in relatively small quantities.

Additionally, the recipes included here have been devised according to
the principles of proper food combining in order to allow for optimal
digestibility, absorption, assimilation, and elimination. Following a diet
using these recipes will provide all the protein and fiber that you need, as
well as a full spectrum of vitamins and minerals.

At first, the idea of avoiding animal products in your regular diet may
seem foreign. But perhaps you have heard the warnings of the American
Heart Association, which link excessive consumption of red meat and
dairy products to heart disease, or those of the American Cancer Society
linking breast, colon, and prostate cancer to these products. Or you may
have heard of the statement issued by the National Academy of Science
containing evidence that the ideal human diet is essentially a vegetarian
one, high in fresh fruits, vegetables, and grains, while low in animal
proteins, fats, and refined foods. You may have grown curious about the
benefits of a vegetarian diet as you've become aware of the risks associated
with a diet high in animal protein foods, but still you hesitate. Don't worry,
you are not alone.

The habit of many years may be fixed in a number of popular beliefs
with a strong hold on many of us. First among these is the myth that you
have to eat meat to get sufficient amounts of protein. Other fixed ideas
include the belief that milk is our best source of calcium, and that only
meat and animal products provide vitamin B_{12}. Meat is commonly associated with sexual potency and virility. On the other side of the coin, vegetarian cooking is commonly considered monotonous and unappetizing.
Very often, there is an underlying fear of disapproval of friends and family
should you become a vegetarian, and the feeling that it is simply too
difficult to eat properly without meat as a mainstay.

The recipes offered in this chapter were designed specifically to dispel
the myths that a vegetarian diet must be boring, unappetizing, and nutritionally inadequate. While a macrobiotic diet has been of benefit to many
people, too often those who are unfamiliar with vegetarianism consider
macrobiotic cuisine, as prepared in many restaurants, to by synonomous
with vegetarian cuising generally. And yet the major cuisines of the world,
including the those of China, India, the Middle East, and Mexico are
essentially vegetarian, using meat only sparingly, as a spice rather than an
entree. Vegetarian cooking can be both tasty and varied.

Being a vegetarian should not be a burden, nor should it alienate you from your friends and family. Of course, at first you may find it neccessary to make a certain number of life-style changes. You will want to look for a good health food store that is convenient to shop in and provides the products that you need. At first you may have to spend a little more time planning and preparing your meals, but with time it will become second nature.

Two important things to remember are flexibility and gentleness. Rigidly held beliefs and dogmas will lead to an accumulation of stress that can deplete your body of essential vitamins and minerals no matter how well you eat. At the same time as you establish your new diet, see if you can relax too. The important thing to remember is to be gentle with yourself. You are learning something new, and initially you may well make mistakes. If, for example, you go off of the diet at a party or if you go on a "binge," it will not help to beat yourself up for it. Simply chalk one up to experience and plan on doing better the next time. If you are out with friends at a restaurant that does not serve brown rice or vegetarian meals, don't panic. You will learn to see your way through such situations without feeling embarrassed or making those around you uncomfortable. For instance, you can order the baked potato instead of the rice, and a grilled piece of fish instead of the red meat.

The ideal diet involves eating a number of small meals throughout the day. Eating just one large meal can interfere with the proper absorption of nutrients and place a burden on digestion. It can also add surplus calories. Generally, you should eat no more than 3 to 4 ounces of a given food at any one meal. In these quantities, you may eat the same food several times during the day, however. This approach will reduce your overall caloric intake and keep your body functioning with optimal energy. Keep in mind that it is best to meet the body's vitamin, mineral, and protein requirements throughout the day.

Reader! If you wish to prepare additional servings of these recipes, increase the amounts of main ingredients (vegetables, fruits, seeds, grains, legumes, flour, etc.) in proportions equal to the existing recipes. Condiments should only be increased by 1/8 tsp. per additional portion.

First Cycle

DAY 1

BREAKFAST

Warm and Sweet Morning Cereal

6 oz. amaranth
3 oz. fresh pineapple,
   if possible; if not,
   pineapple sweetened
   in its own juice
3 oz. raisins
1 tbsp. honey
pinch cardamon
pinch cinnamon

In a medium saucepan, combine amaranth and water. Lower the heat when the water begins to boil. Allow to simmer for approximately 25 minutes. While the amaranth is cooking, cut the pineapple into $1/2''$ pieces. When the amaranth is cooked, add the pineapple and the remaining ingredients. Mix thoroughly. (*Serves 1.*)

LUNCH

Three-Grain Vegetable Bake

3 oz. amaranth
3 oz. basmati rice
3 oz. couscous
3 oz. carrots
$1^1/2$ oz. watercress
3 oz. celery
$1^1/2$ oz. pecans
2 tbsp. safflower oil
2 oz. water
$1/4$ tsp. basil
$1/4$ tsp. rosemary
$1/2$ tsp. fresh mustard
3 oz. golden raisins

Prepare a medium saucepan for each of the grains (amaranth, basmati rice, and couscous). Place 10 oz. of water in the saucepan with the amaranth and cook for 25 minutes. Place 10 oz. of water in the saucepan with the rice and cook for approximately 20 minutes. Place couscous in 10 oz. of water and cook for 10 minutes. Carefully wash carrots and then grate into a small bowl. Rinse watercress and chop. Clean the celery stalks and chop. In a large mixing bowl, combine all the grains and then add remaining ingredients. Mix well. Place mixture in a baking pan. Bake for 20 minutes in a 325-degree oven. (*Serves 2.*)

DINNER

Italian Vegetable Toss

3 oz. carrots
6 oz. zucchini
3 oz. arugula
1 oz. parsley
2 tbsp. safflower oil
1 clove garlic,
   chopped finely
$1/3$ tsp. tarragon
$1/3$ tsp. basil
2 red cabbage leaves
$1^1/2$ oz. pine nuts

Carefully clean the carrots and zucchini. Cut them into bite-sized pieces and steam in either a bamboo steam basket or a stainless steel steamer. Steam for approximately 8 minutes. Rinse arugula and parsley, pat dry with a paper towel and tear into smaller pieces. In a separate small bowl, combine the oil and the herbs. When vegetables are steamed, allow them to cool to room temperature. Transfer them into a large bowl and toss in the arugula and parsley. Pour oil mixture into the bowl as well. Place cabbage leaves on each plate and place mixture on top. Top with pine nuts. (*Serves 2.*)

DINNER (2nd Option)

3 oz. sweet potato
3 oz. amaranth
3 oz. basmati rice
3 oz. zucchini
2 oz. celery
2 tbsp. safflower oil
1/4 tsp basil
2/3 tsp. salt
1/3 tsp. curry
1/2 tsp. tarragon
1/2 tsp. cumin

Aromatic Indian Sweet Potato Bake

Place sweet potatoes in a preheated 400-degree oven for 40 minutes or until done. (You can test it by inserting a fork.) In a medium saucepan, place the amaranth in 10 oz. water. Cook for approximately 25 minutes or until done. In another saucepan, prepare the rice similarly in 10 oz. of water, and then cook for 20 minutes. While the grains are cooking, carefully wash the zucchini and celery. Cut the zucchini into 1/2" cubes. Slice the celery into 1/4" pieces. When the sweet potato is cooked, allow it to cool so you can handle it. Then scoop the sweet potato out of its skin and place it in medium-sized mixing bowl with the cooked rice, amaranth and the remaining ingredients. Turn the mixture into the baking dish. Bake for 15 minutes in a preheated 375-degree oven. (*Serves 2.*)

DAY 2

BREAKFAST

6 oz. brown rice
1 1/2 oz. coconut, shredded and unsweetened
1 1/2 oz. cashews
1 1/2 oz. dates
1/2 tsp. cinnamon
2 oz. water
1 oz. chopped apples
1 1/2 oz. sunflower seeds

Crunchy Sweet Rice

In a medium saucepan, cook brown rice in 14 oz. of water. Lower heat when it comes to a boil. Cooking time is about 30 minutes. When rice is cooked, add coconut. Chop cashews and dates finely and add to rice. Add cinnamon. Take half of the mixture and puree along with 2 oz. of water for a few seconds. Then add the pureed mixture back to the rest of the rice. Sprinkle sunflower seeds and apples on top. (*Serves 1.*)

LUNCH

3 oz. kidney beans
3 oz. cauliflower
3 oz. asparagus
3 oz. celery
2 oz. mushrooms
2 oz. zucchini
1½ oz. filberts
2 oz. water
2 tbsp. sunflower oil
¼ tsp. basil
⅔ tsp. dill
⅓ tsp. chili powder
⅕ tsp. celery seed
1 garlic clove chopped
½ tsp. salt

Vegetable Filbertasia

Soak the beans in a large bowl in 16 oz. of water overnight. In the morning, rinse the beans and replace with 16 oz. of fresh water in a medium pot. Cook for 1¾ hours to 2 hours until done. Carefully rinse the cauliflower, asparagus, celery, mushrooms and zucchini. Steam cauliflower and asparagus for 10 minutes. Chop celery, slice mushrooms and zucchini. Chop filberts medium fine. Put filberts in a blender with water, oil, spices and salt. Place all the vegetables in a serving pan. Top with filbert/kidney bean sauce. Serve at room temperature. (*Serves 2.*)

DINNER

3 oz. butternut squash
1½ oz. shallots
1½ oz. peanuts
2 oz. water
1 garlic clove, finely diced
1 tsp. fresh ginger, diced
½ tsp. basil
½ tsp. salt
2 tbsp. sunflower oil
3 oz. avocado, sliced

Nutty Butternut Squash

Cut squash in half, remove the seeds and discard them. Place squash in a baking pan with ⅓" water, cut side down. Bake for 40 minutes at 400 degrees. When squash is cool enough to handle, remove its skin and cut into 1" pieces. Place in a medium-sized mixing bowl. Chop shallots medium fine and add to the squash. Place peanuts, water, herbs, salt and oil in a blender. Mix well. Add this sauce to the squash and the shallots. Place mixture in a greased, covered baking pan at 350 degrees for 20 minutes. When done, place avocado slices on top as garnish. (*Serves 2.*)

DAY 3

BREAKFAST

6 oz. millet
1½ oz. almonds
pinch cinnamon
1½ oz. brewer's yeast
1 tsp. vanilla
1 tsp. maple syrup

High-Protein Cinnamon Millet

In a medium saucepan, cook millet in 13 oz. of water. When the water comes to a boil, lower heat. Stir occasionally. Cooking time is approximately 30 minutes. In another saucepan, blanche the almonds by placing them in scalding water in order to remove the skins. Then chop them. Add cinnamon, brewer's yeast, vanilla and maple syrup as well as the almonds. (*Serves 1.*)

LUNCH

9 oz. potato
4 c. water
3 oz. tomato
3 oz. green pepper
3 oz. carrots
3 oz. broccoli
1/5 tsp. cumin
1/5 tsp. basil
3 tbsp. sesame oil
1 1/4 tsp. salt
3 oz. scallions,
 chopped

Thick and Spicy Potato Chowder

Scrub or peel potatoes and place in 4 cups of water in a medium saucepan. Boil for approximately 15 minutes. When the potatoes are cooked, place in a blender with the water in which it was cooked, the seasonings and the oil and salt. Wash the tomatoes, pepper, carrots and broccoli. Chop into bite-sized pieces. Transfer the potato mixture back into a saucepan. Add the chopped vegetables. Cook over a low heat for an additional 10 to 15 minutes. Top with scallions. (*Yields 4 to 5 cups approximately.*)

DINNER

3 oz. spaghetti squash
3 oz. scallions
6 oz. tomato
3 oz. green pepper
1 1/2 oz. onion
2 oz. mushrooms
2 tbsp. olive oil
1/4 tsp. basil
1/2 tsp. rosemary
1 tsp. fresh garlic,
 minced
1 tsp. salt

Almost Spaghetti Squash Dinner

Cut squash in half, remove the seeds and discard them. Place the halves in a baking pan with 1/3" of water, cut side down. Bake for 40 minutes at 400 degrees. When the squash is cool enough to handle, remove the pulp or "spaghetti." Carefully wash the scallions, tomato, pepper, onion and mushrooms. Chop them medium fine. In a large skillet, place the oil and sauté the vegetables along with the seasonings and salt for 5 minutes. Combine all the ingredients in a large bowl. Mix carefully and then transfer to a serving dish. (*Serves 2.*)

DAY 4

BREAKFAST

6 oz. barley
2 tbsp. barley malt
3 oz. mashed banana
2 oz. raisins

Banana Barley

In a medium saucepan, cook barley in 14 oz. of water for 20 minutes or until done. Add barley malt, mashed banana and raisins. Mix well. Serve hot. (*Serves 1.*)

LUNCH

3 oz. soy beans
3 oz. kale
3 oz. cauliflower
3 oz. carrots
2 oz. yellow squash
1¹/₂ oz. brazil nuts
1¹/₂ tbsp. soy oil
¹/₃ tsp. garlic, minced
1¹/₂ oz. chives
¹/₄ tsp. coriander
¹/₄ tsp. tarragon
¹/₂ tsp. salt

Rainbow Vegetable Salad

In a large bowl, soak beans overnight in 16 oz. of water. In the morning, rinse the beans and transfer to a medium soup pot with 16 oz. of fresh water. Cook for 2 hours or until done. Carefully rinse kale, cauliflower and yellow squash. Tear the kale and cut the vegetables into bite-sized pieces. Steam in a bamboo steamer basket or stainless steel steamer for 8 minutes. Chop brazil nuts finely. Combine all ingredients in a medium-sized mixing bowl. Mix well. Serve hot or cold. (*Serves 2.*)

DINNER

3 oz. lima beans
3 oz. broccoli
3 oz. tofu
2 oz. onions
1¹/₂ oz. brazil nuts
2 tbsp. soy oil
1 clove garlic, minced
1 tsp. coriander
1 tsp. parsley
¹/₂ tsp. salt
1 tsp. fresh mustard

Brazilian Broccoli Bake

In a large mixing bowl, soak lima beans overnight in 16 oz. of water. In the morning, rinse the beans and transfer them into a medium soup pot with 16 oz. of fresh water. Cook for 1¹/₂ hours or until done. Rinse broccoli and cut into ¹/₂″ flowerettes. Rinse tofu and cut into ¹/₂″ cubes. Peel and slice the onion. Place all ingredients in a large mixing bowl. Add ¹/₂ of the brazil nuts, the oil and seasonings. Add the mustard. Mix well. Place in a greased baking dish with lid. Top with remaining brazil nuts. Bake for 20 minutes in a preheated 350-degree oven. (*Serves 2.*)

BROCCOLI

Second Cycle

DAY 1

BREAKFAST

6 oz. oatmeal
1¹/₂ oz. raisins
1 tbsp. carob powder
pinch nutmeg
¹/₄ tsp. cinnamon

Carob Gruel

In a medium saucepan, boil 15 oz. of cold water. When water begins to boil, add oatmeal and lower heat. Stir frequently. Cooking time is approximately 10 minutes. Add remaining ingredients one minute before the oatmeal is fully cooked. Serve hot. (*Serves 1.*)

LUNCH

3 oz. couscous
3 oz. mushrooms
3 oz. carrots
3 oz. summer squash
1¹/₂ oz. parsley
¹/₂ clove garlic,
    chopped
2 tsp. thyme
¹/₂ tsp. basil
¹/₂ tsp. salt
1¹/₂ oz. pine nuts
4 cherry tomatoes for
    garnish

Light 'n' Easy Squash Salad

In a medium saucepan, cook couscous in 9 oz. of water for 10 minutes or until done. Wash mushrooms, carrots and squash carefully. Slice the mushrooms, carrots and squash into bite-sized pieces. Steam in a bamboo steamer basket or stainless steel steamer until tender but crunchy. Take into consideration that the carrots will take longer to steam than the squash and the mushrooms. Rinse parsley and chop finely. Chop garlic. Combine all ingredients in a large salad bowl. Garnish with cherry tomatoes. (*Serves 2.*)

DINNER

3 oz. black-eyed peas
3 oz. basmati rice
1 oz. hijiki, dry
1¹/₂ oz. watercress
2 oz. parsnip
3 oz. carrot
2 oz. celery
2 oz. onion, chopped
1 tsp. tamari
2 garlic cloves, finely
    diced
3 tbsp. safflower oil
1 tsp. coriander
1 bay leaf
1 tsp. salt

Vegetable Cornucopia Soup with Black-Eyed Peas

In a large bowl, soak peas overnight in 3 cups of water. In the morning, rinse well and transfer to a medium soup pot with 4 cups of fresh water. Bring beans to a boil, lower to medium heat and cover. In a medium saucepan, cook rice in 10 oz. water for 20 minutes. Meanwhile soak hijiki in 8 oz. of water and rinse twice. Rinse the watercress and tear into smaller pieces. Clean the parsnips and carrots well and cut into bite-sized pieces. Clean celery and slice in ¹/₄" pieces. When peas have cooked for 1¹/₂ hours, add the cooked rice and remaining ingredients. Cook over a low heat for 25 to 30 minutes or until beans are tender. (*Yields 4 to 5 cups.*)

Tossed Garden Salad

3 oz. red leaf lettuce
2 oz. endive
2 oz. red pepper
1 oz. alfalfa sprouts

Wash lettuce, endive and pepper. Cut into bite-sized pieces and put into a salad bowl. Top with sprouts. (Serves 2.)

DAY 2

BREAKFAST

6 oz. brown rice
1¹/₂ oz. raisins
1¹/₂ oz. sunflower seeds
1¹/₂ oz. coconut
¹/₂ banana, mashed
2 oz. of your favorite fruit juice, optional

Tropical Rice Breakfast

In a medium saucepan, cook brown rice in 14 oz. of water. When water comes to a boil, lower heat. Cooking time is approximately 30 minutes. During the last ten minutes of cooking, add the raisins, sunflower seeds and coconut. When it is completely cooked, add the mashed banana. When serving, you may add the fruit juice if you wish. (Serves 1.)

LUNCH

3 oz. butternut squash
3 oz. arugula
3 oz. alfalfa sprouts
1¹/₂ oz. currants
2 tbsp. sunflower oil
¹/₂ tsp. dill
¹/₂ tsp. parsley
¹/₂ tsp. salt

Butternut Arugula Salad

Peel the butternut squash. Cut it in half and remove the seeds. Discard the seeds. Place the squash cut side down in a baking pan with ¹/₃" of water. Bake for 40 minutes at 400 degrees. When squash is cool enough to handle, cut it into bite-sized pieces. Place in a medium mixing bowl. Rinse arugula carefully to get all the dirt off. Tear off the stems and discard. Then add the arugula to the squash. Add the remaining ingredients. Toss gently so as not to mash the squash. Serve hot or cold. (Serves 2.)

DINNER

3 oz. brown rice
3 oz. buckwheat
    noodles
3 oz. avocado
3 oz. marinated
    artichokes
2 tbsp. sunflower oil
2 tsp. scallions,
    chopped
1 tsp. parsley,
    chopped
1 garlic clove, minced
$^1/_2$ tsp. basil
$^1/_2$ tsp salt
1 oz. black olives,
    garnish

Herby Italian Noodles with Rice

In a medium saucepan, cook brown rice in 12 oz. of water for 35 minutes or until done. Cook noodles according to directions on package. Chop the avocado and artichokes into bite-sized pieces and place in a medium mixing bowl. Add the remaining ingredients. Toss gently. When the rice and noodles are done, place them on your plates. Top with the avocado mixture. Serve at room temperature. (*Serves 2.*)

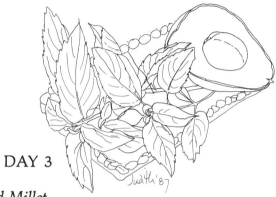

DAY 3

BREAKFAST

6 oz. millet
1 oz. dried banana
$1^1/_2$ oz. almonds
$1^1/_2$ oz. brewer's yeast
1 tbsp. maple syrup

Almond Millet

Cook millet in 13 oz. of water in a medium saucepan for 30 minutes. Add dried banana. Chop almonds. Add them to the millet along with the brewer's yeast and maple syrup. Serve hot. (*Serves 1.*)

LUNCH

3 oz. potato
3 oz. mushrooms
$1^1/_2$ oz. onion
$^1/_2$ oz. sesame seeds
$3^1/_2$ oz. water or
    broth
3 tbsp. olive oil
1 tsp. salt
$^1/_4$ tsp. cayenne
$^1/_2$ tsp. cumin
$^1/_4$ tsp. coriander
vegetable sticks
    (celery, carrots,
    daikon, etc.)

Savory Mushroom Dip

Peel potatoes. Wash them. Slice approximately $^1/_4''$ thick and place in a medium saucepan with enough water to cover. Cook until the potatoes are tender when you stick a fork in them. Rinse and slice mushrooms and onion. Sauté in a medium skillet until the onions are a golden brown. When the potatoes are cooked, place them in a blender with all the other ingredients. Puree well into a diplike consistency. Serve with a variety of vegetable sticks. (*Yield is 12 oz.*)

DINNER

3 oz. onion
1½ oz. olive oil
¼ tsp. basil
¼ tsp. oregano
¼ tsp. cumin
6 oz. tomato
3 oz. yellow pepper
2 oz. zucchini
2 oz. tomato paste
3 oz. water
1 garlic clove, minced
½ tsp. salt
6 oz. spaghetti

Spaghetti Deluxe

Peel and slice onion. Sauté the onion in the oil with the herbs in a 2-quart saucepan for 5 minutes. Chop the tomato, pepper and zucchini finely and then add them to the saucepan along with the tomato paste, water, garlic and salt. Continue to cook, covered, for 15 minutes on low heat. Cook spaghetti in 20 oz. of water in another saucepan for 10 to 12 minutes or until done. Combine with vegetables in a medium mixing bowl. Serve hot. (*Serves 2.*)

TOMATO

DAY 4

BREAKFAST

1½ oz. brazil nuts
4 oz. soy milk
1½ oz. apple cider
1 tbsp. carob powder
½ banana
pinch cinnamon

Chock Full of Protein Drink

Chop brazil nuts finely. Combine all of the ingredients in a blender, including the brazil nuts, and blend well. It tastes really good when the mixture is smooth and creamy. If you like your drinks sweeter, you may use the whole banana. (*Serves 1.*)

LUNCH

3 oz. lentils
2 oz. carrots
3 oz. corn (may be fresh and removed from the husk or frozen)
3 oz. fresh chives
3 tbsp. soy oil
½ tsp. garlic powder
½ tsp. coriander
½ tsp. rosemary
½ tsp. basil
¾ tsp. salt
several parsley sprigs for garnish

Hearty Lentil Soup

Cook lentils in a medium soup pot with enough water to cover. Bring to a boil and then set on medium heat with the lid on. Cooking time is approximately 1 hour. Scrub carrots and cut them into bite-sized pieces. After the lentils have cooked for approximately 20 minutes, drop the carrots into the pot along with the corn and remaining ingredients. When the mixture has cooked for an additional 30 minutes, take half of the mixture out of the pot and put it into a blender. Puree it for 15 seconds and then pour it back into the pot. Cook for an additional 10 minutes. Garnish with parsley sprigs. (*Yields 4 to 5 cups.*)

Nutty Bean Salad

3 oz. black beans
1¹/₂ oz. walnuts
2 oz. celery
2 oz. carrots
1¹/₂ tbsp. soy oil
1 garlic clove, minced
1 tsp. tarragon
¹/₂ tsp. sage
¹/₂ tsp. salt

In a large bowl, soak the black beans overnight in 16 oz. of water. In the morning, rinse the beans and transfer them to a medium saucepan with 16 oz. fresh water. Cook for 1¹/₂ hours or until done. Chop walnuts very finely. Rinse celery and scrub carrots. Cut celery and carrots into bite-sized pieces. Place oil in a wok or skillet and heat. Place all ingredients into the wok or skillet and sauté for 5 minutes. Serve at room temperature. (Serves 1.)

DINNER

Hot and Crunchy Veggie Mix

3 oz. snap green beans
3 oz. cauliflower
3 oz. brussel sprouts
1¹/₂ oz. walnuts
¹/₅ tsp. sage
¹/₂ tsp. dill
¹/₂ tsp. parsley
juice of ¹/₂ lemon
pinch cayenne
2 tbsp. soy oil
³/₄ tsp. salt
2 oz. water

Wash beans and cut them into bite-sized pieces. Steam in a bamboo steam basket or stainless steel steamer for 10 minutes or until tender. Rinse cauliflower and brussel sprouts and cut into bite-sized pieces. Steam for 8 minutes. In a blender, place the steamed beans, walnuts and the remaining ingredients. Pour sauce over the cauliflower and brussel sprouts. You may serve this dish either hot or cold. (Serves 2.)

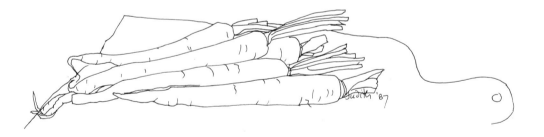

Third Cycle

DAY 1

BREAKFAST

6 oz. couscous
3 oz. apple
2 oz. raisins
$^1/_2$ tbsp. honey
$^1/_2$ tsp. cinnamon
3 oz. favorite fruit
   juice, optional

Sweet Cinnamon Couscous

In a medium saucepan, cook couscous in 14 oz. of water. Bring to a boil, stirring often. Then lower heat. Cook time is approximately 10 to 12 minutes. Wash and slice apples. When couscous has cooked, add apple slices and remaining ingredients. Mix well. Transfer to serving bowls. Add fruit juice if you wish. (*Serves 1.*)

LUNCH

3 oz. mung beans
6 oz. zucchini
$4^1/_2$ oz. summer
   squash
2 oz. Spanish onion
2 oz. carrots
1 oz. parsley
a garlic clove, finely
   diced
3 tbsp. safflower oil
$^3/_4$ tsp. salt
$^1/_2$ tsp. basil
$^1/_4$ tsp. oregano

Milano Bean and Vegetable Soup

Place mung beans in a large bowl with 3 cups of water. Allow the beans to soak overnight. In the morning, rinse the beans well and transfer into a large soup pot, adding 4 cups of fresh water. Bring beans to a boil and lower to medium heat. Keep the lid on. Scrub the zucchini and summer squash, peel the onion and the carrots. Chop the vegetables into bite-sized pieces. Rinse parsley and chop finely. After the beans have been cooking for approximately one hour, add the vegetables and the remaining ingredients. Remove half of the mixture and transfer into a blender. Puree for 15 seconds. Return the puree to the rest of the soup to finish cooking for another 30 minutes. (*Yields 4 to 5 cups.*)

DINNER

3 oz. amaranth
3 oz. basmati rice
1 oz. watercress
1 oz. dill
$1^1/_2$ oz. parsley
$1^1/_2$ oz. carrot
2 tbsp. safflower oil
juice of $^1/_2$ lemon
$^1/_2$ tsp. salt
2 oz. water
$^1/_3$ tsp. tarragon

Superb Vegetable Rice Salad

In a medium pot, cook amaranth for 25 minutes in 10 oz. of water. In another pot, cook the rice in 10 oz. of water for 20 minutes. Rinse the watercress, dill and parsley and chop medium fine. Scrub the carrots well and chop into bite-sized pieces. Place all the ingredients in a medium mixing bowl and mix well. (*Serves 2.*)

DINNER (2nd Option)

Oriental Zucchini Salad

3 oz. amaranth
3 oz. hijiki seaweed
(1 oz. dry; 3 oz.
soaked)
3 oz. carrot
3 oz. zucchini
2 oz. daikon
2 tbsp. safflower oil
2/3 tsp. salt
1/4 tsp. garlic
1/4 tsp. coriander
1/2 tsp. cumin
1 1/2 oz. pecan

In a medium saucepan, cook amaranth in 10 oz. of water for 25 minutes. Rinse hijiki and soak 3 times. Scrub carrots and zucchini. Peel daikon. Cut carrots, zucchini and daikon into bite-sized pieces and steam in a bamboo steamer basket or stainless steamer for 8 minutes. In a skillet or wok, sauté the hijiki with the safflower oil and the herbs for 5 minutes. Combine all the ingredients together in a medium bowl. Add the pecans. Mix well. (Serves 2.)

DAY 2

BREAKFAST

Fruity Rice Breakfast

6 oz. brown rice
1 1/2 oz. coconut
1 1/2 oz. cashews
1 tbsp. your favorite
fruit conserve (no
sugar, just fruit)
1 oz. chopped figs

In a medium saucepan, cook brown rice in 14 oz. of water. When water comes to a boil, lower heat. Cooking time is approximately 30 minutes. When cooked, add the coconut and cashews. Mix well. Remove from the heat. Add the conserves and the figs. Mix again. Transfer to bowl. (Serves 1.)

LUNCH

Curried Vegetable Rice

6 oz. split peas
6 oz. brown rice
3 oz. broccoli
3 oz. carrots
3 oz. zucchini
2 oz. onions
3 tbsp. sunflower oil
1/2 tsp. curry powder
3/4 tsp. salt

In a medium saucepan, cook split peas in enough water to cover. Bring to a boil then lower heat. After peas have cooked for 15 minutes. In another saucepan, cook rice in 14 oz. of water for 30 minutes. Clean vegetables well and cut into bite-sized pieces. After peas have cooked for 15 minutes, add the chopped vegetables, cooked brown rice and remaining ingredients. Cook for an additional 15 minutes. (Yields 4 to 5 cups.)

Sunny Squash

3 oz. butternut squash
3 oz. buckwheat noodles
3 oz. asparagus
2 oz. watercress
1 tsp. parsley
1 clove garlic, minced
5 tbsp. sunflower oil
3/4 tsp. salt

Cut squash in half, remove the seeds and discard them. Place the squash in a baking pan with 1/3″ water, cut side down. Bake for 40 minutes at 400 degrees. When the squash is cool enough to handle, remove the squash from the skin and set aside in a medium-sized bowl. Drop the noodles into salted boiling water and cook for 5 minutes. Set aside. Rinse the asparagus. Steam in a bamboo steamer basket or stainless steel steamer. Cut into 2″ pieces. Rinse watercress and chop. Add noodles to the squash along with the asparagus, watercress, and remaining ingredients. Mix well, tossing gently. (*Yields 4 to 5 cups.*)

Basic Tossed Salad

3 oz. romaine
3 oz. carrots
2 oz. red cabbage
2 oz. tomato

Rinse vegetables and cut into bite-sized pieces. Combine everything together in a salad bowl. (*Serves 2.*)

DAY 3

BREAKFAST

Heart-Warming Breakfast

6 oz. cream of wheat
2 oz. chopped dates
1 oz. coconut
1 1/2 oz. brewer's yeast
1/2 tsp. cinnamon

In a medium saucepan, cook cream of wheat in 12 oz. of water for 10 minutes or until done. Stir occasionally on medium heat. When cooked, add the remaining ingredients. Transfer to bowl. (*Serves 1.*)

LUNCH

Baked Potato Sesame

3 oz. potato
3 oz. spaghetti
1 1/2 oz. scallions
1 tsp. dill
3 oz. tahini sauce
1 1/2 oz. sesame seeds
1 1/2 tbsp. sesame oil
1/4 tsp. coriander
1/2 tsp. salt
1 garlic clove, minced

Bake potato for 40 minutes at 400 degrees. When cool enough to handle, cut into 3/4″ cubes. Cook spaghetti in a medium saucepan in 20 oz. of water for 10 minutes. Rinse scallions and chop them medium fine. Mix potato and spaghetti in a medium mixing bowl. Add the remaining ingredients. Transfer to a baking pan and bake for 15 minutes in a preheated 375-degree oven. (*Serves 2.*)

DINNER

3 oz. adzuki beans
1½ oz. almonds
3 oz. scallions
3 oz. red pepper
1 tsp. parsley
3 oz. tomato
2 tbsp. sesame oil
¼ tsp. oregano
1 tsp. salt
½ tsp. thyme
1 clove garlic, minced
several leaves of
    romaine lettuce

Crunchy Vegetable Bean Salad

In a large bowl, soak beans overnight in 16 oz. of water. In the morning, rinse the beans and place them into a medium pot with 16 oz. of fresh water. Cook for 1 hour or until done. Blanch the almonds by bringing 18 oz. of water in a small saucepan to a boil and dropping the almonds into the water. Remove from the heat. Let the almonds remain in the boiling water for 5 minutes and then run cold water into the saucepan. Squeeze the skins off and let the almonds dry. Sliver the almonds. Rinse the scallions, red pepper, parsley and tomato. Cut them into bite-sized pieces. In a medium mixing bowl, put the beans, almonds and vegetables. Toss gently. Add the remaining ingredients and mix well. Serve cool on a bed of romaine lettuce. (*Serves 2.*)

DAY 4

BREAKFAST

6 oz. banana
2 oz. raisins
3 oz. tofu
4 oz. barley malt
½ oz. carob powder
1 tsp. vanilla
3 heaping tsp. Ener-G-
    Egg Replacer
6 oz. apple juice
pinch cinnamon
pinch nutmeg

Creamy Banana Tofu Pudding

Place all ingredients in a blender. Puree until smooth and creamy. Transfer to a medium saucepan and cook over medium heat for 5 minutes, stirring frequently. Allow to chill for 45 minutes. (*Yields 20 oz.*)

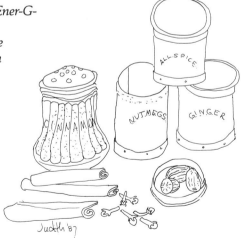

LUNCH

3 oz. chick-peas
1/2 oz. dulse, dry
3 oz. cauliflower
3 oz. tempeh
2 oz. onion
6 oz. tomato sauce
2 tbsp. soy oil
a garlic clove, minced
1/4 tsp. salt
1/2 tsp. basil
2 oz. water

Mid-Eastern Tempeh

In a medium bowl, soak the chick-peas overnight in 16 oz. of water. In the morning, rinse the chick-peas and transfer into a medium soup pot with 20 oz. of fresh water. Cook for 1 3/4 to 2 hours or until done. Rinse dulse 2 or 3 times in cold water. Rinse cauliflower and cut into flowerettes. Cut tempeh into 1/2″ cubes and put all the ingredients together in a medium mixing bowl. Peel and slice the onion and add to the mixture. Toss gently. Add the remaining ingredients and mix well. Transfer to a greased baking pan and bake for 20 minutes in a preheated 350-degree oven. (*Serves 2.*)

DINNER

3 oz. lima beans
3 oz. lentils
3 oz. okra
3 oz. cauliflower
1 1/2 oz. brazil nut
    butter
1 1/2 tbsp. corn oil
1 1/2 oz. water
1/4 tsp. tarragon
1/2 tsp. sage
1/2 tsp. salt
1 garlic clove, minced
Note: Brazil nut butter
    is made with
    "Champion" juicer
    or similar grinder.

Double Bean Delight

In a large bowl, soak beans overnight in 16 oz. of water. In the morning, rinse and replace with 16 oz. of fresh water in a medium soup pot. Cook for 1 1/2 hours or until done. In another pot, cook lentils in 12 oz. of water for 25 minutes. Rinse and cut vegetables into bite-sized pieces. Steam in a bamboo steamer basket or stainless steel steamer for 8 minutes or until tender. Transfer all ingredients into a medium mixing bowl and gently toss. Add the remaining ingredients and mix well. Transfer to a baking pan and bake for 15 minutes in a 350-degree oven. (*Serves 2.*)

Additional Desserts

Multi-Fruit Oatmeal Pudding

3 oz. pears
3 oz. oatmeal
6 oz. pear juice
1 banana
2 heaping tsp. Ener-G-
    Egg Replacer
pinch cinnamon
3 oz. apples

Place all ingredients, except for apples, in a blender. Puree. Transfer puree into small saucepan and cook over medium heat for approximately 5 minutes. Wash and cube apples. Add them to puree and stir frequently. Place in a medium mixing bowl or individual dessert dishes and allow to chill in the refrigerator for at least 45 minutes. (*Yields approximately 18 oz.*)

Tropical Pudding

6 oz. pineapple
6 oz. apple juice
3 tbsp. honey
2 tbsp. Ener-G-Egg
　Replacer
2 tbsp. coconut
pinch nutmeg
4¹/₂ oz. papaya
1¹/₂ oz. pecans

Place all ingredients, except for papaya and pecans, in a blender. Puree. Transfer puree into small saucepan and cook over medium heat for approximately 5 minutes. Peel papaya, remove seeds and cube. Chop pecans. Add both to the puree and stir. Place in medium mixing bowl or individual dessert dishes and allow to chill in refrigerator for at least 45 minutes. (*Yields approximately 16 oz.*)

Mango Strawberry Canton

4 oz. mango
4 oz. strawberries
12 oz. apple juice
2 heaping tbsp. agar-
　agar
1 tsp. vanilla
2 oz. dates, chopped

Peel mango and remove pit. Put in the blender with 2 oz. strawberries. Add apple juice and blend. Transfer to medium saucepan and bring to a boil. Lower heat and add agar-agar. Stir and dissolve agar-agar and simmer for 5 minutes. Add vanilla and chopped dates. Transfer to mixing bowl or individual dessert dishes and place in the refrigerator until juice begins to gel— about 10 minutes. Drop in the remaining strawberries. Chill for 1 hour. (*Serves 2 to 4.*)

Papaya Brown Rice Pudding

3 oz. brown rice
6 oz. papaya
1¹/₂ oz. coconut
1¹/₂ oz. figs
10 oz. pineapple
　coconut juice
2 heaping tsp. Ener-G-
　Egg Replacer
2 oz. blueberries

In a medium saucepan, cook brown rice in about 10 oz. water for 25 minutes. When cooked, place in blender. Peel papaya and remove seeds. Add to blender along with remaining ingredients, except for blueberries. Puree until creamy and smooth. Transfer to medium saucepan and cook over medium heat for approximately 5 minutes. Stir frequently. Transfer to medium mixing bowl or individual dessert dishes and place in refrigerator to chill for 45 minutes. (*Yields approximately 15 oz.*)

Blueberry Kiwi Pudding

3 oz. millet
5 oz. blueberries
2 oz. kiwi
¹/₂ banana
6 oz. apple strawberry
　juice
2 heaping tsp. Ener-G-
　Egg Replacer
1 tsp. lemon juice
1¹/₂ oz. slivered
　almonds

Place millet in a small saucepan with approximately 10 oz. water and cook for 20 minutes. When cooked, put in blender with the remaining ingredients, except for almonds. Puree until smooth and creamy. Transfer puree to medium saucepan and heat for 5 minutes over medium heat, stirring frequently. Transfer to medium mixing bowl or individual dessert dishes and allow to chill in refrigerator for 45 minutes. (*Yields approximately 23 oz.*)

Strawberry Tofu Pudding

4¹/₂ oz. strawberry
6 oz. tofu
3 tbsp. maple syrup
1 tsp. vanilla

Place all ingredients in the blender. Puree until creamy and smooth. Transfer into one medium mixing bowl or individual dessert dishes. Place in refrigerator and allow to chill for 45 minutes. (*Serves 2.*)

Peach Canton

6 oz. peaches
12 oz. apple
  blackberry juice
2 heaping tbsp. agar-
  agar
2 tbsp. Barbados
  molasses
3 oz. pitted black
  cherries

Wash and cut peaches into small pieces. Place half of the peaches in a blender with juice. Place mixture in a medium saucepan and bring to a boil. Lower heat and add agar-agar. Stir and dissolve agar and simmer for 5 minutes. Add molasses. Transfer to a medium mixing bowl or individual dessert dishes and place in refrigerator until juice begins to gel—around 10 minutes. Add remaining peaches and cherries. Chill for 1 hour. (*Serves 2.*)

Peachy Tofu Pudding

6 oz. peaches
3 oz. tofu
3 oz. barley malt
1 tsp. vanilla
6 oz. peach juice

Wash and cut peaches. Place all ingredients in blender and puree until smooth. Transfer to medium saucepan and place on medium heat for 5 minutes, stirring frequently. Transfer to medium mixing bowl or individual dessert dishes and allow to chill in refrigerator for 45 minutes. (*Yields 18 oz.*)

Blueberry Banana Pudding

6 oz. blueberries
1 banana
3 oz. tofu
3 oz. apple juice
4 oz. nectarines, sliced
2 oz. almonds

Place blueberries, banana, tofu and apple juice in a blender. Puree until smooth and creamy. Transfer to medium mixing bowl or individual dessert dishes. Top with nectarine slices and almonds. (*Serves 2.*)

Part Four

Perfecting
Your
Technique

14 · WEIGHT MANAGEMENT

"Counting calories is not as important as thoughtfully choosing the kinds and amounts of food you eat. The typical American diet needs to be adjusted to include more complex carbohydrates, fewer proteins, and less fat. Begin your new eating plan by eliminating the three whites from your diet: white sugar, white flour, and salt. Then eliminate processed food including most canned, frozen, or prepared convenience foods. Read labels and do not eat anything you can't pronounce."

THERE ARE VIRTUALLY HUNDREDS of diet programs available today. Most are based on high-protein, low-calorie regimens, or involve products that are supposed to melt away fat, change the metabolism or stimulate muscle development. Before embarking upon any of these, first examine the notion of what is proper weight, making sure your perception of what constitutes your ideal weight is not mistaken.

THE SCOPE OF THE PROBLEM

You may not realize it, but it requires from two to four years of being over-fat before you become overweight. Excess fat will first infiltrate the muscle tissue before it spills out as subcutaneous tissue, that which you can see underneath the folds of skin. By the time the fat is visible on your arms and face, the problem has already reached the advanced stages and the buttocks, thighs, belly, upper arms, and back have already been saturated. To assume that a crash diet based on fasting, or calorie restriction is going to reverse this process can be a dangerous assumption to make. The end result of easy solutions may only be repeated failures. The key to weight management, and ideal weight control, is not diet alone but exercise in combination with diet.

THE ROLE OF EXERCISE

Exercise is more important in maintaining proper weight than counting calories. You have heard that for every 3,500 calories in excess of your body's metabolic requirements you will gain a pound, while for every 3,500 calories under that requirement you would lose a pound. These were both cumulative figures. So that, for example, if you were eating one extra slice of bread per day, you would have gained over ten pounds by the year's end, at the rate of 70 extra calories per slice, 490 calories per week. But this represents a gross misunderstanding of how our bodies work. Diets based on such a seemingly rational, logical, though mechanistic view of the body sound simple. Yet they don't work—because the body does not work that way—so rationally, logically and, worst of all, so mechanically. Look at all the thin people who eat great quantities of food and never gain an ounce. Look at all the fat people who just have to think about food, or smell food, and gain pounds.

We need to determine what causes weight problems and treat the causes, not the symptoms. The way to do this is to understand how the body works, and then use its own natural mechanisms to produce the desired results. Exercise is the key.

THE SETPOINT

Primitive man gorged when food was available and starved when there was none. His body had built-in survival mechanisms that stored fat when he gorged and then conserved energy when food was scarce. The conservation mechanism slowed down his metabolism, making use only of enough energy to keep him alive and functioning. That mechanism is still with us and still working. Decreasing your caloric intake, skipping a meal or even eating irregularly may trigger the starvation mechanism. Your body's protective response is to go into its conservation mode—to conserve energy and preserve the fat, just in case starvation is really imminent. When the body gets food, it puts it in a "bank," to ensure against any possible further deprivation. Each of our bodies seems to have a certain natural level, or setpoint, that it strives to maintain to keep itself functioning.

Researchers are now looking at how the body gains and retains weight and are redefining their understanding of weight control. What are the causes of weight gain? The answer seems to lie in a weight-regulating mechanism located in a control center in the brain called the hypothalamus. It determines the level of fat that it considers ideal for the body. It proceeds to maintain that level, come what may. That level, selected by the weight-regulating mechanism, then becomes the setpoint. The setpoint is analogous to a thermostat. A thermostat set at 70° kicks off and activates the heating system when the temperature falls below 70°. Similarly, a setpoint of 140 pounds activates the weight-regulating mechanism to store more fat if the body weight falls below that 140-pound level. In its effort to maintain the setpoint, the weight-regulating mechanism works in two ways: It controls the appetite and it regulates our metabolism and the storage of energy.

First, appetite control determines when you feel hungry. It sends you a message to eat. You may have no control over the urge to eat—the hypothalamus makes sure of that—but you do have complete control over your response. You can choose when and how to respond. What you eat and how much you eat are totally up to you. The hypothalamus will continue to stimulate the feeding mechanism and decrease satiety, you will continue to feel hungry and eat, until the desired setpoint level is achieved, and your weight is back to where it was.

Second, a weight-regulating mechanism signals the body when to conserve energy and store it, or use it up. If you eat a large amount of food, it increases the rate at which the body burns calories. If you eat a small amount, the body decreases the rate. In each case, the goal is to preserve the setpoint. This explains why people on diets may lose weight temporarily, but ultimately regain it, and then keep their weight at close to the former, albeit unsatisfactory level. It's called the yo-yo syndrome, and every dieter is familiar with it. Usually that weight has been typical for them for many years. It is their setpoint. The body is accustomed to it, feels safe and secure at that level, and consequently does what it can to maintain it. People who are overweight commonly observe that they don't really eat that much. Indeed, studies have confirmed that underweight people comonly eat more than overweight people. What we distill from this is that overweight people may have a body chemistry geared to making fat even from a low-calorie diet. It seems that they are just better at storing fat than at burning fat. Their bodies are programmed to make fat and protect their setpoints. This also explains why some other people never seem to gain weight. Their setpoints are low, their ability to use energy is efficient, and so they don't store fat. You cannot cheat the setpoint. You can, however, change the setpoint, but only through aerobic exercise.

THE AGING FACTOR

From the age of 30 on, your metabolism decelerates about 5 percent every seven years. In other words, if you were eating the same number of calories at 50 years of age that you ate at 30, you would be gaining several pounds every year. But weight itself is not an indication of optimal body health. A person weighing 200 pounds, who lifts weights and exercises, may have only 3 to 4 percent body fat. Many football players, for example, would fall into this category. But if these individuals stopped all their physical activity and one year later they weighed the same, their entire body structure would be different. They would look and feel obese, because their muscle would have turned to fat. Muscle that is not used, atrophies. Weight itself should not be taken as the primary indicator of health. What is important is the percentage of lean muscle tissue and the percentage of fat to total body mass. Ideally, most men should be approximately 15 percent body fat, most women no more than 18 to 20 percent. However, most studies indicate that most men are between 22 and 24 percent, most women between 26 and 34 percent.

LEAN BODY MASS

Lean body mass increases when intramuscular fat is replaced with muscle. Muscles have special enzymes that burn calories during exercise. The more muscle you have, the more enzymes you have that burn calories. As the amount of muscle increases, the amount of fat decreases, and the capacity for burning more calories is further enhanced. So when muscles move, they burn calories and increase lean body mass. It's a new cycle, but this time it's not vicious!

AEROBIC EXERCISE AND THE FIT CYCLE

Although there are probably genetic tendencies that predetermine that one of us will have a low setpoint and be thin, or a high setpoint and be overweight, it is still possible for most people to "re-set" their fat thermostat. The key to reprogramming your setpoint lies in understanding and acting on the relationship between the kind and amount of exercise you do (your energy output) and the kind and amount of food you eat (your energy input). The trick lies in changing from a fat cycle to a fit cycle.

Running and other aerobic exercises can help you enter the fit cycle. Aerobic exercises uses large muscles in a repetitive rhythmic pattern.

To measure the effect of aerobic exercise on your body you will need to "watch"—or more appropriately—"feel" your heart rate, by measuring your pulse. There are three different heart rates to monitor.

RESTING HEART RATE

The resting heart rate is the rate at which your heart has been pumping after you sit quietly for at least 15 minutes. It is usually 15–20 beats per minute slower than your "normal" heart rate.

Measure by taking your pulse for 10 or 20 seconds and then multiplying the result by 6 or 3, respectively. The average resting heart rate for men is 72–78 beats per minute, for women it's faster: 78–84. The better your aerobic circulation, the lower this rate will be.

Studies seem to indicate that people with resting heart rates above 70 have a greater risk of heart attack. By beating fewer times per minute, an efficient heart has more time to rest between beats. Hence, at each contraction or beat, it may be pumping more oxygen to the body's cells.

TARGET HEART RATE

To produce a beneficial cardiovascular effort during exercise, you should elevate your heart rate sufficiently to strengthen heart muscles while at the same time avoiding any damage to the heart or cardiovascular system.

Take your pulse throughout your aerobic workout to make sure you are neither under- nor over-exerting yourself. Generally, your target rate is determined by taking 220 and subtracting your age and then multiplying the result by 70 percent. So a 31-year-old person would have a rate of 220 minus 31 times 70 percent or 132.

Whatever you do you should not exceed 140 beats per minute when you're just starting an aerobic exercise program.

RECOVERY HEART RATE

This rate records your heart beat five minutes after you've stopped exercising. It gives you some indication about whether you have gone one or more beats too far. If this rate is 120 beats per minute (150 in those over 50 years old), you need to cut back during your next workout.

To achieve a training effect on cardiovascular functioning or to lower your setpoint toward "thinness," you must do the exercise continuously for 20 to 60 minutes at your target heart rate at least three times a week.

During aerobic exercise, the body uses free fatty acids primarily and glycogen secondarily as fuel. While exercising, you do not use many calories. For example, you would have to walk $11^1/_2$ miles to burn up 3,500 calories or one pound. Weight loss is the effect of a *cumulative* process in which calories are being used on a more regular and frequent basis. This cumulative use of calories produces ongoing changes in the body's chemistry, lowering the setpoint, increasing the lean muscle mass with its fat-burning enzymes, and increasing the metabolism so the body burns calories at a higher rate. For hours following the exercise period, the body continues to burn calories at a higher rate. The effects of exercise on the body last long after the exercise period has ended. This will be true as long as you continue to do aerobic exercise at least three days a week. Remember, duration is more important than distance or intensity.

Although many people may intellectually recognize the need for and benefit of aerobic exercise, too often they would rather spend their time doing other things, or hope to take a pill to reduce because it requires no particular effort or ongoing commitment. Making a change in your lifestyle to accomodate exercise *does* require effort and commitment. Your health and well-being are worth the price.

Exercise increases muscle, which has fat-burning enzymes. The more you exercise and develop muscles, the more lean body mass and less fat. All this will happen in addition to the much heralded cardiovascular and psychological advantages of aerobic exercise. Lowering the setpoint is a bonus.

Your individual exercise program will start the same way whether your goal is overall fitness or weight management. The proper sequence for a holistic workout is outlined in Chapter 15, starting with relaxation techniques and measurement of the pulse at rest. In addition, you will want to take your body measurements before starting any exercise program.

If you step on the scale after a few weeks of exercising, you may notice an increase in pounds. Don't be dismayed. That is a good sign. It means you are increasing muscle in relation to intramuscular fat (muscle weighs more than fat). Interpret the increase as getting better and stronger, not heavier. Then throw away the scale. Pounds do not measure fitness. Your tape measure and your clothes are better indicators of changes in your body. You will lose inches, usually in the "right" places.

EATING PLANS

Counting calories is not as important as thoughtfully choosing the kinds and amounts of food you eat. The typical American diet needs to be adjusted to include more complex carbohydrates, fewer proteins, and less fat. Begin your new eating plan by eliminating the three whites from your diet: white sugar, white flour, and salt. Then eliminate processed food including most canned, frozen or prepared convenience foods. Read labels and do not eat anything you can't pronounce.

There is one point that most books on dieting fail to mention. That is the importance of getting in touch with your appetite thermostat. Your body tells you when to eat and when to stop, and you don't always hear it or listen to it.

The best eating plan is to eat more frequently—smaller meals, every four to six hours, so that both hunger and satiety can be experienced. Do eat breakfast, just keep down fat and sugar consumption. More people who skip breakfast are overweight than underweight. Get in touch with your eating drives. Keep lunch light, preferably eating complex carbohydrates, which are low in calories and high in satiety. Soup is a satisfying lunch, especially a water-based soup full of vegetables, grains, and legumes. Salads are good for lunch, but after eating one you could feel hungry again quite soon. Add whole grain bread to complement it. Beware of salad dressings; most are high in fat, sugar, and calories. Eat enough breakfast and lunch to take away the strong hunger drive, but not enough to feel full. If you are hungry before the next meal, have a snack. Eat only in response to hunger, not for entertainment.

Another divergence from traditional diets, but designed to pay attention to your body's natural eating drive, is to eat one meal a day to complete satiety, until you do not want to eat anymore. The evening meal is preferred, so it will hold you throught the evening until bedtime. This is the most difficult time to avoid snacks.

Beware: The weight you eventually reach may not necessarily be the weight you desire. Be realistic and be philosophical. The genetic determinants of setpoint may limit what you can realistically accomplish. If you follow the principles of exercise and diet for a reasonable period of time, and your weight stabilizes at a point higher than your fantasy weight, accept it and enjoy being yourself, as you are.

If you continue to exercise aerobically and eat a healthful diet, your weight-regulating mechanism will stabilize your weight and keep it at the new setpoint. Eating and exercising in this way will soon become a natural way of living for you. You won't need a maintenance diet or some other interim discipline to follow. Once you've set your own course, there will be no other course to follow and no need for fad approaches to dieting.

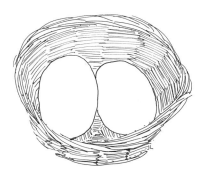

15 · NUTRITION AND EXERCISE

"Walking can be done by almost anyone, almost anywhere. For some, including the elderly, pregnant, arthritic, or those with heart disease, it is the only form of reasonable cardiovascular exercise. All you need is some comfortable old clothes, a good pair of running (walking) shoes, and a hat to protect you if the weather is hot and sunny or cold and windy. About 1½ hours of walking will give you the same aerobic effect as 30 minutes of running."

ANY DIET SHOULD BE tailored to each person's specific requirements, with attention paid to your body's specialized needs as well as to the type and amount of exercise to which you are accustomed. The additional stress of exercise requires adjusting your nutritional intake to replenish the fuel used up during exercise.

FOOD ALLERGIES AFFECTING EXERCISE

Food allergies are discussed at length in the allergy chapters of the book. Few things can adversely affect our energy level during exercise more than allergies. An allergy will weaken your immune system, making you more vulnerable to infection and deterioration. If you overexercise, you will probably incur joint and muscle inflammation, yet a properly functioning immune system will allow your body to quickly repair itself.

FAT AND PROTEIN

When you exercise regularly, your body burns a higher than normal percentage of fats, even while you sleep. To give your body an adequate supply of essential fatty acids, steer clear of animal fats and eat extra oils selected from a variety of available vegetable sources. Rely primarily on unrefined oils found in foods such as raw seeds, raw nuts, avocados, and grains. Refined oils increase your risk of consuming too many free radicals—unstable molecules that can attack your cells, speed up the aging process, and weaken your body.

Protein is an inefficient fuel that is pressed into service only after preferred fuels are depleted. It is digested slowly and tends to dehydrate your body by using lots of water for its digestion and elimination. Under normal circumstances, you can only digest and utilize three ounces of food at a time, so regulate your protein intake to avoid the taxing waste of energy that follows overconsumption. Complex carbohydrates are much more efficient and should serve as your key foods for replenishing glycogen, the energy fuel.

CARBOHYDRATE LOADING

Carbohydrate loading is an eating regimen followed by some athletes in preparation for a long competition, such as a running marathon. A typical schedule for a runner begins seven days before the event with an exhausting bout of exercise, depleting the stores of glycogen in the body. To further aid the glycogen depletion, the runner eats a low-carbohydrate, high-protein and high-fat diet. Three days before the event, he packs in as many carbohydrates as possible to replenish the glycogen, keeping protein and fat at moderate levels. The body is stressed by this deprivation of carbohydrate fuel, and it responds to that stress by overcompensating and storing extra supplies of glycogen in the muscles. Thus, the marathon runner has more energy and can run longer before tiring.

One modification of this classic loading technique is to substitute tapered rest for the exhaustive bout of exercise during the week preceding the event. Also, the last week might feature a high complex carbohydrate diet. A further modification sometimes suggested is for the runner to rest and eat a high complex carbohydrate diet 48 to 72 hours before the event.

What was just described is preparation for an extraordinary event that few of us would even participate in. For regular exercise, or competition in general, guidelines for eating are: 1) Eat enough so as not to feel hungry during the event. Eat modest amounts of complex carbohydrates up to $2^1/2$ hours before exercising. Stay away from fat and protein. Avoid salty or spicy foods, simple sugars, and unfamiliar foods that could irritate or upset you. 2) Allow time for your stomach and small intestines to empty. 3) Drink water or diluted fruit juice until one hour before the event, then continue to drink water only.

You may wonder if, after drinking so much water, a runner, walker, or biker will need to stop and urinate. The fact is the kidneys slow down during exercise, so the body will retain fluids for use by other tissues to reduce heat build-up that comes with exercise and produce sweat. The body, in effect, turns off the water-eliminating system and turns on the water-retention system.

SUPPLEMENTS

In general a person who eats a well-balanced diet will not need vitamin or mineral supplements for their exercise needs. However, not all the vitamins and minerals naturally available in foods will be available to everyone, due to food sensitivities, poor absorption, chemical imbalances and improper food combining. Persons affected by these factors may need supplements, even megadoses, of vitamins and minerals to bring a particular deficiency up to par or to strengthen a weak point.

Exercise stresses the body, with B complex vitamins in particular burned off by stress. It is recommended that B complex vitamins as well as vitamin A, which helps stimulate the immune system, be taken as part of an exercise regimen. The antioxidants, vitamins C and E, and selenium, are also recommended before and after exercise. Calcium and magnesium, in a 1:1 ratio, are commonly used to benefit muscles. Iron deficiency is common among women and athletes, and runners should be tested for iron deficiency before training begins.

SALT INTAKE AFTER EXERCISE

A common misconception is that your body loses salt through perspiration after exercise. In fact, it loses only water, leaving the body's salt in higher concentrations than before. You need more water after exercise, not more salt, to help prevent fatigue, irritability, and exhaustion. Salt pills are not recommended.

A BIG DINNER OR A BEDTIME SNACK?

If you are serious about exercise, dinner should be your smallest meal of the day. In the late afternoon or early evening, your body is in a state of recuperation and repair from exercise. Burdening it with a heavy meal hampers this process.

You shouldn't eat anything substantial for at least two hours before you go to sleep because little will leave your stomach within an hour after eating. Once you're in a prone position, whatever is in your stomach has difficulty moving into the intestine. If you are hungry late in the evening, try a very light food such as fruit, or have a liquid refreshment like an herbal tea.

POST-EXERCISE NUTRITION

During exercise, you use up water and fuel. You need to replenish them—in that order. Water, the recommended beverage, helps alleviate feelings of exhaustion. Give your body an opportunity to return to normal before eating.

Even if you are not consciously thirsty, drink an 8- to 10-ounce glass of water after exercising, and again at 20-minute intervals for the next hour. You cannot restore the water you lost in exercise simply by drinking a lot at one time. Your body's tissues, after all, can only absorb water at a certain rate; the rest is eliminated. The average water consumption per day for a healthy adult who exercises is eight 8- to 10-ounce glasses. What you do not use, the body will eliminate.

If you are ravenous after exercising, it may mean you have run out of fuel. You have depleted your supply of glucose and/or glycogen and your body wants to start replenishing it immediately. Pay attention to the amount of complex carbohydrates you are eating. You may want to start eating more as a part of your regular diet to build up glycogen levels.

While pre-exercise nutrition should consist of a high complex carbohydrate diet, post-exercise nutrition should include protein as well. Since you will need protein to rebuild or repair muscles and other tissues.

EXERCISE ALTERNATIVES

Doing the same exercises all the time develops certain of our muscles to the exclusion of others. Runners, for example, typically have very healthy internal body systems and well-developed legs, but they lack proportional upper-body strength. Combining different forms of exercise can help achieve a good balance of muscle activity throughout the body. Below are some aerobic alternatives to running.

Any aerobic exercise should be done three or four times a week for 20 to 30 minutes each time for maximum benefit. Start slowly, increasing the amount of time and intensity by about 10 percent every two weeks. Use good quality equipment, including proper foot gear. All sports require both pre- and post-game stretching.

After completing *any* aerobic exercise you should:
1. Check your pulse. See if you have achieved your target heart rate. If you haven't, exercise a bit harder next time.
2. Avoid hot showers, saunas, or whirlpools. Heat keeps the peripheral capillaries dilated, making it difficult for your blood to return to your heart right after exercise.
3. Avoid strength exercises like weightlifting after doing aerobics. Weightlifting constricts blood capillaries so the blood does not return to your heart. Do them before the aerobic exercises or at another time.
4. Rehydrate yourself, replacing body fluids lost doing exercise.

Cross-Country Skiing

Since weather or location may make this alternative difficult, indoor cross-country machines are available and can be used year round. Some experts even think that cross-country skiing is better aerobically than running, since in cross-country skiing you use more muscles than just those in your legs. The more muscles involved in exercise, the better the aerobic effect you get.

Swimming

Swimming is an outstanding cardiovascular exercise. It is rhythmic, uses all the major muscle groups, stretches the muscles and keeps you limber. The water's buoyancy reduces the pressure on bones and joints, pressure that can cause injuries in other sports. As a result, people unable to walk or jog because of a skeletal or structural problem often still can take up swimming.

If you are a nonswimmer, you can still take up a water sport. You can begin by taking your pulse while walking back and forth slowly in the waist-deep area of a pool. Swing your arms naturally when walking. Build up the intensity of this regimen to reach and maintain your target heart rate.

If you are a swimmer, take you pulse and do warm-up exercises. Once in the pool, start slowly and easily with a restful stroke, like the breast stroke or the side stroke. Build up slowly until you reach your target heart rate. You may eventually change to more intense strokes, such as the crawl or butterfly. Aim to swim for a full 20 minutes, even if you have to swim on your back for a while when you tire.

As with other aerobic exercises, swim for 20 to 30 minutes, three to four times a week. But be careful; daily swimming can lead to strained or pulled muscles. Skip a day to allow your body to recover. Periodically, try to increase your swimming speed by sprinting for up to 30 seconds at a time. As soon as you feel yourself winded, return to your normal pace. Repeat this three to five times in a row with a 30-second recovery interval between sprints. This type of interval training can enhance your cardiovascular conditioning.

Swimming builds powerful shoulders and arm muscles, as well as rear leg muscles. After swimming, stretch your rear leg muscles. And since the back stroke uses the anterior leg muscles more, they may also require additional stretching afterwards.

Wear a comfortable suit that will stay on without constant fuss and attention. The ideal pool water temperature is 77° to 81°F. Warmer water makes it difficult for the body to eliminate heat; colder water makes it difficult to warm up muscles.

There are some drawbacks to swimming. The biggest problem may be finding a pool. If you choose swimming, choose an alternate sport as well, for those times when a pool is not available.

Another disadvantage is the possibility of getting conjuctivitis or ear infections. You can protect yourself against both by wearing goggles and either a bathing cap or ear plugs. Select only good goggles—the cheap varieties are ineffective. Be sure not to use a nose plug if your nose is inflamed in any way, since that condition actually is better served by allowing the free circulation of moisture. Some people react badly to the chlorine in the water, especially, as is often the case, if the concentration is high.

Walking

Walking can be done by almost anyone, almost anywhere. For some, including the elderly, pregnant, arthritic, or those with heart disease, it is the only form of reasonable cardiovascular exercise. All you need is some comfortable old clothes, a good pair of running (walking) shoes, and a hat to protect you if the weather is hot and sunny or cold and windy.

Walking is a low-intensity exercise, so you have to do it for a longer time than a sport like running to get maximum cardiovascular conditioning. About 1 1/2 hours of walking will give you the same aerobic effect as 30 minutes of running.

Walk with an even, rhythmic heel-to-toe gait; swing your arms from side to side in a natural way. Don't keep them pressed tightly against your body or in your pockets. Try not to carry anything since it will weigh you down and upset your balance.

Start by taking your pulse and doing the warm-up exercises. For the first two to three weeks, walk 20 to 30 minutes a day. Increase that to 1 1/2 hours a day in 10 percent increments every two or three weeks. Begin each session by walking slowly, building up to your target heart rate, and then tapering off to a slow pace. Check your pulse every 10 minutes. If you feel tired, slow down or stop altogether until you recover. Then start slowly and build up your speed and heart rate again.

You can walk anywhere. First choice, and the most fun, is outdoors on a soft surface of grass or earth. If you walk in the street, be sure to face the traffic by walking on the left side. If the weather or your health do not permit you to go outdoors, walk indoors, up and down the hallway in your apartment building, or snake in and around the rooms in your home.

Cycling

Bicycle riding is excellent for the long distance runner. It works out the anterior leg muscles in the front of the leg, muscles that tend to weaken since running works the rear leg muscles more. By strengthening the anterior leg muscles, you can prevent knee and rear leg muscle injuries.

If you ride a bicycle very slowly, you need more time on it to gain proper cardiovascular conditioning. At the same time, if you sprint all the time you will lose any aerobic benefit as well, so never try to ride a bicycle to the point that you are exercising at over 80 percent of your maximum heart rate. However, you can do interval training, much like swimming, while you bike ride. Ride the bicycle as fast as you can for 30 seconds at a time.

Then rest for 30 seconds by riding at a normal pace. Do this three to five times in a row. Such interval training will help increase your aerobic capacity and stamina.

Remember to stretch out properly after bike riding. It is best to wear good biking shoes, since they transmit force to the pedals more efficiently. Walking and running shoes will do well, if you can't find biking shoes. You should use foot clips to secure your shoes to the pedals.

Bicycling causes less trauma to the joints and muscles than jogging or running. Still, problems can occur. In addition to collisions, the most common injuries are outer calf pain, knee pain, and chronic soreness of the hands.

Whether you use a 3-speed or 10-speed bicycle does not really matter. What does matter is that the bike is sturdy, that the frame is suited to your size and that it is kept in safe operating condition. Structurally, men's bikes are often sounder than women's, and for this reason many women buy them. Adjust the seat height so that you can pedal. Your knee should be almost straight when the pedal is closest to the ground, but even at that position, the leg should be slightly bent. Use pant clips or rubber bands to keep your pants from tangling in the chain. At night, dress so that you can be seen. A red leg light provides a moving signal of your presence on the road.

For exercising, you might want to use a bike with handlebars tilted upward, so you can sit up straight. Your bones will be in alignment, and such bikes are friendlier to your lower back than bikes with racing handles. For distance or racing, you will want to use downward tilted handlebars.

Riding indoors on a stationary bicycle is also beneficial. The same basic principles apply. The more interesting the exercise bicycle is, (for example, with built-in computers), the more the exercise will help hold your interest, reducing some of the boredom that you might otherwise experience.

Anybody who is able to ride a bicycle and at the same time read a novel or a magazine is not riding the bicycle hard enough to gain a cardiovascular benefit. Your concentration should always be on the sport itself.

Rope Jumping

Rope jumping, or jumping *without* a rope, gives you cardiovascular conditioning with a bonus: you can burn more calories per minute jumping rope than running, swimming, or bike riding. Jumping rope, however, can have a disastrous effect on the legs and lower back. Never start jumping for a *long* period of time. In the beginning, even a few minutes can be too long.

To begin properly, run in place, or walk in place, faster and faster, until your legs are coming off the ground at a very fast rate. Stay light on your feet. Avoid pounding them into the ground. Then, for a period of 10 to 20 seconds, start to jump very lightly on both feet at the same time. It is not necessary to jump high. Just keep jumping, and then after 30 seconds (with or without a rope), start walking or jogging in place again. Do this for a minute or two. As soon as you feel your breath return, start jumping again. Spend no more than 2 to 4 minutes jumping the first day. The older or heavier you are, the less you should do the first few times.

Never jump rope on a daily basis. It can lead to a lot of serious problems, since it can just be too stressful for the body. Increase your jumping time by about 10 percent every two weeks. This will allow your bones and musculature to develop proper stress build-up, as opposed to the overstress that would likely be caused by a too rapid increase, leading not only to calf pain and lower back pain, but to stress fractures of the bones in the leg and foot. Your ultimate aim is to jump for 20 to 30 minutes continuously. Interval training can be used with jumping rope, in much the same way described for swimming or bicycling.

Remember, duration is more important than intensity.

Rope jumping can be done in a small space, like a patio or small yard. In inclement weather, it can be done in a garage, basement or any room with a ceiling high enough for a rope to clear. A jump rope travels well; it packs easily and permits a workout almost anywhere.

To make a fine jump rope, you need a 3/8" nylon rope that measures double the length from the floor to your nipple, and two 6" PVC 1/2 pipes. You do not need bearings or digital counters. Simply monitoring your heart rate with a watch will tell you all you need to know.

Other Aerobic Alternatives

Other aerobic exercise alternatives include rowing (using a boat or rowing machine), roller skating, aerobic dancing, minitrampolining (or rebound jogging), and using a treadmill. You can also get aerobic effects from tennis, handball, racquet ball, squash, and basketball.

Chair stepping is an aerobic exercise, but we do not recommend it for *beginners*. It overstresses both your knees and heart.

POPULAR ANAEROBIC ALTERNATIVES

Each of the sports discussed below, as well as most others, actually fall somewhere between aerobic and anaerobic. They require explosive bursts of energy followed by longer periods of lower energy output or rest. They are anaerobic because they build one or all of the following in a concentrated effort: strength, power, endurance, or the skill of specific muscles or muscle groups.

Weight Training

Weight training can provide an excellent way for the runner to maintain strength and flexibility. By increasing the strength of all your muscles, not just those in your legs, you can increase your ability to withstand the stresses of long distance running. Also body parts that are weak tend to get injured much faster.

Arm, shoulder, and anterior leg muscle exercises should be emphasized in weight training. It is important, however, not to try to build up big muscles through weight training; this will only add to the weight and exercise burden you have to carry during running. While it is important to be strong, weight training can also tighten you up. Thus, flexibility and a range of motion programs as well as a good stretching program are needed to loosen you up.

Remember, allow a full 48 hours between weight-training sessions for the muscles to repair and heal since weight training breaks down muscle.

Start with low weights that are easy to lift. Do three sets of 8 to 12 repetitions. The last two repetitions should be difficult; your muscles strengthen only when they fatigue. The initial repetitions (or reps) result in muscle tone, the final reps give muscle strength. As soon as the last two reps become easy, it means it is time to increase the weights by a minimum of $2^{1}/_{2}$ pounds to a maximum of 10 pounds.

To build muscle mass, or "beach" muscles, use heavy weights and do fewer reps, about eight to ten. To improve tone, use light weights, and do more reps, about 12 to 15 per set.

As a rule, weight trainers think that athletes need to eat huge amounts of protein to rebuild and repair the muscle tissue broken down by exercise. In fact, athletes typically eat too much protein, and not enough complex carbohydrates (which are also excellent sources of protein).

Different forms of weight training will help increase general muscle strength. One involves the use of free weights. A second utilizes universal machines, and a third uses isokinetic, or Nautilus-type, training procedures. All three systems basically do the same thing. They help muscle become completely fatigued and so increase the size of the muscle fibers.

Free weights can be used at home as well as in an athletic club. But since it takes some time to prepare for each of the different exercises, it may seem to take a long time to get the effect you want. Free weights have to be used very carefully; they pose the most risks of all weight-training procedures.

They help develop better coordination, however, than other weight-training procedures.

Racket Sports

Tennis, racketball, squash, paddleball, and handball are basically discontinuous, stop-and-go sports. Players need power for explosive bursts of energy and stamina to run around the court. They come closest to aerobic activity when there are long volleys that result in the continuous use of large muscles.

Racket sports are very popular. Indoor and outdoor courts are abundant and many are accessible year round. To begin, find a place to play, and a good instructor who will guide you on proper technique, equipment and clothing.

Try to play with people who are at your level to avoid unnecessary tension and embarassment. Remember, exercise is supposed to benefit you—physically and spiritually.

Golf

Golfers need good neuromuscular coordination and focused concentration. The game is characterized by short bursts of energy interspersed with longer periods of slow activity or rest. Unfortunately, a good deal of stress builds up around each shot. Your caloric expenditure will depend totally on whether you walk (how far and how fast), or ride an electric cart around the five- or six-mile golf course. If you walk briskly between holes, you can approach some aerobic conditioning for brief periods of time.

To start, find a golf instructor who will guide you to appropriate equipment and clothing. It is best to learn proper stance and movement from the beginning, rather than later having to unlearn improper techniques.

If you are playing golf for exercise and pleasure, it can give you both. If you bring your business or social problems to the course, however, you lessen these benefits. Golfing in hot or humid weather can lead to dehydration. Drinking water before, during, and after play therefore becomes essential.

A 28-DAY EXERCISE PLAN

This comprehensive exercise program is designed for the runner or anyone serious about regular exercise who wants to develop and maintain good health. But for it to work, you must be willing to make a commitment to incorporate this gentle, realistic, exercise routine into your life-style. Exercise should be viewed in the same way as brushing your teeth, something to develop as a daily habit whose importance you recognize. Don't regard it as something extra you'll do if you have time after you do everything else. Exercise is part of everything else. Yet also understand you won't die if you miss a day.

The Basic 28-Day Exercise Plan calls for your choice of running or some other aerobic exercise on Days 1, 3, and 5. For the first 4 weeks, do the exercise for 20 minutes. Increase the duration by 10 percent every two weeks if you are under 35 years of age and have no history of heart disease. Increase the duration by 10 percent every 4 weeks if you are over 35 or have a history of heart disease.

These exercise plans are designed in one-week cycles, since most people plan their time that way. Day 1 of the exercise plan may be any day of the week. The sequence is what matters.

Your exercise program, to be viable, needs to reflect your goals, attitudes, strengths, weaknesses, and life-style. Use these suggested plans as guidelines; feel free to alter them to suit individual requirements.

When choosing aerobic alternatives, use both sides of your brain. Use the left side to choose activities that will enable you to get and keep your body functioning at your target heart rate for 20 to 30 minutes at least three days a week. Also be realistic in your expectations. So use the right side of your brain to evaluate activities that appeal to you.

Different exercises affect different muscles. You can combine two complementary exercises in your total program and rotate them according to whim or weather. You could have one indoor and one outdoor choice. For example, skiing and biking build up the anterior leg muscles while providing good aerobic conditioning. If you run outdoors and use a stationary bicycle indoors, you have come up with a set of complementary exercises good for all seasons. Either one could also be combined with swimming. There are outdoor and indoor pools. Weight training is a beneficial form of anaerobic exercise that augments any aerobic exercise. It can be done with free weights or an isokinetic machine, like the Nautilus.

When you purchase equipment, choose sturdy, safe, well-built, quality equipment. Junk breaks down quickly. Appropriate clothes and footgear are also important. Be particular about your running shoes. Perfect fit is critical.

Prior to starting any serious exercise or conditioning program, most people should have a complete physical exam, including a stress test. A cardiovascular stress test entails hooking you up to an electrocardiograph, which monitors your heart and blood pressure as you walk or run on a treadmill. The workload is increased at regular intervals. The results can indicate hidden or small conditions that could lead to trouble. Stress tests are done in various centers, hospitals, and some cardiologists' offices. If you are under 35 years of age, not overweight, and have no family history of heart disease, you probably do not need a stress test. A routine physical examination will do.

If for some reason you cannot or do not wish to have such an exam, the important point is to start and proceed very slowly. If any unusual signs manifest themselves, stop right away and check them out immediately with your doctor.

What time of day is best to exercise? If you guessed either morning, noon or night, you'd be right. There are three more facts to consider:

a. Most people are more flexible and looser (also more fatigued after a day's work) at about 6 P.M. So exercising in late afternoon takes advantage of the flexibility, pumps up energy to revitalize a tired body and reduces the tensions of the day. Exercising in early morning, on the other hand, takes advantage of a well-rested and fresh state of mind.

b. Each person needs to be in tune with his or her own body, following the monthly rhythms that seem to affect our intellect, mood, and physical energy levels. Do it when it feels good.

c. The right time for exercise is any time you manage to find in your busy schedule. It is best to plan your exercise.

If you feel exhausted, reduce the intensity and duration of any exercise by 50 percent. Your body is talking to you. Listen to it. That's good preventive sports medicine. The only legitimate reason for skipping your exercise is illness. Business is the worst excuse. You probably could use exercise most when you are under stress from work.

Relaxation, warm-ups and cool-down exercise should be used with all types of exercise: physical activity, aerobic, anaerobic, and all those in between. They maintain flexibility in muscles, tendons, ligaments, and joints, and help to prevent injury.

Too much, too fast, or too soon are the most common reasons for sport injuries. DO NOT OVERDO. Less is better—at the beginning—at least until your body adapts. Be in touch with your body to avoid injury and disillusionment because of some bad, though probably avoidable experience. Test yourself to see what affects your body. If you overdo, you will lose your sensitivity to the small clues your body will provide. So before beginning your Basic 28-Day Plan, review all cautions.

You are now ready to begin your Basic 28-Day Plan. It is a one-size-fits-all plan, and it is good for the rest of your life. The exercises will work for you as long as you do. There is a variation of the Basic Plan presented here if you wish to go beyond good health toward excellence, or have special fitness goals. Option A provides an opportunity for anaerobic exercise or sports. Option B adds interval training to aerobic exercise.

Steps 1 through 5 are the warm-up sequence: Relaxation, Nonspecific Warm-Up, Joint Warm-Up, Pre-sport Stretching, Specific Warm-Up. Together with Steps 7 and 8, the cool-down sequence (Post-sport Stretching and Cool-Down), they should be done every single day of your life to maintain good flexibility, circulation, balance, and a sense of well-being.

Step 6 is the slot in which you should put your running or chosen aerobic alternative. It is the one part of the sequence that will change from day to day, or from time to time, as your needs and goals change.

BASIC 28–DAY PLAN
(weeks 1–4)

DAY	STEPS	TIME
1	warm-ups (#1–5) choice of aerobic exercise (#6) cool-downs (#7–8)	20 min.
2	#1–5 & #7–8	
3	#1–8	
4	#1–5 & #7–8	
5	#1–8	
6	#1–5 & #7–8	
7	#1–5 & #7–8	

Repeat the 7–day sequence four times for a total of 28 days. Beginning on Day 1 of the fifth week (roughly the beginning of the second month), increase the time you exercise by 10 percent. Instead of 20 minutes, exercise aerobically for 22 minutes. Follow the increment schedule as described above until you reach the time limits listed below:

EXERCISE	TIME LIMIT
Walking	1½ hours
Running	30 minutes (unless you want to compete)
Swimming	45 minutes to 1 hour
Bicycling	30 minutes (unless you want to compete)
Jumping	30 minutes (due to high intensity of jumping, it is detrimental to go beyond this limit)

Monitor your pulse to be certain you are exercising within your target heart range. As you become more fit, and your body handles the stress of exercise more efficiently, you will have to work harder to get up to and stay at your target heart rate. Do this first by increasing duration until you reach the defined time limit, then by increasing intensity as measured by your heart rate.

This is a lifetime exercise plan. As such, it accomodates itself to you each year. On your birthday, recalculate your target heart range. The formula again is 220 minus your age times 70%.

If for reasons of your own you desire a more demanding schedule, do Step 6, your aerobic exercise, a fourth time during each week. A good choice is Day 6 or Day 7. If you decide to train for a marathon, you could train three days, rest one, train three days and rest one.

OPTION A

The 28-Day Plan's Option A suggests you choose an anaerobic exercise or sport to alternate with your aerobic exercise. Step 6 will be an aerobic exercise or sport one day a week. Option A is designed for persons who enjoy a particular sport, like tennis or golf, and want to incorporate it into their exercise regimen. It will also appeal to persons who want to develop stronger and more balanced musculature through weight training or calisthenics.

If you are enthusiastic about your sport and want to play twice a week, below is a suggested schedule to accomodate that. *Remember, you need to space bouts of anaerobic exercise at least 48 hours apart.* The intensity of such exercise breaks down tissue and it takes two full days to repair and recover from that stress.

The Basic Plan is sufficient to achieve and maintain optimal conditioning. Option A is only for those who want more.

Option A suggests an anaerobic exercise or sport on Days 2 and 5 (or only one day if you prefer). This allows you to include tennis or any other racket sport, golf, weight training, etc. You may choose to do calisthenics: 1) push-ups for the arms, shoulders, back, stomach and most of the body, 2) bent-knee sit-ups for the abdominal muscles, and 3) jumping jacks for the legs and shoulders. Start with a few of each and build up. Use proper form and technique with every repetition. If you get sloppy, you will get tired and then quit.

For the first four weeks of Option A, follow the Basic Plan. Begin here on Day 1 of week 5. Notice that on Days 2 and 5, Step 6 is anaerobic. On Days 1 and 3 continue your usual aerobic exercise—this time for 22 minutes each session.

Option A
(week 5)

DAY	STEPS	TIME
1	warm-ups (#1–5) choice of aerobic exercise (#6) cool-downs (#7–8)	22 min.
2	#1–8 #6 anaerobic	
3	#1–8 #6 aerobic	
4	#1–5 & 7–8	
5	#1–8 #6 anaerobic	
6	#1–5 & 7–8	
7	#1–5 & 7–8	

(week 6)

8	#1–8 aerobic	22 min.
9	#1–8 anaerobic	
10	#1–8 aerobic	
11	#1–5 & 7–8	
12	#1–8 anaerobic	
13	#1–5 & 7–8	
14	#1–5 & 7–8	

During weeks 7 and 8, increase the sessions by 10 percent if you are under 35 and have had no heart condition. The Step 6 aerobic exercises on Days 2, 5, 9, and 12 will be performed for 24 minutes. Repeat Days 1–14 for week 7 and 8 (Days 15–28).

At the beginning of week 9, increase the time again by 10 percent to:

a. 26 minutes of aerobic exercise if you are under 35 and do not have a heart condition;

b. 24 minutes of aerobic exercise if you are over 35 or have a history of heart problems.

If you feel like having a heavy workout, you may do your aerobic exercise AFTER your anaerobic exercise or sport. For example, you may want to swim after tennis. That's fine. *But do not do anaerobic after aerobic. It interferes with the body's ability to recover properly.*

If you reach a plateau, or a point in your regimen you cannot get past, yet you feel you have not reached your physiological limit, seek professional guidance. Something you are doing (or not doing properly) could be imposing a limitation. You could be getting in your own way. Or it may just be that your body can't work any harder.

OPTION B

This option adds interval training one or two days a week to the aerobic exercise in Step 6 of the Basic 28–Day Plan. This option is for those who strive for excellence in cardiovascular fitness, beyond what it takes to stay in good physical condition. This is not training for marathoners, but for those who want to do a bit more to improve their stamina, endurance and conditioning.

Interval training can be done with any aerobic exercise. For example, if you were running, you would run at your target heart rate for 10 minutes. Then run to get your pulse to beat as close to your maximum heart rate as possible (220 minus age times 85%) for 30 seconds. Then run at your target heart rate (220 minus age times 70%) for 30 seconds. Repeat 4 consecutive times during one exercise period. Increase by one repetition every month to a limit of 10 times.

There are cautions to be observed in interval training. The high-intensity nature of this kind of training can lead to injury, and *it is not recommended for persons who have heart desease or other serious medical problems unless they have a doctor's approval.*

Interval training is anaerobic, so the cautions regarding anaerobic exercise hold. A full 48 hours is required between anaerobic exercise periods to allow for recovery from the stress it causes.

Once a week for this kind of conditioning is recommended. If you have specific fitness goals, you may choose to do interval training twice a week. The plan schedules it twice to demonstrate the ideal spacing. Four sets are enough to fatigue most people. A set consists of a 30-second sprint plus a 30-second rest.

Do not attempt to *combine* the Basic Plan with Option A and Option B. It is too much to add both anaerobic and interval training to aerobic exercise without professional guidance.

Option B
(week 5)

DAY	STEPS	TIME
1	warm-ups (#1–5) choice of aerobic exercise (#6) cool-downs (#7–8)	22 min.
2	#1–5 & #7–8	
3	#1–8 with interval	
4	#1–5 & 7–8	
5	#1–8 without interval	
6	#1–8 without interval	
7	#1–5 & #7–8	

Repeat above for Days 8–14 (week 6).

Thereafter increase time by 10 percent every two weeks until you reach the time limit for that particular exercise as listed under the Basic Plan.

RUNNING A MARATHON

If you are really serious about exercise and about running in particular, you may someday go the final distance—like the ancient Greek Olympic athletes—and train to run a marathon. Here are a few sensible and practical tips for those who want to go that extra distance.

Top marathon runners seem to follow training routines in which they run 110-150 miles a week. This does not constitute normal training. If the average runner attempted this kind of regimen, it would probably end up totally wrecking his or her body.

The best way to train for a marathon is to do it gradually. Start with three miles, five days a week for the first month. Increase it one mile a day for the next three months, taking off one day and adding a longer run on Sunday. Increase until you are able to do six miles a day, let's say, Tuesday, Wednesday, Thursday, and Friday, rest Saturday, and do 12 miles on Sunday, for 36 miles a week. When you run 24 miles during the week and 22 miles on Sunday, you have a total of 46 miles a week. If one of the days during the week is for interval training (faster training), you will get both speed and endurance.

Consistency is very important when you train. So is getting enough rest. If you run seven days a week, your body never gets a chance to recuperate. If, on the other hand, you do a 20-mile run on Sunday, rest on Monday, loosen up with four miles on Tuesday, do eight miles on Wednesday, skip Thursday, run ten miles on Friday, and skip Saturday, you would be doing the same mileage with three day's rest. You should definitely rest the day before a marathon. Remember you will also need about approximately one day of rest for every mile after you race.

It's also important to keep a diary while you train. There are many factors that will impact your performance, including biorhythms and circadian rhythms, and keeping track of the way you feel can help you understand these subtle cycles.

Pacing

Try to focus in on your pacing. Keep a stopwatch so that you know, within two or three seconds every mile how well you're doing. Shifting pace throughout a long race can be very stressful on the body. If you start out slower and get faster in six-mile increments, you will be doing much better. Because of changes in blood and brain chemistry, proper pacing will improve the way you feel during a long run.

A marathon is tricky. You may feel like you have energy right up to the 23rd mile, and then suddenly, it's gone. Your muscles are tight, and you feel lucky even to be able to walk. Suddenly at the 24-mile mark, your legs might say, "I quit," and then you find yourself, with thousands of others, starting to walk. It happens because those people, in all likelihood, didn't do one or some of the following: They didn't eat properly; they didn't properly pace themselves in their training; they started their exercise program too vigorously, or they peaked weeks before the race.

Water

It is crucial to properly hydrate yourself before, during, and after a marathon. Drink at least a pint of water before the race. During a marathon, you need to have water *every* mile.

The best thing to do is have a plastic water container with a sipper in it. When you pick it up, you can sip it as you run for a mile. People who run races in areas where they have friends generally have two or three people throughout the course of the race helping them with water.

Diluted grape juice in your water gives you extra glucose, so that you're delaying the time that your body will have to rely upon the extra glycogen it has stored up. In effect, you're always keeping your reserve in reserve. When other people hit the 20-mile mark and their glycogen and glucose are gone, they're out of energy, not you.

Form

Keep your head high, breathe through your mouth, and keep your shoulders loose. Your hands and arms should not be swinging; the wristbone should be at the level of the hipbone. If you hold your arms higher, you'll cause a muscle contraction that will cause fatigue in that muscle group. When muscle fatigue in the shoulders causes the arms to be raised higher, the shoulders slump forward, the neck drops down, and you'll get less air and your cells will get less oxygen. Try to keep your feet close to the ground, almost in a shuffle motion, with your knees slightly bent. You don't want to be running stiff-legged because that can jar the knees. Your body should be slightly bent forward at the waist. When you're running uphill, elbows should be elevated slightly behind you; run more toward the ball of the foot and take shorter steps. Again, your knees should be bent. Your shoulders should be forward to take advantage of the momentum you'll get coming down.

Gear

Most runners tend to wear a pair of running shoes for a longer time than those shoes are able to provide good support. Run-down heels can lead to the displacement of musculo-skeletal structure and subsequent hip problems, tendonitis and strains. Yet they are not the only sign of the end of a shoe's serviceability. A good athletic supply store can help determine the condition of your running shoes.

Make sure that the back lip of the shoe, where the heel is, has been cut off. It serves no purpose, and it can actually dig into the Achilles tendon every time you move, bruising it.

Make sure you wear tight, thin socks. Heavy socks tend to bunch up because of sweat, giving you blisters. Improperly worn socks, more than anything else, also will give you blisters. Put vaseline around all your toes, around the ball of your foot, and around the heel. Also put vaseline in your crotch, around your breasts, under your armpits.

In cold weather, it's important to avoid overdressing, because trapped perspiration can lead to severe chills.

In warmer weather, wear clothes that permit free perspiration. Never wear sweat suits.

Diet

On the sixth, fifth, and fourth days before a marathon, you should eat only protein, three times a day. Animal protein is not recommended. You could have soybean powder, or protein powder, or tofu—in other words, a high-quality protein.

On the three days immediately prior to the race, you should have no protein, just complex carbohydrates. On the day before the race, cut out fruits and salads. Try to eat something that will be only partially through your intestines during the race.

That night, have something about an hour before you go to sleep. Try to retire around midnight. This will be a major meal because you want to really saturate your body with glycogen. You could have buckwheat pasta, or brown rice, and if you're not allergic to wheat, you could have whole grain pasta or whole grain bread. Avoid greasy, highly seasoned and sugary foods.

In the morning, if it's at least four hours before the race, you could blend two bananas with grape juice. This will give you additional carbohydrates that will help you through the race, digested in your system before the race. Eat no solid food before the race. Your body's system will be too nervous. When you're nervous and anxious, your body doesn't digest normally. Electrolyte replacers are very important. Try to have two of the electrolytes (like potassium or magnesium) prior to a marathon, one every five miles during the race, and two at the end.

Before and After

Try and get a full-body massage, a Shiatsu massage, or a reflexology massage the day before the marathon. It's also important to float, if possible. Do an isolation tank float one or two days during the week before the marathon, preferably the day before, along with guided imagery.

When you've finished your race, don't just stop running and walk. Take at least 12 minutes to cool down by going from your running pace to a jog, a slower jog, and then a brisk walk. *Never* go directly into a sauna, hot tub, hot bath, or hot shower.

Always enjoy what you're doing and what you've accomplished.

16 · SELECTING AN ALTERNATIVE HEALTH PRACTITIONER

"Frequent colds, recurring infections, and fatigue are all part of the warning mechanisms used by the body to signal an under-functioning immune system. But they are rarely recognized as such. The phenomenal sales of cold remedies, for example, reflect how little attention is paid to strengthening the immune system—an approach that would far more effectively reduce the incidence of these disorders."

ULTIMATELY, YOU ARE RESPONSIBLE for your own well-being, but having access to proper health care practitioners is an important element in health maintenance. Their educated guidance and treatment can be invaluable, both in times of uncertainty and crisis and for prevention and awareness building during times of complete well-being.

Alternative health practitioners can help define the weak links in your body's structure and function and then direct you toward optimal personal care. There are many different approaches, but some general guidelines are worth mentioning here.

A good holistic medical practitioner will perform at least these three basic types of analysis before prescribing any treatment plan:

1) Take a detailed medical history.

2) Perform a physical examination that goes beyond conventional methodologies.

3) Study carefully the results of appropriate laboratory tests taken at the time of the history taking and the physical examination.

In addition, you have the right to expect that the practitioner includes in his or her repertory, some or all of the following:

• as many noninvasive diagnostic techniques as possible;

• an awareness of the potential diagnostic value of even very minor signs and symptoms in the prevention of major dysfunction;

• a preference for noninvasive over invasive techniques (For example, substances will be administered orally rather than intravenously, except when a condition calls for the more direct route.);

• a recognition of the importance of strengthening the body's resistive capacities and an interest, wherever possible, in attempting to repair any malfunctioning organ or gland rather than to replace its function through the administering of its secretions;

• a tendency, whenever possible, to treat the primary weak link first if more than one has been discovered (For example, if the stomach is producing insufficient hydrochloric acid, resulting in the malabsorption of calcium, among other substances, the resulting calcium deficiency could lead to osteoarthritis, periodontal disease, or skin problems; by treating the hydrochloric acid insufficiency, the physician would be treating the primary weak link.);

• an approach that treats the person as a whole person, not just a collection of ailing parts;

• the demonstrated ability to listen carefully and to skillfully classify any relevant symptoms in order to arrive at the best possible diagnosis;

• an orientation toward optimal health and sensitivity to dysfunctions that signal an imbalance in the individual;

• familiarity with a combination of approaches to help the person regain balance (For example, in addition to orthodox treatments, the physician's recommendations may include advice about stress reduction and life-style changes to reduce or elminate causative factors in the environment.);

• a willingness to refer the individual, when the condition warrants, to other medical practitioners whose specialized knowledge in a given area may be necessary to provide the most valuable restorative program; and

• a demonstrated awareness of the importance of the individual's own attitudes toward health and disease, and a willingness to communicate openly with the individual.

The alternative health practitioner should expect you to be an active, committed participant in the process, and not a passive, disinterested patient who accepts everything the doctor recommends.

ASKING THE RIGHT KINDS OF QUESTIONS

One form of this active participation may be the questions you ask with a view to getting the important information you need to help you in your contributions to the healing process. Some examples are:

• What, specifically, is being treated?
• How do you know that that's the problem?
• What are some realistic goals in my situation?
• What is the time frame?
• Does every individual with this condition get exactly the same tests, the same treatments?
• What are my weak links?
• Are these tests and this treatment relevant to my body and my condition?

THE IMPORTANCE OF COMMONPLACE SYMPTOMS

Many people are living with symptoms that, because they are mild and do not constitute a full-blown disease state, are accepted, needlessly, as being an inevitable consequence of getting older. In fact, such people are often told by their conventional physicians: "Nothing is wrong with you. Everything is normal." And yet, the symptoms may be early warnings that something is out of balance.

Gas in the lower bowel (flatulence), belching, heaviness in the stomach, heartburn and bloating, for example, may all be indicators of a malfunctioning digestive system, depending on their frequency and severity. These conditions are not normal in a healthy state, and they are often correctable.

Similarly, many of the symptoms that accompany delayed allergic reactions (the masked, cyclical allergies) are widely accepted as normal, and therefore to be tolerated for no better reason than "that's the way it is." The failure to recognize a connection between these symptoms and allergies may be due to the fact that they do not appear for upwards of thirty hours after the ingestion of the offending food or chemical substance. Typical symptoms are headache, irritability, anxiety, sudden changes of mood, and excessive fatigue, as well as unexplained body aches and pains. These symptoms may not be severe enough to be labeled as disease states, so the underlying cause is repeatedly overlooked or denied by traditional practitioners. Even when the disorders are recognized, their true significance may still be missed by those who try to reverse the symptoms without addressing the underlying causes for their appearance. Thus frequent colds, recurring infections, and fatigue are all part of the warning mechanisms used by the body to signal an under-functioning immune system. But they are rarely recognized as such. The phenomenal sales of cold remedies, for example, reflect how little attention is paid to strengthening the immune system—an approach that would far more effectively reduce the incidence of these disorders.

TYPES OF PRACTITIONERS

It has never been my policy to make specific recommendations, to suggest to a person that a specific practitioner is the best doctor for them to see. The quality of a doctor's health care may depend on both the physician and the patient, as well as on their mutual compatibility. This is not something I, or anyone else, could predict in advance. But I still feel that people should be given some direction. So, what I have done here is supplied a directional guide. It is not meant to be a recommendation. Rather, I have offered some general guidelines and a sampling of available practitioners. I have concentrated on modalities that the reader may not have easy access to. Chiropractors and osteopaths, for example, are not listed here; their names or addresses may be gotten with relative ease from many sources. Nor are nutritionists listed here, although the experienced holistic or New-Age nutritionist may be enormously helpful in helping you get the most from your diet. The listings in the following appendix are merely meant to provide an opportunity for the reader to see how many alternative approaches are available near at hand as an alternative to conventional modalities. In some instances I have listed urban practitioners—because more readers would have access to them—and not those in rural areas, although the latter may be excellent as well. These listings are certainly not exhaustive and should be considered only a sampling to encourage your own selection process.

The appendix includes, first, a general listing of some useful names and addresses of alternative health organizations and resources. This is followed by a state-by-state compilation of a selection of practitioners throughout the country in the following modalities: Homeopathy, Chelation Therapy, Orthomolecular Medicine, Acupuncture, Clinical Ecology, and Naturopathy. For more extensive information in your area, check the listings in the Yellow Pages of the phone directory. Each of these modalities may be extremely useful when used properly, representing viable alternatives to conventional medical orthodoxies. Selecting the right health care professional can be an important decision that will benefit you for rest of your life. In this chapter I have tried to provide the overview and in the appendix some specifics on how to go about finding and evaluating such a person. If I have succeeded in putting you on the right track, this may be one of the most important chapters in this book. But before listing the practitioners themselves, here are some general points about each of these different approaches.

HOMEOPATHY

Homeopathy is based on the principle that what causes illness may follow a law of similars, meaning that by giving a healthy person a dilute amount of that which is a causative agent can in fact help the body rebalance itself. If a person has a head cold, you would give the person a substance that would cause cold symptoms in a healthy person, but in a sick person it helps to cure them. Homeopathy is limited in scope at this time in the United States, although one hundred years ago it was the prevailing form of medicine—until allopathic medicine and the American Medical Association in particular launched an intensive drive against it, which culminated in its being virtually banned in this country. Very recently, there has been a renewed interest in homeopathy, and growing numbers of physicians are using its principles. The homeopath must be a medical doctor in addition to his or her homeopathic specialization. Homeopathy is particularly useful in the treatment of fevers, bacterial infections, toxicity, and the cumulative effects of alcohol, drugs, tobacco, caffeine, or sugar. It is not recommended for cancer, AIDS (acquired immune deficiency syndrome), or heart disease.

CHELATION THERAPY

Chelation Therapy is a relatively new medical science, having started only about a quarter of a century ago. There are at this time nearly 1,000 doctors, including many board-certified cardiologists, who are using chelation therapy. The modality involves an intravenous drip of a substance known as EDTA, a chelating agent. The agent helps stimulate the destruction of free radicals, which seem to be a primary causative agent of the aging process itself. By slowing down the destructive potential of these free radicals, it allows the cells to heal themselves. As the cells heal, they are more able to fight off whatever infection or disease affects us. Claims have been made that chelation therapy can open up the arteries. Moreover, objective data has substantiated this. Improvement of vascular circulation in people who had obstructed arteries, especially those to the brain and to the extremities, has been demonstrated following treatment with this modality.

Chelation therapy runs about $100 per visit and patients generally have from 20 to 40 visits, depending on the severity of the condition. People are also begun receiving chelation therapy as a preventative treatment to slow down the aging process, based on the view that free radicals are a primary factor of the aging process. The treatment may be problematic, however, for patients with kidney disease, and renal monitoring is crucial. A physician must be certified as a practicing chelating therapist to perform the therapy.

ORTHOMOLECULAR MEDICINE

Orthomolecular physicians and orthomolecular psychiatrists are conventionally trained medical doctors with an additional specialization. The purpose of orthomolecular medicine is the establishment of the right balance of the chemicals naturally occurring in the body. They try to rebalance the chemicals within the body without using synthetic drugs that might interfere with natural processes. Their goal is homeostasis, or balance. Frequently, orthomolecular physicians use a high-dosage vitamin regimen, far higher than what the average physician would ever presume would be needed. But it is their experience that only with these very high amounts, these megadoses, do they see the best results. For example, orthomolecular psychiatrists have had striking success in the treatment of schizophrenics, putting the condition into remission by using massive doses of Niacin (B_3), B_6, and vitamin C—amounts that you would never give a healthy person. Orthomolecular psychiatrists are also better able to treat depression, by examining possible chemical imbalances in the brain.

Moreover, orthomolecular physicians have the benefit of being able to use psychoanalysis or psychotherapy if deemed necessary, but that would be as a last resort. The cost of treatment is comparable to that for conventional physicians.

ACUPUNCTURE

Acupuncturists work by opening up blocked energy pathways, or meridians, so that healing energy can go directly to a particular point in the body where it is needed, therefore stimulating the innate natural healing capacity of the body. The acupuncturist, in this country, must also be a medical doctor. Acupuncturists are particularly good for nerve problems, pain, musculo-skeletal problems, but not for cancer or heart disease. The cost of treatment may range from $75 to a $100 per visit.

CLINICAL ECOLOGY

Clinical ecologists are unique in that they are able to closely examine the relationship between the elements of a person's diet and any symptoms they may be experiencing. For example, a person's irritable bowel may be due to consumption of milk. The clinical ecologist will be able to identify this causative factor. He or she examines all the different foods, inhalants, and liquids that a person consumes to see which one of these, or which combinations, may be causing a physical or mental reaction. This modality has been particularly successful, for example, in the treatment of symptoms of arthritis. One clinical ecologist, Dr. Marshall Mandell, has been able to eliminate all arthritic symptoms in about 80 percent of his patients using a four-day rotating and elimination diet, preceded by an initial five-day fast in a clinically controlled environment. Clinical ecologists tend to use a far broader arsenal of treatments than the traditional allergist. Outside of the initial visit, the cost of seeing a clinical ecologist is no more than for a conventional physician, ranging from $40 to $75, depending on the state. The initial visit may vary from $125 to $500, depending on which tests are performed and the time required.

NATUROPATHY

Naturopathic physicians can treat most conditions. They are not, however, allowed to perform major surgery (although they can perform minor surgery). Their very extensive background is centered in the botanical sciences, including the use of herbs and tinctures, with a wide variety of natural immune-stimulating properties. The naturopath practices a natural form of health care the traditions of which precede the advent of modern medicine, not unlike the traditional Tibetan physician who must be able to identify nearly a thousand different healing herbs, mineral sources, and animal sources. The naturopath has years of extensive study in the healing potential of such substances. He or she is also able to understand muscular and skeletal bodily adjustment. Naturopaths use a much broader basis for diagnosis than do conventional allopathic physicians. Finally, the naturopath is usually a very good teacher as well. Not only do you get a therapy, you also generally get an education about the nature of your condition and the rationale behind the therapy. Naturopaths tend to be relatively inexpensive, generally in the neighborhood of $40 to $60 per visit.

Appendix: A Resource Listing
of Alternative Health Professionals

I. ORGANIZATIONS

Academy of Orthomolecular Psychiatry, P.O. Box 372, Manhassett, NY 11030,
  (800) 847–3802
Alliance of Massage Therapists, 875 6th Avenue, New York, NY 10011, (212) 736–1100
ALS Society of America, 15300 Ventura Blvd., Suite 315, Sherman Oaks, CA 91403,
  (818) 990–2151
Alzheimer's Disease and Related Disorders Association, 360 N. Michigan Avenue, Suite
  1102, Chicago, IL 60601, (312) 853–3060
American Academy of Medical Preventics, 6151 W. Century Blvd., Suite 1114, Los
  Angeles, CA 90045, (213) 645–5350
American Alliance of Massage Professionals, 3108 Rt. 10W, Denville, NJ 07834,
  (201) 989–8939
American Anorexia Nervosa Association, Inc., 133 Cedar Lane, Teaneck, NJ 07666,
  (201) 836–1800
American Herb Association, P.O. Box 353, Rescue, CA 95672
American Holistic Medical Association, 6932 Little River Tpke., Annandale, VA 22003
American Holistic Nurses Association, P.O. Box 116, Telluride, CO 81435
American Massage Therapy Association, 1329 W. Pratt Blvd., Chicago, IL 60626,
  (312) 761–AMTA

American Tinnitus Association, P.O. Box 5, Portland, OR 97207

The American Veterinary Holistic Medical Association, 2214 Old Emmorton Rd., Bel Air, MD 21014

ANAD (National Association of Anorexia Nervosa and Associated Disorders), P.O. Box 271, Highland Park, IL 60035, (312) 831-3438

Association for Cardiovascular Therapy, P.O. Box 706, Bloomfield, CT 06002

Association for Heart Patients, P.O. Box 54305, Atlanta, GA 30308, (404) 523-0826

Association for the Promotion of Herbal Healing, 2000 Center St., Suite 1475, Berkeley, CA 94704

Cancer Control Society, 2043 N. Berendo, Los Angeles, CA 90027, (213) 663-7801

Center for the Study of Anorexia and Bulimia, 1 W. 91st Street, New York, NY 10024

Coalition for the Medical Rights of Women, 2845 24th Street, San Francisco, CA 94110

Ginseng Research Institute, P.O. Box 42, Roxbury, NY 12474

Heal (Human Ecology Action League), P.O. Box 1369, Evanston, IL 60204

Health Associates, 1990 Broadway, Suite 1206, New York, NY 10023, (212) 307-1399

Hearing and Tinnitus Help Association, P.O. Box 97, Skillman, NJ 08558

Help Anorexia, Inc., 5143 Overland Avenue, Culver City, CA 90230, (213) 558-0444

Herb Research Foundation, 1780 55th Street, Boulder, CO 80301, (303) 449-3779

Hippocrates Health Institute, 25 Exeter Street, Boston, MA 02116

Huxley Institute for Biosocial Research, 900 N. Federal Highway, Suite 330, Boca Raton, FL 33432

International Academy of Holistic Health & Medicine, 218 Avenue B, Redondo Beach, CA 90277, (213) 540-0564

International Academy of Preventive Medicine, 34 Corporate Woods, Suite 469, Overland Park, KS 66210

International Association of Cancer Victims and Friends, Inc., 7740 W. Manchester Avenue, Suite 110, Playa del Rey, CA 90291

International College of Applied Nutrition, P.O. Box 386, La Habra, CA 90631, (818) 697-4576

International Foundation for Homeopathy, 1141 NW. Market, Seattle, WA 98107, (206) 789-7237

International Society for Bioelectricity, P.O. Box 82, Boston, MA 02135

La Leche League International, Inc., 9616 Minneapolis Avenue, Franklin Park, IL 60131, (312) 455-7730

National Association of Naturopathic Physicians, 2613 N. Stevens, Tacoma, WA 98407, (206) 752-2555

National Center for Homeopathy, 1500 Massachusetts Ave., NW., Suite 163, Washington, DC 20005, (202) 223-6182

National Council of Stutterers, P.O. Box 8171, Grand Rapids, MI 49508, (616) 241-2372

National Health Federation, 211 W. Foothill Blvd., Monrovia, CA 91016, (818) 357-2181

National Hypoglycemia Association, P.O. Box 885, Ithaca, NY 14850

National Women's Health Network, 224 7th Street, SE., Washington, DC 20003

Natural Hygiene Society, 698 Brooklawn Ave., Bridgeport, CT 06604

Nutrition for Optimal Health Association, P.O. Box 380, Winnetka, IL 60093

Society for Clinical Ecology, 2005 Franklin Street, Suite 490, Denver, CO 80205

The Stroke Foundation, Inc., 898 Park Avenue, New York, NY 10021, (212) 734-3434

Temporomandibular Joint Research Foundation, 3043 Foothill Blvd., Suite 8, La Crescenta, CA 91214, (213) 248-9767

Tourette Syndrome Association, 41-02 Bell Blvd., Bayside, NY 11361, (212) 224-2999

Women for Sobriety, P.O. Box 618, Quakertown, PA 18951, (215) 536-8026

II. HOMEOPATHIC PRACTITIONERS

ARIZONA

Abram Ber, M.D., 3134 N. 7th St. #4, Phoenix, AZ 85014, (602) 279-3795

Cheryl Harter, M.D., 2636 N. Dayton St., Phoenix, AZ 85006, (602) 241-1441

John C. Reed, M.D., 4739 N. 40th, Phoenix, AZ 85018, (602) 956-4444

Harvey Bigelsen, M.D., 7333 E. Monterey Way, #5, Scottsdale, AZ 85251, (602) 994-3788

Jessie E. Jacobs, M.D., 4300 N. Miller Rd., Suite 102, Scottsdale, AZ 85251, (602) 994-1951, 949-8186

CALIFORNIA

Hahnemann Medical Clinic, Christine C. Ciavarelle, P.A.C., Gregory R. Manteuffel, M.D., 1918 Bonita Ave., Berkeley, CA 94704, (415) 849-1925

David H. Powelson, M.D., D.Ht., 570 The Almeda, Berkeley, CA 94707, (415) 525-6193

Larry Snyder, M.D., 3844 Brayton Ave., Long Beach, CA 90807, (213) 427-5153

Sarem Singh Khalsa, M.D., Cedars-Sinai Medical Office Towers, 8631 W. Third St., Suite 1135E, Los Angeles, CA 90048, (213) 659-0620

Richard A. Baddour, M.D., 2454 C St., San Diego, CA 92102, (714) 239-7996

David J. Anderson, M.D., D.Ht., 1947 Divisadero St., San Francisco, CA 94115, (415) 929-1682

Leo Bakker, M.D., 830 Felton St., San Francisco, CA 94134, (415) 239-4954

Corey W. Weinstein, M.D., 1063 Plymouth, San Francisco, CA 94112, (415) 334-6212

Donald S. Rich, M.D., 706 Western Dr., Santa Cruz, CA 95060, (408) 423-2078

Joe D. Goldstrich, M.D., P.O. Box 5445, Santa Monica, CA 90405, (213) 454-7514

A. Joel Rice, M.D., 41651 Sierra Dr., Three Rivers, CA 93271, (209) 561-4683

Alan S. Charles, M.D., 1414 Maria La., Walnut Creek, CA 94596, (415) 937-3331

COLORADO

Nicholas J. Nossaman, M.D., 1750 High St., Denver, CO 80218, (303) 388-7730

CONNECTICUT

William F. McCoy, M.D., D.Ht., 25 Mooreland Rd., Greenwich, CT 06830, (203) 661-4340

Joseph L. Kaplowe, M.D., 131 Dwight St., New Haven, CT, (203) 624-8694

Ahmed N. Currim, M.D., 153 East Ave., Norwalk, CT 06851, (203) 866-1319

Thyparambil C. Cherian, M.D., 141 Sound Beach Ave., Old Greenwich, CT 06870, (203) 928-7729

William E. Shevin, M.D., 245 School St., Putnam, CT 06260, (203) 928-7729

DELAWARE

Robert H. Hall, M.D., 1207 Delaware Ave., Wilmington, DE 19806, (302) 656-5123

DISTRICT OF COLUMBIA

H. E. Sartori, M.D., M.P.H., 4501 Connecticut Ave., NW. (#306), Washington, DC 20008, (202) 244-6327

FLORIDA

Joya Schoen, M.D., 1900 N. Orange Ave., Orlando, FL 32804, (305) 898–2951
Salvador A. Williams, M.D., D.Ht., 4413 Southern Blvd., West Palm Beach, FL
33406, (305) 683–4333

IDAHO

Samuel Wayne Smith, M.D., Rt. #3 South, Pocatello, ID 83204, (208) 775–4937

ILLINOIS

Ruth C. Martens, M.D., 950 Lee St., Suite 200, Des Plaines, IL 60016, (312) 635–7240
Joel Shepperd, M.D., 7249 N. Western Ave., Chicago, IL 60645, (312) 274–3127

INDIANA

Willis A. Fromhold, M.D., 510 Willard Ave., Indianapolis, IN 46227, (317) 783–4543

KENTUCKY

Bernard J. Baute, M.D., 214 S. Proctor Knott, Lebanon, KY 40033, (502) 692–3159

LOUISIANA

David L. Dugger, M.D., 1308 Nashville Ave., New Orleans, LA 70115,
(504) 895–8424

MAINE

David Getson, M.D., 999 Forest Ave., Portland, ME 04103, (207) 797–8813

MARYLAND

Wyrth Post Baker, M.D., D.Ht., 4701 Willard Ave., Chevy Chase, MD 20815,
(301) 656–8940
William J. Cates, M.D., 17515 Redland Rd., Derwood, MD 20855, (301) 921–0350
Anthony M. Aurigemma, M.D., 8201 16 St., Silver Spring, MD 20910, (301) 495–
3060

MASSACHUSETTS

Jesse A. Stoff, M.D., 182 Maple Ave., Great Barrington, MA 01230, (413) 528–3114
Christine F. Luthra, M.D., 54 Rockview St., Jamaica Plain, MA 02130, (617) 524–3892
Ronald W. Dushkin, M.D., Jeffrey A. Migdow, M.D., Box 793, Lenox, MA 01240,
(413) 637–3280
Edward H. Chapman, M.D., 91 Cornell St., Newton Lower Falls, MA, (617) 923–4601
Richard Moskowitz, M.D., D.Ht., The Turning Point, 173 Mt. Auburn St., Water-
town, MA 02172, (617) 923–4601

MICHIGAN

Dennis K. Chernin, M.D., 2225 Packard, Suite 1, Ann Arbor, MI 48104,
(313) 665–6747

Patricia E. Kelly, M.D., 326 W. Liberty, Suite 300, Ann Arbor, MI 48103, (313) 995-5982

Edward J. Linker, M.D., 3200 W. Liberty, Ann Arbor, MI 48103, (313) 761-2581

Prosper D. White, M.D., D.Ht., 545 David Whitney Bldg., 1553 Woodward, Detroit, MI 48226, (313) 965-0256

Michael A. Santoro, M.D., 319^1/$_2$ S. Washington, Royal Oak, MI 48067, (313) 543-1055

MINNESOTA

G. William Jones, M.D., 122 W. Lake St., Anoka, MN 55408, (612) 753-1377

Michael G. Carlston, M.D., 945 W. Hoyt St., St. Paul, MN 55117, (612) 824-5570

NEVADA

Willem H. Khoe, M.D., D.Ac., 3880 S. Jones Blvd., Suite 214, Las Vegas, NV 89103, (702) 871-5599

Elizabeth Lodge Rees, M.D., 1523 Foster Ave., Reno, NV 89509, (702) 883-8902

NEW JERSEY

Pratap C. Singhal, M.D., D.Ht., 431 Washington Ave., Belleville, NJ 07109, (201) 759-2241

Arvi Jurgens, M.D., N.D., 49 Grant St., Fairview, NJ 07022, (201) 945-7545

Paul P. Bahder, M.D., D.Ht., P.O. Box 552, 10 Lakeview Ave., Kingston, NJ 08528, (609) 924-3132

George R. Henshaw, M.D., D.Ht., 228 Midland Ave., Montclair, NJ 07042, (201) 744-4506

Ellis H. Allar, M.D., 6618 Ventnor Ave., Ventnor City, NJ 08406, (609) 823-1473

NEW MEXICO

Karl E. Robinson, M.D., 122 Darmouth St., Albuquerque, NM 87106, (505) 265-0607

Martin P. Goldman, M.D., 100 Cienega St., Suite D, Santa Fe, NM 87501, (505) 988-4386

NEW YORK

Jack Cooper, M.D., 2 Marvin Ave., Brewster, NY 10509, (914) 279-9300

George Congram, M.D., 24 Arbor Lane, Dix Hills, NY 11746, (516) 271-8016

William L. Bergman, M.D., 2 E. 37th St., New York, NY 10016, (212) 684-2290

Ronald A. Grant, M.D., 303 E. 83rd St., New York, NY 10028, (212) 734-5789

William Gutman, M.D., D.Ht., 3 E. 85th St., New York, NY 10028, (212) 288-0758

Kay S. Lawrence, M.D., 386 Broadway, 6th Fl., New York, NY 10013, (212) 431-1372

Warren F. Metzler, M.D., 80 Fifth Ave., Suite 1504, New York, NY 10011, (212) 807-8691

James H. Stephenson, M.D., D.Ht., 66 E. 83rd St., New York, NY 10028, (212) 794-0150

NORTH CAROLINA

George Guess, M.D., D.Ht., 15 Pine Ridge Rd., Asheville, NC 28804, (704) 252-5376

Winifred Jo Pringle, M.D., Route 5, Box 395, Hillsborough, NC 27278, (919) 732-6947

OHIO

David C. Fabrey, M.D., 800 Compton Rd., #24, Cincinnati, OH 45231,
(513) 521-5333

Harold J. Wilson, M.D., 28 W. Henderson Rd., Columbus, OH 43214, (614) 261-0151

Charles E. Bolinger, M.D., 315 W. 5th St., Marysville, OH 43040

Maesimund B. Panos, M.D., D.Ht., 5418 S. State Route 202, Tipp City, OH 45371,
(513) 667-2222

OREGON

John E. Gambee, M.D., 66 Club Rd., #140, Eugene, OR 97401, (503) 686-2536

PENNSYLVANIA

Walter F. Kepler, Jr., M.D., D.Ht., 100 Lexington Ave., Havertown, PA 19083,
(215) 446-4357

Rudolph M. Ballentine, M.D., RD. 1, Box 88, Honesdale, PA 18431, (717) 253-5551

Henry N. Williams, M.D., D.Ht., 556 W. James St., P.O. Box 153, Lancaster, PA
17603, (717) 394-3776

Arland Lebo, M.D., RD. 3, Mt. Joy, PA 17552, (717) 653-2572

Barney A. Stegura, M.D., 630 S. Hanover St., Nanticoke, PA 18634, (717) 735-0234

N. M. Warner, M.D., Parkesburg Health Center, 689 Strasberg Ave., Parkesburg, PA
19365, (215) 857-5300

Z. Stuart Chance, M.D., 110 North Camac St., Philadelphia, PA 19107,
(215) 568-5934

J. Murl Johnston, M.D., 694 Washington Rd., Pittsburgh, PA 15228, (412) 531-3076

TENNESSEE

Robert C. Owen, M.D., 210 25th Ave. North, Suite 1016, Nashville, TN 37203,
(615) 327-3291

TEXAS

Andrew C. Stenhouse, M.D., 5211 W. 9th St., Amarillo, TX 79106, (806) 353-7417

Robert M. Schore, M.D., D.Ht., 10405 E. Northwest Highway, Dallas, TX 75238,
(214) 340-5557

Donald E. Pentecost, M.D., 2919 Markum Dr., Fort Worth, TX 76117, (817) 831-0321

Selic Soroka, M.D., 6206 Dashwood, Houston, TX 77081, (713) 778-1904

VERMONT

Dhyano Pierson, M.D., 323 Pearl St., Burlington, VT 05401, (802) 862-0836

Horace O. Reider, M.D., 100 Lakeview Terrace, Burlington, VT 05401, (802) 864-5003

VIRGINIA

Sandra M. Chase, M.D., D.Ht., 3541 Chain Bridge Rd., Suite 5-A, Fairfax, VA 22030,
(703) 273-5250

Iona A. Razi, M.D., David G. Wember, M.D., D.Ht., 400 N. Washington St. #202,
Falls Church, VA 22046, (703) 237-9393

WASHINGTON

Antonius W. Imkamp, M.D., 30620 Pacific Highway S., Federal Way, WA 98003, (206) 839-1433

M. Dean Crothers, M.D., Jennifer Jacobs, M.D., Evergreen Center for Homoeopathic Medicine, 1141 N.W. Market, Seattle, WA 98107, (206) 789-7237

Michael R. Glass, M.D., 2503 24th Ave. West, Seattle, WA 98199, (206) 789-7237

WISCONSIN

Alan S. Levine, M.D., D.Ht., Rosemary Rau-Levine, M.D., 1914 Monroe St., Madison, WI 53711, (608) 251-0861

Dale Buegel, M.D., 6310 N. Port Washington Rd., Milwaukee, WI 53217, (414) 332-9145

III. CHELATION THERAPY PRACTITIONERS

ALABAMA

Gus J. Prosch, Jr., M.D., 759 Valley St., Birmingham, AL 35226, (205) 823-6180

H. Ray Evers, M.D., P.O. Drawer 587, Cottonwood, AL 36320, (205) 691-2161, 1-800-621-8924

Pat Hamm, M.D., 3804 Sixth Ave., Huntsville, AL 35807, (205) 534-8115

ALASKA

F. Russell Manuel, M.D., 3330 C. St., Suite 100, Anchorage, AK 99503, (907) 562-6070

Robert Rowen, M.D., 615 E. 82nd Ave., #300, Anchorage, AK 99518, (907) 344-7775

Robert E. Martin, M.D., P.O. Box 870710, Wasilla, AK 99687, (907) 376-5284

ARIZONA

Francis Jonathan Woo, Jr., M.D., 60 Riviera Dr., Lake Havasu City, AZ 86403, (602) 453-3330

Hubbard Fellows, M.D., 3604 Wells Fargo, Suite M, Scottsdale, AZ 85251, (602) 994-3799

Stanley R. Olsztyn, M.D., 3200 N. Hayden Rd., Suite 162, Scottsdale, AZ 85251, (602) 945-4501

ARKANSAS

Norbert J. Becquet, M.D., 115 W. 6th St., Little Rock, AR 72201, (501) 375-4419

Maurice L. Stephens, M.D., Rt. 5, Box 168, N. Monroe & Old Hwy. 17 N., Mena, AR 71953, (501) 394-6300

Doty Murphy, III, M.D., 812 Dorman, Springdale, AR 72764, (501) 756-3251

CALIFORNIA

Emil Levin, M.D., 450 S. Beverly Dr., Beverly Hills, CA 90210, (213) 556-2091

Carl V. Lansing, M.D., 705 N. Pebble Beach, Crescent City, CA 95531, (707) 464-2144

Robert S. Ellyn, M.D., 4684 White Oak Ave., Encino, CA 91316, (818) 788-8917
A. Leonard Klepp, M.D., 16311 Ventura, #725, Encino, CA 91436, (818) 981-5511
David J. Edwards, M.D., 360 S. Clovis Ave., Fresno, CA 93727, (209) 251-5066
James J. Julian, M.D., 1654 Cahuenga Blvd., Hollywood, CA 90028, (213) 467-5555
H. Richard Casdorph, M.D., Ph.D., 1703 Termino Ave., Suite 201, Long Beach, CA
    90804, (213) 597-8716
Ward Dean, M.D., 8760 Sunset Blvd., Los Angeles, CA 90069, (213) 652-5731
M. Jahangiri, M.D., 2156 S. Santa Fe. Ave., Los Angeles, CA 90058, (213) 587-3218
Joseph A. Ramljak, M.D., 921 Westwood Blvd., Suite 233, Los Angeles, CA 90024,
    (213) 208-4880
Josuha H. Ritchie, M.D., 1462 Glendale Blvd., Los Angeles, CA 90026,
    (213) 413-6161
Edward E. Winger, M.D., 400 29th St., Oakland, CA 94609, (415) 839-6477
Charles B. Farinella, M.D., University Executive Park, 69-730 Hwy. 111, S-106 A,
    Rancho Mirage, CA 92270, (619) 324-0734
Garry F. Gordon, M.D., William G. Toy, M.D., 1816 Tribute Road, Sacramento, CA
    95815, (916) 925-7811
T. Dosumu-Johnson, M.D., 5222 Balboa Ave., Suite 62, San Diego, CA 92117,
    (619) 492-9101
Joseph Jackson Downing, M.D., 2300 California St., Suite 302, San Francisco, CA
    94115, (415) 346-9923
Robert Haskell, M.D., 5133 Geary Blvd., San Francisco, CA 94118, (415) 668-1300
Paul Lynn, M.D., 345 W. Portal Ave., San Francisco, CA 04127, (415) 566-1000
Eddie F. Barr, M.D., 930 Town & Country Village, San Jose, CA 95128,
    (408) 247-7521

COLORADO

Rob Krakovitz, M.D., P.O. Box 9618, Aspen, CO 81612, (303) 925-3748
James R. Fish, M.D., 3030 N. Hancock, Colorado Springs, CO 80907, (303) 471-2273
Edward G. Anderson, 180 Adams, Suite 200, Denver, CO 80206, (303) 388-2411

DISTRICT OF COLUMBIA

George Mitchell, M.D., 2112 F. St., NW., Suite 404, Washington, DC 90006,
    (202) 429-9456

FLORIDA

Lester I. Tavel, M.D., D.O., 401 Manatee Ave., E., Bradenton, FL 33508,
    (813) 748-7943
Robert R. Roth, M.D., 811 SE. 13th Ave., Deerfield Beach, FL 33441, (305) 426-8532
Ricardo J. Sabates, M.D., 1818 Sheridan St., Hollywood, FL 33020, (305) 922-7333
Robert J. Rogers, M.D., 15 W. Avenue B, Melbourne, FL 32901, (305) 723-2360
I. Randall Ross, M.D. 375 S. Courteray Pkwy., Merritt Island, FL 32952,
    (305) 453-3420
Richardo J. Sabates, M.D., 1990 SW. 27th Ave., Miami, FL 33145, (305) 441-2145
Robert E. Willner, M.D., 909 N. Miami Beach Blvd. North Miami Beach, FL 33162,
    (305) 949-6331
Surindar Singh Bedi, M.D., 8726 County Rd. 54, New Port Richey, FL 33552,
    (813) 376-0082

Joya Lynn Schoen, M.D., 1900 N. Orange Ave., Orlando, FL 32804, (305) 898-2951

Dan Christian Roehm, M.D., 3400 Park Central Blvd., W., Suite 3450, Pompano Beach, FL 33064, (305) 977-3700

Ray C. Wunderlich, Jr., M.D., 666 6th St., S., St. Petersburg, FL 33701, (813) 866-3612

Eugene H. Lee, M.D., 706 W. Pratt, Suite D, Tampa, FL 33606, (813) 251-3089

GEORGIA

Oliver L. Gunter, M.D., P.C., P.O. Box 347, 24 N. Ellis St., Camilla, GA 31730, (912) 336-7343

Terril J. Schneider, M.D., 3312-D Northside Dr., #200, Macon, GA 31210, (912) 783-1363

William C. Douglass, M.D., 2470 Windy Hill Rd., #440, Marietta, GA 30067, (404) 953-0710

HAWAII

Clifton Arrington, M.D., 73-1249 Lihau St., Kailua-Kona, HI 96740, (808) 322-9400

IDAHO

Charles T. McGee, M.D., 1717 Lincolnway, #108, Coeur d'Alene, ID 83814, (208) 664-1478

John O. Boxall, M.D., 824 17th Ave. S., Nampa, ID 83651, (208) 466-3518

ILLINOIS

Razvan Rentea, M.D., 3354 N. Paulina, Chicago, IL 60657, (312) 549-0101

Robert S. Waters, M.D., 739 Roosevelt Rd., Bldg. 8, Suite 314, Glen Ellyn, IL 60137, (312) 790-8100

Raymond A. Alexander, M.D., #1 Doctors Park Road, Mount Vernon, IL 62864, (618) 242-5770

John R. Tambone, M.D., 102 E. South Street, Woodstock, IL 60098, (815) 338-2345

INDIANA

George McComas Wolverton, M.D., 647 Eastern Blvd., Clarksville, IN 47130, (812) 282-4309

David A. Darbro, M.D., 2124 E. Hanna Ave., Indianapolis, IN 46227, (317) 787-7221

Sandra C. Denton, M.D., 430 N. Park Ave., #104, Indianapolis, IN 46202, (312) 787-7221

Floyd B. Colemen, M.D., 405 S. Wayne, Waterloo, IN 46793, (219) 837-2371

KANSAS

Roy N. Neil, M.D., 105 W. 13th St., Hays, KS 67601, (913) 628-8341 or 628-3215

Stevens B. Ackers, M.D., 1100 N. Francis, Suite 400, Wichita, KS 67214, (316) 263-7002

Hugh D. Riordan, M.D., 3100 N. Hillside St., Wichita, KS 67219, (316) 682-3100

KENTUCKY

John C. Tapp, M.D., 414 Old Morgantown Rd., Bowling Green, KY 42101,
(502) 781-1483

Walt Stoll, M.D., ABFP, 1412 N. Broadway, Lexington, KY 40505, (606) 233-4273

Kirk D. Morgan, M.D., 3101 Breckenridge Ln., Suite 2-B, Louisville, KY 40220,
(502) 491-6240

LOUISIANA

Steve Kuplesky, M.D., 7324 Alberta Dr., Baton Rouge, LA 70808, (504) 769-8503

James P. Carter, M.D., 1430 Tulane Ave., New Orleans, LA 70112, (504) 588-5136

MARYLAND

Paul V. Beals, M.D., Nicholas J. Tavani, Jr. M.D., Ph.D., 9101 Cherry Lane Park,
#205, Laurel, MD 20708, (302) 490-9911

MASSACHUSETTS

Michael Janson, M.D., 2557 Massachusetts Ave., Cambridge, MA 02140,
(617) 661-6225

MICHIGAN

Robert G. Thomas, M.D., 21 N. Elm St., Three Oaks, MI 49128, (616) 756-9531

MINNESOTA

Jean Eckerly, M.D., 5851 Duluth St., Suite 110, Minneapolis, MN 55422,
(612) 593-9458

MISSISSIPPI

Robert Thomas Hollingsworth, M.D., Drawer 87, 901 Forrest St., Shelby, MS 38774,
(601) 398-5106

MISSOURI

Harvey Walker, Jr., M.D., Ph.D., 138 N. Meramec Ave., Clayton, MO 63105,
(314) 721-7227

Lawrence D. Dorman, M.D., 9120 E. 35th St., Independence, MO 64052,
(816) 358-2712

Charles J. Rudolph, M.D., Ph.D., 2800-A Kendallwood Pkwy., Kansas City, MO
64119, (816) 453-5940

MONTANA

David V. Kauffman, M.D., 110 Central Ave., Whitefish, MT 59937, (406) 862-3543

NEVADA

W. Douglas Brodie, M.D., Michael L. Gerber, M.D., 3670 Grant Dr., Reno, NV
89509, (702) 826-1900

Donald E. Soli, M.D., 975 Ryland Ave., Reno, NV 89520, (702) 786-7101

NEW JERSEY

Ralph Lev, M.D., 952 Amboy Ave., Edison, NJ 08837, (201) 738–9220
Milan J. Packovich, M.D., 585 Winters Ave., Paramus, NJ 07652, (201) 967–5081
Faina Muits, M.D., Ph.D., 15 Rosemont Terrace, West Orange, NJ 07052, (201) 736–3743

NEW YORK

Reino F. Hill, M.D., 230 W. Main St., Falconer, NY 14733, (716) 665–3505
Robert C. Atkins, M.D., 400 E. 56th St., New York, NY 10022, (212) 758–2110
Martin Feldman, M.D., 132 E. 76th St., New York, NY 10021, (212) 744–4413
Leo Galland, M.D., Warren M. Levin, M.D., 444 Park Ave. S., New York, NY 10016, (212) 696–1900
Richard Izquierdo, M.D., 1057 Southern Blvd., New York, NY 10452, (212) 589–4541 or 589–2440
Harold Markus, M.D., 161 Ave. of the Americas, 14th Floor, New York, NY 10013, (212) 675–2550
Stanley H. Title, M.D.,171 W. 57th St., New York, NY 10019, (212) 581–9532
Neil L. Block, M.D., Michael Schachter, M.D., Mountainview Medical Bldg., Mountainview Ave., Nyack, NY 10960, (914) 358–6800
Stanley Skollar, M.D., 130 Rt. 59, Suffern, NY 10901, (914) 368–0046

NORTH CAROLINA

Logan T. Robertson, M.D., Rt. 2, Canton, NC 28716, (704) 235–8312
John Lindsay Laird, M.D., Rt. 1, Box 7, Leicester, NC 28748, (704) 683–3101

NORTH DAKOTA

Richard H. Leigh, M.D., 1600 University Ave., Grand Forks, ND 58210, (701) 775–5527
Brian E. Briggs, M.D., 718 6th St., Minot, ND 58701, (701) 838–6011

OHIO

Josephine Aronica, M.D., 1867 W. Market St., Akron, OH 44313, (216) 867–7361
L. Terry Chappell, M.D., 122 Thurman St., Bluffton, OH 45817, (419) 358–4627
James P. Frackelton, M.D., 24700 Center Ridge Road, Cleveland, OH 44145, (216) 835–0104
William C. Schmelzer, M.D., 3219 Sullivant Ave., Columbus, OH 43204, (614) 272–5244
Harold J. Wilson, M.D., 28 W. Henderson Rd., Columbus, OH 43214, (614) 261–0151
Don K. Snyder, M.D., Rt. 2, Box 1271, Paulding, OH 45879, (419) 263–2722
Stavros, E. Meimaridis, M.D., 4550 Liberty Avenue, Vermilion, OH 44089, (216) 967–0151

OKLAHOMA

Jerald M. Gilbert, M.D., 7530 NW. 23rd, Bethany, OK 73008, (405) 789–9500
Vicki J. Conrad, M.D., 1616 S. Boulevard, Edmond, OK 73034, (405) 341–5691
Charles H. Farr, M.D., 11330 N. May Ave., Suite A, Oklahoma City, OK 73120, (405) 752–0070

OREGON

John Gambee, M.D., 66 Club Rd., #140, Eugene, OR 97401, (503) 686–2536
An C. Vu, M.D., 520 SW. 6th St., Suite 806, Portland, OR 97204, (503) 228–5158
Terrace Howe Young, M.D., 21 Oaks, Suite 240, 525 Glencreek Rd., NW., Salem, OR 97304, (503) 371–1558

PENNSYLVANIA

Ronald M. Repice, M.D., FAAFP, 1502 Upland St., Chester, PA 19013, (215) 874–1500
Lloyd Grumbles, M.D., 1601 Walnut St., #1323, Philadelphia, PA 19103, (215) 567–0938
P. Jayalakshmi, M.D., K. R. Sampathachar, M.D., 6366 Sherwood Rd., Philadelphia, PA 19151, (215) 473–4226
Lance S. Wright, M.D., 3901 Market St., Philadelphia, PA 19104, (215) 387–1200
Harold Buttram, M.D., RD. #3, Clymer Rd., Quakertown, PA 18951, (215) 536–1890

SOUTH CAROLINA

Allen Edwards, M.D., Theodore C. Rozema, M.D., 1000 Rutherford Rd., Landrum, SC 29356, (803) 457–4141

TENNESSEE

Maurice S. Goldman, M.D., 2850 Westside Dr., Suite K, Cleveland, TN 37311, (615) 476–6578
Sheila W. Robertson, M.D., 6195 Macon Rd., Suite 5, Memphis, TN 38134, (901) 373–3400
Donald Thompson, M.D., P.O. Box 2088, Morristown, TN 37814, (615) 581–6367

TEXAS

William Irby Fox, M.D., 1227 N. Mockingbird Lane, Abilene, TX 79603, (915) 672–7863
Roy W. Dowdell, M.D., 1109 W. Baker Rd., Baytown, TX 77521, (713) 422–3576
Ralph E. Smiley, M.D., 8345 Walnut Hill Lane, Dallas, TX 75231, (214) 368–4132
Charles F. Bailey, Jr., M.D., 125 Longhorn Rd., Ft. Worth, TX 76179, (817) 232–4991
Robert M. Battle, M.D., 9910 Long Point Rd., Houston, TX 77055, (713) 932–0552
J. L. Borochoff, M.D., 8830 Long Point Rd., Suite 504, Houston TX 77055, (713) 461–7517
Luis Edward Guerrero, M.D., 6550 Tarnef, Suite 204, Houston, TX 77074, (713) 981–4901
Issac L. Morrison, M.D., 8762 Long Point Rd., Houston, TX 77055, (713) 464–2775
Vladimir Rizov, M.D., 6550 Tarnef, #4, Houston, TX 77071, (713) 771–5506
Wesley R. T. Metzner, M.D., 234 San Pedro, San Antonio, TX 78205, (512) 223–1876
Edmond Scavone, M.D., 8607 Wurzbach Rd., Suite U 102, San Antonio, TX 78240, (512) 694–4091
Thomas Roger Humphrey, M.D., 2400 Rushing, Wichita Falls, TX 76308, (817) 766–4329

VIRGINIA

Sohini P. Patel, M.D., 5275 Lee Hwy., Suite 104, Arlington, VA 22207–1619, (703) 237–0303

Harold Huffman, M.D., P.O. Box 155, Hinton, VA 22831, (703) 867–5242

Elmer Cranton, M.D., Ripshin Rd., Box 44, Trout Dale, VA 24378, (703) 677–3631

WASHINGTON

Robert Kimmel, M.D., 1800 "C" St., Suite C-8, Bellingham, WA 98225,
(206) 734–3250

Leo Bolles, M.D., 15611 Bellevue Redmond Rd., Bellevue, WA 98008, (206) 881–2224

Jonathan Collin, M.D., 11903 NE. 128th St., Kirkland, WA 98033, (206) 823–0808

Charles T. McGee, M.D., 1717 Lincoln Way, #108, Spokane, WA 83814,
(208) 664–1478

Quentin, G. R. Schwenke, M.D., 321 Wellington, Walla Walla, WA 99362,
(509) 525–4070

WEST VIRGINIA

Prudential Corro, M.D., Rt. 4, Box 630, Beckley, WV 25801, (304) 252–0775

Steve M. Zekan, M.D., 1208 Kanawha Blvd., E., Charleston, WV 25301,
(304) 925–0579

Ebb K. Whitley, Jr., M.D., Box 540 Whitley Clinic, Rt. 52, Iaeger, WV 24844,
(304) 938–5357

WISCONSIN

Philip F. Mussari, M.D., P.O. Box 409, 235 Main St., Necedah, WI 54646,
(608) 565–7401

Rathna Alwa, M.D., Box 990, 93 W. Geneva St., Williams Bay, WI 53191,
(414) 245–5566

IV. ORTHOMOLECULAR PRACTITIONERS

ALASKA

Russell Manuel, M.D., Doris Williams, Ph.D., 3330 "C" St., Anchorage, AK 99503,
(907) 562–6070

ALABAMA

H. Ray Evers, M.D., P.O. Drawer 587, Cottonwood, AL 36230, (205) 691–2161

ARIZONA

Charlene, DeHaven, M.D., 941 S. Dobson, Suite 209, Mesa, AZ 85202,
(602) 834–1700

Abram Ber, M.D., 3134 7th St., Suite A, Phoenix, AZ 85014, (602) 279–3795

Ruth H. Capp, M.D., 5801 E. Paseo Cimarron, Tucson, AZ 85715, (602) 557–2452

ARKANSAS

Harold Hedges, M.D., 424 N. University, Little Rock, AR 72205, (501) 664–4810

A. M. Worrell, Jr., M.D., 3900 Hickory, Pine Bluff, AR 71603, (501) 535–8200

CALIFORNIA

Sidney Alder, M.D., 1820 Lincoln Ave., Anaheim, CA 92081, (714) 774–4474

George Borrell, M.D., 1842 W. Lincoln Ave., Anaheim CA 92801, (714) 991–5061

Douglas Ernst, M.D., 900 Alvarado Rd., Berkeley, CA 94705, (415) 548–6464

George Karalis, M.D., 2161 Allston Way, #7, Berkeley, CA 94704, (415) 843–6791

Stephen Langer, M.D., 3031 Telegraph, Berkeley, CA 94705, (415) 548–7384

Michael Lesser, M.D., 2340 Parkker St., Berkeley, CA 94704, (415) 845–0700

Tod Mikuriya, M.D., 41 Tunnel Rd., Berkeley, CA 94705, (415) 548–1188

Phyllis Saifer, M.D., 3031 Telegraph Ave., Suite 21, Berkeley, CA 94705,
(415) 849–3346

Arnold Fox, M.D., 416 N. Bedford Dr., #307, Beverly Hills, CA 90210, (213) 278–6447

Leonard Klepp, M.D., 16311 Ventura Blvd. Suite 725, Encino, CA 91436,
(213) 981–5511

Seymour Myers, M.D., 16917 Ventura Blvd., Encino, CA 91316, (213) 788–5231

David Edwards, M.D., 360 S. Clovis Ave., Fresno, CA 93727, (209) 251–5066

Horst Weinberg, M.D., 3505 E. Shields, Fresno, CA 93726, (209) 224–2500

Bruce Battleson, M.D., 18124 Culver Dr., Suite H, Irvine, CA 92715, (714) 551–3433

Rob Krakovitz, M.D., 12719 Washington Pl., Los Angeles, CA 90066, (213) 390–6633

Joseph Ramljak, M.D., 921 Westwood Blvd., Suite 233, Los Angeles, CA 90024,
(213) 208–4880

Harvey Ross, M.D., 7080 Hollywood Blvd. #1015, Los Angeles, CA 90028,
(213) 466–8330

Priscilla Slagle, M.D., 12301 Wilshire Blvd., Suite 300, Los Angeles, CA 90025,
(213) 826–0175

John Michael, M.D., 6536 Telegraph Ave., A-201, Oakland, CA 94609,
(415) 547–8111

Anita Millen, M.D., 301 E. Colorado Blvd., #801, Pasadena, CA 91101,
(213) 578–0531

Kenneth Hodge, M.D., 2322 Butano Dr., Suite 208, Sacramento, CA 95825,
(916) 485–4844

Carl Markwood, M.D., 1736 Professional Dr., Sacramento, CA 95825,
(916) 481–9921

Orville Davis, M.D., 4224 Ohio St., San Diego, CA 92104, (619) 283–6033

Zane Gard, M.D., 6386 Alvarado Ct., S-326, San Diego, CA 92120, (619) 583–5963

John Henderson, M.D., 3805 Front St., San Diego, CA 92103, (619) 293–7747

Karl Maret, M.D., 3330 Sixth Ave., San Diego, CA 92103, (619) 698–9504

Harriet McInnes, M.D., 3655 Adams Ave., San Diego, CA 92116, (619) 280–4570

Lawrence Taylor, M.D., 4167 Ohio St., San Diego, CA 92104, (619) 296–2952

Richard Kunin, M.D., 2698 Pacific, San Francisco, CA 94115, (415) 346–2500

John M. Ackerman, M.D., 2417 Castillo St., Santa Barbara, CA 93105,
(805) 682–1011

Wyman Sanders, M.D., 2901 Wilshire Blvd., #345, Santa Monica, CA 90403,
(213) 828–6471

COLORADO

Harold Whitcomb, M.D., 100 E. Main, Aspen, CO 81611, (303) 925–5440

Mabel Brelje, M.D., 6900 W. Alameda, Denver, CO 80226, (303) 936–7466

Kendall Gerdes, M.D., 1617 Vine St., Denver, CO 80206, (303) 377–8837

Nicholas Nonas, M.D., 601 E. Hampden, Suite 475, Englewood, CO 80110,
(303) 781–9416

CONNECTICUT

John Beaty, M.D., 40 E. Putnum Ave., Cos Cob, CT 06807, (203) 869–6302
Sidney Baker, M.D., Robert McLellan, M.D., 310 Prospect St., New Haven, CT 06511, (203) 789–1911
Marshall Mandell, M.D., 3 Brush St., Norwalk, CT 06850, (203) 838–4706
Alan Dattner, M.D., RR 1, Box 69, N. Grosvenordale, CT 06255, (203) 923–9596
Walter Lehmann, M.D., 27 Cricket Lane, Wilton, CT 06897, (203) 762–3387

DISTRICT OF COLUMBIA

John Lofft, M.D., 3301 New Mexico Ave., NW., #22, Washington, DC 20016 (202) 686–0300
George Mitchell, M.D., 2112 F St., NW., #404, Washington, DC 20016, (202) 429–9456
H. E. Saatori, M.D., 4501 Connecticut Ave., #306, Washington, DC 20008, (202) 244–6327

FLORIDA

Moke Williams, M.D., 4545 N. Federal Hwy., Ft. Lauderdale, FL 33305, (305) 771–2711
Donald Carrow, M.D., 147 N. Belcher Rd., Suite 4, Largo, FL 33541, (813) 536–3531
Robert Rodgers, M.D., 15 W. Ave. B., Melbourne, FL 32901, (305) 723–2360
Joya Schoen, M.D., 1900 N. Orange Ave., Orlando, FL 32804, (305) 898–2951
Rodman Shippen, M.D., 615 E. Princeton St., Orlando, FL 32803, (305) 896–3551
William Philpott, M.D., 6101 Central Ave., St. Petersburg, FL 33710, (813) 381–4673
Ray Wunderlich, M.D., 666 Sixth St. S., St. Petersburg, FL 33701, (813) 822–3612

GEORGIA

Milton Fried, M.D., 5675 Peachtree Dunwoody Rd., Atlanta, GA 30342, (404) 252–0235
Howard Yager, M.D., 3109 E. Shadowlawn Ave., N., Atlanta, GA 30305, (404) 261–1165
William Saunders, M.D., 5054 Austell Rd., Austell, GA 30001, (404) 941–1383
Robert Webster, M.D., 2665 Acadia St., East Point, GA 30213, (404) 766–0239
Young Shin, M.D., 1135 Hudson Bridge Rd., Stockbridge, GA 30281, (404) 474–3666

IDAHO

Charles McGee, M.D., 411 Coeur d'Alene Ave., Coeur d'Alene, ID 83814, (208) 664–1478
Eugene Trout, M.D., 421 Coeur d'Alene Ave., Coeur d'Alene, ID 83814, (208) 664–9151

ILLINOIS

Theron Randolph, M.D., 505 N. Lake Shore Dr., Chicago, IL 60611, (312) 828–9480
G. R. Oberg, M.D., 4911 Rt. 31, Crystal Lake, IL 60014, (815) 455–1990
Robert Waters, M.D., 7310 W. North Ave., Suite 4A, Elmwood Park, IL 60635, (312) 452–0017
Theodore TePas, M.D., 1012 Lake Shore Blvd., Evanston, IL 60202, (312) 328–5826
George Shambaugh, M.D., 40 S. Clay, Hinsdale, IL 60521, (312) 887–1130

Tipu Sultan, M.D., 1050 N. Center, Maryville, IL 62062, (618) 288-3233
Robert Filice, M.D., 24 W. 500 Maple Ave., Naperville, IL 60540, (312) 369-1220
Paul Dunn, M.D., 715 Lake St., Oak Park, IL 60301, (312) 383-3800
Thomas Stone, M.D., 1811 Hicks Rd., Rolling Meadow, IL 60008, (312) 934-1100
John Olwin, M.D., 4711 Golf Rd., Skokie, IL 60076, (312) 676-4030

INDIANA

John O'Brien, M.D., 3217 Lake Ave., Fort Wayne, IN 46805, (219) 422-9471
David Darbro, M.D., 2124 E. Hanna, Indianapolis, IN 46227, (317) 787-2221

IOWA

Dale Harding, M.D., 115 S. Park, Eagle Grove, IA 50533, (515) 448-4703
Vernon Varner, M.D., 328 E. Washington St., Iowa City, IA 52240, (319) 337-6483

KANSAS

Charles Hinshaw, M.D., 1133 E. 2nd St., Wichita, KS 67214, (316) 262-0951
Hugh Riordan, M.D., 3100 N. Hillside, Wichita, KS 67219, (316) 682-3100

KENTUCKY

Walt Stoll, M.D., 1412 N. Broadway, Lexington, KY 40504, (606) 233-4273

LOUISIANA

C. E. Blunck, M.D., 1705 Belleview Dr., Plaquemine, LA 70764, (504) 383-9852

MARYLAND

Wyrth Baker, M.D., 4701 Willard Ave., Chevy Chase, MD 20215, (301) 656-8940
James Brodsky, M.D., 4701 Willard Ave., Suite 224, Chevy Chase, MD 20215, (301) 652-6760
William Cates, M.D., 17515 Redland Rd., Derwood, MD 20855, (301) 921-0350
Paul Beals, M.D., 9101 Cherry Lane, Suite 205, Laurel, MD 20708, (301) 490-9911
Robin Ely, M.D., 10411 Gorman Rd., Laurel, MD 20707, (301) 953-1662
Ahamad Shamim, M.D., 200 Fort Meade Rd., Laurel, MD 20707, (301) 776-3700

MASSACHUSETTS

Jeanne Hubbach, M.D., Michael Janson, M.D., 2557 Massachusetts Ave., Cambridge, MA 02140, (617) 661-6225
G. Vinton Hallock, M.D., 305 Belmont St., Worcester, MA 01604, (617) 752-4681

MICHIGAN

Thomas Hoffer, M.D., 5825 Allen Rd., Allen Park, MI 48101, (313) 383-0393
Dennis Chernin, M.D., 2225 Packard, Ann Arbor, MI 48104, (313) 665-6747
H. C. Tien, M.D., 820 N. Capital Ave., Lansing, MI 48906, (517) 372-4660
Gurudarsha Khalsa, M.D., 27330 Southfield Rd., Lathrup Villa, MI 48076, (313) 552-8848
Bill Nagler, M.D., 16500 N. Park Dr., Suite 51, Southfield, MI 48075, (313) 559-5817

Henry Turlel, M.D., 19145 W. Nine Mile Rd., Southfield, MI 48075, (313) 357–5588
Willard Beebe, M.D., 16333 Trenton Rd., Suite 1009, Southgate, MI 48195,
  (313) 281–0144

MINNESOTA

Marcia Franklin, M.D., Karlstad Clinic, Karlstad, MN 56732, (218) 436–2251
Pamela Morford, M.D., 2545 Chicago Ave., Suite 515, Minneapolis, MN 55404,
  (612) 824–5250
Thomas Wittkipp, M.D., 606 24th Ave., S., Suite 803, Minneapolis, MN 55454,
  (612) 339–4066

MISSOURI

Robert Deitchman, M.D., 141 N. Meramec Ave., Clayton, MO 63105, (314) 862–4455
Tipu Sultan, M.D., 14585 Washington St., Florissant, MO 63033, (314) 921–5600
Garry Vickar, M.D., 1245 Graham Rd., Suite 506, Florissant, MO 63031,
  (314) 837–4190
Barbara Herjanic, M.D., 4940 Audubon Ave., St. Louis, MO 63110, (314) 455–4851
Marihan Herjanic, M.D., 1420 Grattan St., St. Louis, MO 63104, (314) 291–7600
William Lamb, M.D., Jeannette Schoonmaker, M.D., Cherry at Kimbrough, Suite
  224, Springfield, MO 65806, (417) 865–0914

MONTANA

Ralph Campbell, M.D., 4 Third Ave., Polson, MT 59860, (406) 883–2232

NEBRASKA

Eugene Oliveto, M.D., 8031 W. Center Rd., Omaha, NE 68124, (402) 392–0233
Stuart Schlanger, M.D., 7330 Maple, Omaha, NE 68134, (402) 391–6713

NEVADA

Elizabeth Rees, M.D., 1511 N. Carson St., Carson City, NV 89701, (702) 883–8902
Robert Milne, M.D., F. Fuller Royal, M.D., 6105 Tropicana, Las Vegas, NV 89103,
  (702) 871–2700
Michael Gerber, M.D., 316 California St., #20, Reno, NV 89509, (712) 827–2223
Yiwen Tang, M.D., 290 Brinkby Ave., Reno, NV 89509, (702) 826–9500

NEW JERSEY

Catherine Spears, M.D., 25 Red Road, Chatham, NJ 07928, (201) 635–8795
Richard Podell, M.D., 29 South St., New Providence, NJ 07974, (201) 464–3800
Barbara Handman, M.D., Cherry Hill Rd. #5, Princeton, NJ 08540, (601) 466–2563
Harry Panjwani, M.D., 106 Prospect St., Ridgewood, NJ 07451, (201) 447–2033
Carl Pfeiffer, M.D., 862 Rt. 518, Skillman, NJ 08558, (609) 924–8613
Philip Bonnet, M.D., 1203 Parkside Ave., Trenton, NJ 08618, (609) 883–6616
Jack Ward, M.D., 333 W. State St., Trenton, NJ 08618, (609) 392–7174
Kenneth Hall, M.D., 55 Wendt Lane, Wayne, NJ 07470, (201) 694–0405
Faina Munits, M.D., 15 Rosemont Terr., West Orange, NJ 07052, (201) 736–3743

NEW YORK

Peter Andrus, M.D., 1021 Western Ave., Albany, NY 12203, (518) 482–7343

Frank Nochimson, M.D., 416 74th St., Brooklyn, NY 11209, (718) 630–7195

Harold Weiss, M.D., 8002 19th Ave., Brooklyn, NY 11214, (718) 236–2202

Doris Rapp, M.D., 1412 Colvin Blvd., Buffalo, NY 14223, (716) 875–5578

George Congram, M.D., 24 Arbor Lane, Dix Hills, NY 11746, (516) 271–8016

Juan Wilson, M.D., 1900 Hempstead, East Meadow, NY 11554, (516) 794–0404

Harry Sackren, M.D., 6 Orchard Rd., Great Neck, NY 11021, (516) 487–8893

Jose Yaryura-Tobias, M.D., 560 Northern Blvd., Great Neck, NY 11021, (516) 487–7116

Serafina Corsello, M.D., 152 E. Main St., Huntington, NY 11743, (516) 271–0222

Alfred Zamm, M.D., 111 Maiden Lane, Kingston, NY 12401, (914) 338–7766

Richard Carlton, M.D., 68 E. 86th St., New York, NY 10028, (212) 737–4496

Hyman Chartock, M.D., Karl Humiston, M.D., 104 E. 40th St. #906, New York, NY 10016, (212) 986–9385

Allan Cott, M.D., 160 E. 38th St., New York, NY 10016, (212) 679–5593

Leo Galland, M.D., 41 E. 60th St., New York, NY 10022, (212) 308–6622

Warren Levin, M.D., Steven Rachlin, M.D., 444 Park Ave. S., New York, NY 10016, (212) 696–1900

Morton Teich, M.D., 930 Park Ave., New York, NY 10028, (212) 988–1821

Stanley Title, M.D., 171 W. 57th St., New York, NY 10019, (212) 581–9532

Sherry Rogers, M.D., 2800 W. Genesee St., Syracuse, NY 13219, (315) 488–2856

Miklos Boczko, M.D., 12 Greenridge Ave., White Plains, NY 10605, (914) 949–8817

NORTH CAROLINA

Logan Robertson, M.D., Rt. 2, Canton, NC 28716, (704) 235–9112

T. M. Bullock, M.D., F. M. Carroll, M.D., 104 Seventh Ave., Chadbourn, NC 28431, (919) 654–4614

J. Gray McAllister, M.D., 151½ E. Franklin, Chapel Hill, NC 27514, (919) 968–4651

NORTH DAKOTA

Brian Briggs, M.D., 718 SW. 6th St., Minot, ND 58701, (701) 838–6011

OHIO

Paul Siegel, M.D., 3619 Park East Rd., Beachwood, OH 44122, (216) 464–7677

Heather Morgan, M.D., 138 S. Main St., Centerville, OH 45459, (513) 439–1797

James Frackelton, M.D., Derrick Lonsdale, M.D., 24700 Center Ridge Rd., Cleveland, OH 44145, (216) 835–0104

Richard Bahr, M.D., 999 Brewbaker, Dayton, OH 45420, (513) 298–8661

OKLAHOMA

Howard Hagglund, M.D., 2227 W. Lindsey, Suite 1401, Norman, OK 73069, (405) 329–4457

OREGON

Philip Stonebrook, M.D., 472 Scenic Dr., Ashland, OR 97520, (503) 482–2032

John Gambee, M.D., 66 Club Rd., #140, Eugene, OR 97401, (503) 686–2536

Milton Hartzell, M.D., #2 Valley River Center, Eugene, OR 97401 (503) 345–7110
John Green, M.D., 3674 Pacific Hwy. 99E, Hubbard, OR 97032, (503) 981–1175
Joseph Hart, M.D., 6201 SW. Capitol Hwy., Portland, OR 97201, (503) 246–3397
Lendon Smith, M.D., 2233 SW. Market St., Portland, OR 97201, (503) 222–2365

PENNSYLVANIA

Howard Posner, M.D., 111 Bala Ave., Bala Cynwyd, PA 19004, (215) 667–2927
Leland Green, M.D., S. Broad St. at Allentown, Lansdale, PA 19446, (215) 855–9501
Milan Packovich, M.D., 2601 Fifth Ave., McKeesport, PA 15132, (412) 673–3900
Leander Ellis, M.D., 4401 Conshohocken Ave., Philadelphia, PA 19131,
    (215) 447–6444
P. Hayalakshmi, M.D., 6366 Sherwood Rd., Philadelphia, PA 19151, (215) 473–4226
Howard Lewis, M.D., 1241 Peermont Ave., Pittsburgh, PA 15216, (412) 531–1222
Harold Buttram, M.D., RD #3, Clyer Rd., Quakertown, PA 18951, (215) 536–1890

SOUTH CAROLINA

Allan Lieberman, M.D., 7510 Northforest Dr., Charleston, SC 29418, (803) 572–1600
Bruce Ford, M.D., 943 N. Church St., Spartanburg, SC 29303, (803) 585–2214
Albert Anderson, M.D., 19 Gallery Centre, Taylors, SC 29687, (803) 244–9020

TENNESSEE

William Crook, M.D., 657 Skyline Dr., Jackson, TN 38301, (901) 423–5100
Donald Thompson, M.D., 856 W. 4th North St., Momstown, TN 97814,
    (615) 581–6367
Richard Wanderman, M.D., 6584 Poplar Ave., Suite 420, Memphis, TN 38138,
    (901) 683–2777

TEXAS

R. W. Noble, M.D., 6757 Arapaho Rd., Suite 757, Dallas, TX 75248, (214) 458–9944
William Rea, M.D., 8345 Walnut Hill Lane, Suite 2, Dallas, TX 75231, (214) 368–4132
Don Mitchell, M.D., 6565 DeMoss, #107, Houston, TX 77074, (713) 771–2493
Jacob Siegel, M.D., 7410 Long Point Rd., Houston, TX 77055, (713) 682–2553
John Trowbridge, M.D., 9816 Memorial Dr., Suite 205, Humble, TX 77338,
    (713) 540–2329
Don Mannerberg, M.D., 375 Municipal Dr., Richardson, TX 75080, (214) 669–8707
John Seals, M.D., 4499 Medical Dr., San Antonio, TX 78229, (512) 696–7810
Eva Lee Snead, M.D., 959 SW. 34th St., San Antonio, TX 78237, (512) 434–4381

UTAH

Dennis W. Remington, M.D., 3707 N. Canyon Rd., #8C, Provo, UT 84604,
    (801) 224–9000

VERMONT

Stuart Freyer, M.D., 343 Dewey St., Bennington, VT 05201, (802) 442–3127
Peter Albright, M.D., 30 Western Ave., St. Johnsburg, VT 05819, (802) 174–5392

VIRGINIA

Elmer Cranton, M.D., P.O. Box 44, Trout Dale, VA 24373, (703) 677–3631

WASHINGTON

Sean Killoran, M.D., 900 Sheridan Rd., Bremerton, WA 98310, (206) 479–6694
Jonathan Wright, M.D., 13210 SE. 240th St., Kent, WA 98031, (206) 631–8920
David Buscher, M.D., 121 Third Ave., Kirkland, WA 98033, (206) 827–2151
Daniel Pletsch, M.D., 11012 NE. Fouth Plain Rd., Vancouver, WA 98662,
    (206) 256–4118
John Potts, M.D., 1109-B S. Second, Walla Walla, WA 99362, (509) 525–6120
Randall Wilkinson, M.D., Richard Wilkinson, M.D., 302 S. 12th Ave., Yakima, WA
    98902, (509) 453–5506

WEST VIRGINIA

A.V. Jellen, M.D., 2097 National Rd., Wheeling, WV 26003, (304) 242–5151

WISCONSIN

Eleazar Kadile, M.D., 1901 S. Webster, Green Bay, WI 54301, (414) 423–2204
Michael Sanfelippo, M.D., 2219-E Capitol Dr., Milwaukee, WI 53211, (414) 962–0155

V. ACUPUNCTURE PRACTITIONERS

ALABAMA

Acupuncture Clinic, 3245 Lorna Rd., Birmingham, AL 35216, (205) 979–4079

ALASKA

Anchorage Center of Family and Oriental Medicine, 4115 Lake Otis Pkwy., Anchor-
    age, AK 99508, (907) 562–2418

ARKANSAS

E.V. Monson, Jr., Boone County Medical Center, Harrison, AR 72601, (501) 741–9300

CALIFORNIA

Kims Acupuncture Clinic, 300 N. State College Blvd., Anaheim, CA 92806,
    (714) 778–1661
Mas Acupuncture Center, 1842 W. Lincoln Ave., Anaheim, CA 92801,
    (714) 535–5677
Parks Acupuncture Clinic, 508 S. Beach Blvd., Anaheim, CA 92804, (714) 828–3993
Peking Acupuncture Group, 509 S. Euclid Ave., Anaheim, CA 92802, (714) 772–7080
Shins Acupuncture Center, 1720 W. Ball Rd., Anaheim, CA 92804, (714) 533–4710
Wangs Acupuncture Clinic, 410 S. Euclid Ave., Anaheim, CA 92802, (714) 991–3145
Acupressure Workshop, 1533 Shattuck Ave., Berkeley, CA 94709, (415) 845–1059
Acupuncture Clinic of Beverly Hills, 300 S. Beverly Dr., Beverly Hills, CA 90212,
    (213) 551–0828

Barco Medical Clinic, 9400 Brighton Way, Beverly Hills, CA 90210, (213) 270-5933
Certified Acupuncture Group, 9735 Wilshire Blvd., Beverly Hills, CA 90212, (213) 275-9016
Crossworlds Acupuncture, 16542 Ventura Blvd., Encino, CA 91316, (818) 906-0808
Acupuncture Center, 709 N. Hill, Los Angeles, CA 90012, (213) 680-2849
Acupuncture Clinic, 1011 N. Broadway, Los Angeles, CA 90012, (213) 222-5090
Acupuncture Clinic, 975 S. Vermont Ave., Los Angeles, CA 90006, (213) 383-2726
Acupuncture Clinic, 7080 Hollywood Blvd., Los Angeles, CA 90028, (213) 462-6795
Auhs Acupuncture Center, 906 Crenshaw Blvd., Los Angeles, CA 90019, (213) 932-8421
China Acupuncture Clinic, 5318 Whittier Blvd., Los Angeles, CA 90022, (213) 266-8205
Chinese Acupuncture Center, 987 N. Broadway, Los Angeles, CA 90012, (213) 626-1381
Hollywood Acupuncture Medical Clinic, 1741 Ivar Ave., Los Angeles, CA 90028, (213) 469-3433
Los Angeles Acupuncture, 942 S. New Hampshire Ave., Los Angeles, CA 90006, (213) 389-1572
Oriental Acupuncture Center, 3201 N. Figueroa, Los Angeles, CA 90065, (213) 227-1054
Professional Acupuncture Group, 8635 W. 3rd St., Los Angeles, CA 90048, (213) 854-7799
Acupuncture Center, 4000 Broadway, Oakland, CA 94611, (415) 655-0668
Oakland Acupuncture Center, 4691 Telegraph Ave., Oakland, CA 94609, (415) 655-2299
Acupuncture & Acupressure Clinic, 1316 26th St., Sacramento, CA 95822, (916) 447-8267
Acupuncture Medical Clinic of Sacramento, Inc., 6945 Fair Oaks Blvd., Sacramento, CA 95825, (916) 485-4556
Acupuncture Center, 7325 Clarmemont Mesa Blvd., San Diego, CA 92111, (619) 292-9209
Acupuncture Clinic of San Diego, 3955 First Ave., San Diego, CA 92103, (619) 299-3654
California Acupuncture Clinic, 420 Walnut Ave., San Diego, CA 92103, (619) 291-0048
Acupuncture Associates, 1418 Stockton St., San Francisco, CA 94133, (415) 397-6100
Acupuncture Center, 269 Dorland St., San Francisco, CA 94114, (415) 863-1480
Chinese Acupuncture Clinic, 818 Clay, San Francisco, CA 94108, (415) 397-9299
Traditional Acupuncture Clinic, 3641 Sacramento, San Francisco, CA 94118, (415) 921-4808

CONNECTICUT

Acupuncture and Pain Center of Greenwich, 40 E. Putnam Ave., Cox Cob, CT 06807, (203) 661-4233

DISTRICT OF COLUMBIA

Institute of Preventive Medicine, 2139 Wisconsin Ave., NW., Washington, DC 20007, (202) 333-8880

FLORIDA

Boca Raton Health Center, 5601 N. Federal Hwy., Boca Raton, FL 33431,
(305) 994-3055

Acupuncture Center of Clearwater, 1710 Drew, Clearwater, FL 33515, (813) 441-9541

Acupuncture Center Suncoast, 2566 Simset Point Rd., Clearwater, FL 33575,
(813) 797-1161

Chinese Acupuncture Clinic, 1815 Hwy. 19 S., Clearwater, FL 33546, (813) 796-7851

Acupuncture Center, 4834 N. Federal Hwy. Fort Lauderdale, FL 33308,
(305) 491-5660

Chinese Acupuncture Institute, Inc., 3045 Federal Hwy., Fort Lauderdale, FL 33306,
(305) 561-5775

Chinese Acupuncture Institute, 1876 N. University Dr., Fort Lauderdale, FL 33322,
(305) 474-7666

Acupuncture Center, 3604 University Blvd. S., Jacksonville, FL 32216, (904) 737-5555

Acupuncture & Medical, Inc., 10621 N. Kendall Dr., Miami, FL 33176, (305) 596-0858

Acupuncture & Physical Therapy, 1680 Meridian Ave., Miami, FL 33139,
(305) 673-1060

Acupuncture & Physical Therapy, 13710 SW. 56th St., Miami, FL 33140,
(305) 385-7272

Acupuncture Medical Center, 6950 N. Kendall Dr., Miami, FL 33156, (305) 661-0572

Center for Traditional Chinese Acupuncture, 470 Biltmore Way, Miami, FL 33134,
(305) 446-3550

Center of Traditional Chinese Acupuncture, 15251 NE. 18th Ave., Miami, FL 33162,
(305) 940-7763

Acupuncture & Pain Control Center, 1230 Hillcrest St., Orlando, FL 32803,
(305) 896-3005

Acupuncture Center, 401 Pasadena Ave. S., St. Petersburg, FL 33707, (813) 381-3644

Acupuncture Center, 5473 66th St. N., St. Petersburg, FL 33709, (813) 541-2666

Chinese Acupuncture Clinic, 1535 Ninth St. N., St. Petersburg, FL 33705,
(813) 823-6472

Acupuncture Center of Hillsborough, 355 Hillsborough Ave. W., Tampa, FL 33604,
(813) 237-1174

Acupuncture Center of Florida, 706 W. Platt, Tampa, FL 33606, (813) 251-3089

Acupuncture Center of Tampa, 501 E. Buffalo Ave., Tampa, FL 33603, (813) 228-7129

Acupuncture Center Suncoast, 8405 N. Florida Ave., Tampa, FL 33604,
(813) 932-2610

HAWAII

Acupuncture Assoc. of Hawaii, 1185 Bethel, Honolulu, HI 96813, (808) 533-3131

Chinese Acupuncture Center, 100 N. Beretania, Honolulu, HI 96817, (808) 533-6778

Acupuncture Clinic, Sunset Plaza, Kailua Kona, HI 96740, (808) 329-1044

ILLINOIS

Acupuncture Center, 5214 N. Western Blvd., Chicago, IL 60625, (312) 271-5900

North Shore Acupuncture Associates, 1236 W. Chase, Chicago, IL 60626,
(312) 262-6276

Acupuncture Clinic, 6525 North Ave., Oak Park, IL 60302, (312) 848-0330

Kansas

Acupuncture & Chiropractic Center, 3724 Everett, Kansas City, KS 66102,
(913) 281-3035

Acupuncture Bio-Nutrition Chiropractor, 7811 Floyd, Shawnee Mission, KS 66204,
(913) 381-5541

Boerr Acupuncture Chiropractic Clinic, 1406 SW. Topeka Ave., Topeka, KS 66612,
(913) 235-0873

Maryland

Acupuncture Associates of Annapolis, Cape St. Claire Shopping Ctr., Annapolis, MD
21401, (301) 757-7665

Acupuncture Associates, 4803 Yellowwood Ave., Baltimore, MD 21209,
(301) 367-0606

Acupuncture Clinic of Towson, 7600 Osler Dr., Baltimore, MD 21204, (301) 825-6667

Acupuncture Center of Washington, 4400 E. West Hwy., Bethesda, MD 20814,
(301) 652-2828

Acupuncture Traditional Chinese, 5413 W. Cedar Lane, Bethesda, MD 20814,
(301) 493-0029

Acupuncture Clinic of Medicine, 11125 Rockville Pike, Rockville, MD 20852,
(301) 881-7866

Acupuncture Health Center, 5942 Hubbard Dr., Rockville, MD 20852, (301) 881-0364

Acupuncture Associates, 8830 Cameron St., Silver Spring, MD 20910, (301) 565-2700

Massachusetts

Acupuncture & Shiatsu Therapy, 359 Boylston St., Boston, MA 02116, (617) 247-0707

Acupuncture Associates, 304 Boylston St., Boston, MA 02116, (617) 536-7816

Acupuncture Associates of Cambridge, 843 Massachusetts Ave., Cambridge, MA
02139, (617) 491-4410

Acupuncture of Cambridge, 10 Pleasant St., Cambridge, MA 02139, (617) 864-4600

New England Acupuncture Center, 58 John F. Kennedy, Cambridge, MA 02138,
(617) 354-6304

Acupuncture Center of New England, 77 Maple St., Springfield, MA 01105,
(413) 733-0007

Acupuncture, 21 West St., Worcester, MA 01609, (617) 755-5557

Traditional Acupuncture Office, 20 Institute Rd., Worcester, MA 01609,
(617) 752-1354

Michigan

Health Clinic for Pain & Stress PCJ, 1110 S. Linden Rd., Flint, MI 48504,
(313) 732-7820

Western Michigan Pain Control Center, 751 Kenmoor SE., Grand Rapids, MI 49506,
(616) 949-9401

Minnesota

Acupuncture, Health Rehabilitation and Pain, 3312 W. 45th St., Minneapolis, MN
55410, (612) 925-9008

The Acupuncture Center, 6519 Nicollet Ave., Minneapolis, MN 55423, (612) 866–3818
Chinese Acupuncture, Inc., 4331 Excelsior Blvd., Minneapolis, MN 55416,
(612) 920–4556
Acupuncture Center, Inc., 3590 Owasso, St. Paul, MN 55112, (612) 484–8449

MISSOURI

Acupuncture Society of America, 4140 Broadway, Kansas City, MO 64111,
(816) 931–2127

MONTANA

Acupuncture & Chiropractic Clinic, 1505 Avenue D., Billings, MT 59102,
(406) 245–9333
Acupuncture Wai-Man Woo Clinic, 503 Wicks Lane, Billings, MT 59105,
(406) 245–2910
Acupuncture Eastern Medical Center, 2205 Broadwater Ave., Billings, MT 59102,
(406) 652–3820
Acupuncture East-West Medical Center, 13 Eleventh St. N., Great Falls, MT 59401,
(406) 761–4911
Acupuncture Clinic of Missoula, 715 W. Kensington Ave., Missoula, MT 59801,
(406) 728–1600

NEVADA

Acupuncture Center of Korea, 919 E. Charleston Blvd., Las Vegas, NV 89104,
(702) 382–1335
Acupuncture Center of Orient, 2029 Paradise Rd., Las Vegas, NV 89104,
(702) 735–7242
Chinese Acupuncture Medical Center, 1718 S. Eastern Ave., Las Vegas, NV 89104,
(702) 457–4677

NEW MEXICO

Acupuncture & Chiropractic Center, 1000 San Maleo Blvd. SE., Albuquerque, NM
87108, (505) 266–3305
Acupuncture Center, 1820 Juan Tabo Blvd. NE., Albuquerque, NM 87112, (505) 293–
6011
Acupuncture Center, 1544 Cerillos Rd., Santa Fe, NM 87501, (505) 988–3538
Chinese Acupuncture Clinic, 124 Sombrio Dr., Santa Fe, NM 87501, (505) 988–2316

NEW YORK

Brooklyn Acupuncture Center, Inc., 1270 E. 19th St., Brooklyn, NY 11230,
(718) 377–7981
Acupuncture Clinic of Fort Erie, 566 Center St., Buffalo, NY 14218, (716) 871–4941
Kings Acupuncture Center, Inc., 3185 Eggert Rd., Buffalo, NY 14223, (716) 833–6687
Acupuncture Center of Flushing, 42–62 Kissena Blvd., Flushing, NY 11355,
(718) 866–4431
Acupuncture Clinic of the East, 43–45 Broadway, Flushing, NY 11373, (718) 699–7086
Acupuncture Center of Long Island, 75 E. Deer Park Rd., Huntington, NY 11743,
(516) 499–4569

Acupuncture Information Center, 25 Tudor City Place, New York, NY 10017, (212) 599–0437

Acupuncture Information Center, 141 E. 55th St., New York, NY 10022, (212) 759–9440

Acupuncture Medical Center, 37 Union Square W., New York, NY 10003, (212) 989–6505

Acupuncture Medical Center, 290 Fifth Ave., New York, NY 10001, (212) 714–0140

Acupuncture Treatment Group of New York, 1449 Lexington Ave., New York, NY 10128, (212) 534–6800

New York Traditional Chinese Acupuncture, 147 W. 42nd St., New York, NY 10036, (212) 575–9373

OREGON

Acupuncture Center of Portland, Medical Dental Building, Portland, OR 97205, (502) 233–2845

Acupuncture Center of Oregon, 2210 Lloyd Center, Portland, OR 97232, (503) 281–6767

Acupuncture Pain Control Center, 4055 SW. Garden Home Rd., Portland, OR 97219, (503) 245–3156

East Portland Acupuncture Clinic, 3703 SE. 39th St., Portland, OR 97202, (503) 231–4101

Far East Acupuncture Center, 1424 NE. 109th St., Portland, OR 97220, (503) 254–9869

Metro Acupuncture Clinic, 511 SW. Tenth St., Portland, OR 97205, (503) 242–1969

Oriental Acupuncture Clinic, Portland Medical Center, Portland, OR 97205, (503) 228–4309

RHODE ISLAND

Acupuncture Center of Rhode Island, 1425 Main St., Warwick, RI 02886, (401) 821–6613

SOUTH CAROLINA

Acupuncture & Pain Control Clinic, 678 St. Andrews Blvd., Charleston, SC 29407, (803) 763–3311

Acupuncture & Pain Control Clinic, 2753 Laurel St., Columbia, SC 29204, (803) 799–7755

TENNESSEE

Carlota Clinic & Medical Acupuncture, 5300 Cottonwood Rd., Memphis, TN 38118, (901) 795–7900

TEXAS

Acupressure Reflex Health Clinic, 1538 E. Anderson Lane, Austin, TX 78752, (512) 837–6282

Austin Acupuncture Clinic, 5404 Ram Creek Parkway, Austin, TX 78759, (512) 346–0503

Austin Acupuncture Clinic, 1910 Justin Lane, Austin, TX 78757, (512) 451–3645

Acupuncture Therapy Clinic, Medical City, Dallas, TX 75230, (214) 233–5343

Acupuncture Association of the Southwest, 7320 Brentwood Stair Rd., Fort Worth, TX 76112, (817) 451-4728
Acupuncture Center International, 6550 Tarnef, Houston, TX 77074, (713) 776-3442
Acupuncture Speciality, Inc., 3201 Hillcroft, Houston, TX 77057, (713) 783-1319
Acupuncture Therapy Clinic, 4119 Montrose, Houston, TX 77006, (713) 527-0128
East-West Acupuncture Clinic, 6243 Bissonnet, Houston, TX 77081, (713) 981-8889

VIRGINIA

Acupuncture & Pain Treatment Center, 3046 Berkmar Rd., Charlottesville, VA 22901, (804) 973-3356
Dr. Trans Acupuncture Clinic, 8303 Arlington Blvd., Fairfax, VA 22031, (703) 573-1313
Acupuncture Center, 3705 George Mason Dr., Falls Church, VA 22041, (703) 671-3220

WASHINGTON

Acupuncture & Chinese Medicine, 7388 23rd St., NE., Seattle, WA 98115, (206) 527-2431
Acupuncture Association of Washington, 144 NE. 54th St., Seattle, WA 98105, (206) 522-0906
Acupuncture Clinic of Seattle, 4709 Ninth, NE., Seattle, WA 98105, (206) 632-6348
Acupuncture Clinic, 1412 NE. 88th St., Vancouver, WA 98665, (206) 574-4074

VI. CLINICAL ECOLOGY PRACTITIONERS

ALABAMA

James H. Walker, Sr., M.D., 1501 15th Ave. S., Birmingham, AL 35233, (205) 934-9770
Andrew M. Brown, M.D., 515 S. Third St., Gadsden, AL 35901, (205) 547-4971
Joseph B. Miller, M.D., 5901 Airport Blvd., Mobile, AL 36608, (205) 342-8540

ARKANSAS

Rheeta M. Stecker, M.D., 1315 Central Ave., Hot Springs, AR 71901, (501) 624-5206
Harold H. Hedges, M.D., 424 N. University, Little Rock, AR 72205, (501) 644-4810

ARIZONA

Talmage W. Shill, M.D., 2520 N. Mesa Dr., Mesa, AZ 85201, (602) 898-0698
Ralph F. Herro, M.D., 5115 N. Central Ave., Phoenix, AZ 85012, (602) 266-2374
James A. Smidt, M.D., 5115 N. Central Ave. #C, Phoenix, AZ 85012, (602) 252-9731
Guy S. Fasciana, D.M.D., 7601 Calle sin Ensidia #14, Tucson, AZ 85718, (602) 742-4594

CALIFORNIA

Phyllis L. Saifer, M.D., 3031 Telegraph Ave. #215, Berkeley, CA 94705, (415) 849-3346

Cathie Ann Lippman, M.D., 292 S. LaCienega Blvd. #202-20, Beverly Hills, CA 90211, (213) 659-9187

Joseph J. McGovern, Jr., M.D., 389 30th St., Oakland, CA 94609, (415) 444-5721

John D. Michael, M.D., 6536 Telegraph Ave. #A201, Oakland, CA 94609, (415) 547-8111

Robert J. Sinaiko, M.D., 389 30th St., Oakland, CA 94609, (415) 444-5721

George R. Fricke, M.D., 1355 Florin Rd., Sacramento, CA 95822, (916) 427-8988

Zane R. Gard, M.D., 6386 Alvarado Ct. #5326, San Diego, CA 92120, (619) 583-5863

Milton Millman, M.D., 2602 First Ave., Suite 104, San Diego, CA 92103, (714) 232-3159

Iris R. Bell, M.D., 1902 Webster St., San Francisco, CA 94115, (415) 563-9384

Ronald R. Chappler, M.D., 909 Hyde St. #401, San Francisco, CA 94109, (415) 885-4343

Don L. Jewett, M.D., Ph.D., Rm. U-471, University of California, San Francisco, CA 94143, (415) 666-5132

COLORADO

Harold C. Whitcomb, Jr., M.D., 100 E. Main St., Aspen, CO 81611, (303) 925-5440

Vincent A. Lagerborg, M.D., Ph.D., 29 Crestmoor Dr., Denver, CO 80220, (303) 482-6001

Del Stigler, M.D., 2005 Franklin St. #490, Denver, CO 80205, (303) 831-7335

Lawrence J. Dickey, M.D., 109 W. Olive St., Fort Collins, CO 80524, (303) 482-6001

S. Crawford Duhon, M.D., 373 W. Drake Rd., Fort Collins, CO 80526, (303) 223-3970

CONNECTICUT

Frederick Kessler, M.D., 71 Turtle Bay Dr., Branford, CT 06405, (203) 481-9957

Sidney M. Baker, M.D., 310 Prospect St., New Haven, CT 06511, (203) 789-1911

Marshall Mandell, M.D., Three Brush St., Norwalk, CT 06850, (203) 838-4706

DISTRICT OF COLUMBIA

George H. Mitchell, M.D., 2112 F St., NW., Suite 404, Washington, DC 20037-2712, (202) 429-9456

FLORIDA

Neil C. Henderson, M.D., 30 SE. Seventh St., Boca Raton, FL 33432, (305) 368-2915

Martin Brody, M.D., D.D.S., 7100 W. 20th Ave., Hialeah, FL 33016, (305) 822-9035

Morris Beck, M.D., 7400 N. Kendall Dr. #507, Miami, FL 33156, (305) 271-4711

Stanley J. Cannon, M.D., 9085 SW. 87th Ave., Miami, FL 33176, (305) 279-3020

Douglas Sandberg, M.D., 1500 NW. 12th Ave., Miami, FL 33136, (305) 547-6511

Alan J. Serrins, M.D., Sydney D. Wruble, M.D., 7400 N. Kendall Dr., Miami, FL 33156, (305) 595-1597

Hobart T. Feldman, M.D., 16800 NW. Second Ave. #301, North Miami Beach, FL 33169, (305) 652-1062

William H. Philpott, M.D., 6101 Central Ave., St. Petersburg, FL 33710, (813) 381-4673

Ray C. Wunderlich, Jr., M.D., 666 Sixth St., S., St. Petersburg, FL 33701, (813) 822-3612

GEORGIA

Morton D. Boyette, M.D., 804 14th Ave., Albany, GA 31708, (912) 435-7161
Milton Fried, M.D., 4426 Tilley Mill Rd., Atlanta, GA 30360, (404) 451-4857
Ann A. Bailey, M.D., P.O. Box 8, Warm Springs, GA 31830, (404) 655-3331

IDAHO

Jack A. Seeley, M.D., 10798 W. Overland, Boise, ID 83709, (208) 377-3368
Charles T. McGee, M.D., 1717 Lincoln Way #108, Coeur d'Alene, ID 83814-2537,
(208) 664-1478

ILLINOIS

Allan B. Aven, M.D., 1120 E. Central Rd., Arlington Heights, IL 60005,
(312) 253-1070
Mary F. Quarto, M.D., 830 W. Newport Ave., Chicago, IL 60657, (312) 883-0052
Theron G. Randolph, M.D., 505 N. Lakeshore Dr. #6506, Chicago, IL 60611,
(312) 828-9480
Michael E. Rubin, M.D., 1585 Ellinwood, Des Plaines, IL 60016, (312) 297-5500
George E. Shambaugh, Jr., M.D., 40 S. Clay St., Hinsdale, IL 60521, (312) 887-1130
Robert C. Filice, M.D., 24 W. 500 Maple Ave. #216, Naperville, IL 60540,
(312) 369-1220
Norene B. Hess, M.D., Robert T. Marshall, M.D., Ph.D., 700 Oak, Winnetka, IL
60093, (312) 446-1923

INDIANA

John F. O'Brian, M.D., 3217 Lake Ave., Fort Wayne, IN 46805, (219) 422-9471
David A. Darbro, M.D., 2124 E. Hanna, Indianapolis, IN 46227, (317) 787-7221
James K. Hill, M.D., 8803 N. Meridian St., Suite 340, Indianapolis, IN 46260,
(317) 846-7341

IOWA

Robert W. Soll, M.D., Ph.D., 105 N. Main St., Denison, IA 51442, (712) 263-6166
Rafael Tarnopolsky, M.D., 3200 Grand Ave., Des Moines, IA 50312, (515) 271-1400

KANSAS

Charles T. Hinshaw Jr., M.D., 1133 E. Second, Wichita, KS 67214, (316) 262-0951

LOUISIANA

Jacob Tasher, M.D., Highland Park Plaza, Suite 201, Covington, LA 70433,
(504) 892-4677
James Moore Foster, M.D., 1927 Hickory Ave., Harahan, LA 70183, (504) 738-5375
Hartwig M. Adler, M.D., 408 Vendome Pl., New Orleans, LA 70125, (504) 865-1767

MARYLAND

Barbara A. Solomon, M.D., 8109 Harford Rd., Baltimore, MD 21234, (301) 668-6511
William J. Cates, M.D., 17515 Redland Rd., Derwood, MD 20855, (301) 921-0350

MASSACHUSETTS

James A. O'Shea, M.D., 50 Prospect St., Lawrence, MA 01841, (617) 683-2632
Sheldon S. Goldberg, M.D., 120 Maple St., Springfield, MA 01103, (413) 732-7426
Richard B. Yules, M.D., 475 Pleasant St., Worcester, MA 01609, (617) 791-6305

MICHIGAN

Paula G. Davey, M.D., 425 E. Washington, Ann Arbor, MI 48104, (313) 662-3384
John J. Kelly, M.D., 14726 Champaign, Allen Park, MI 48101, (313) 386-5500
Jack W. De Long, M.D., 111 W. 24th St., Holland, MI 49423, (616) 396-2325
Harry R. Butler, M.D., 1821 King Rd., Trenton, MI 48183, (313) 676-2800
Cornelius F. Derrick, M.D., 1821 King Rd., Trenton, MI 48183, (313) 675-0678

MINNESOTA

Mark A. Muesing, M.D., 303 Kingwood, Brainerd, MN 56401, (218) 829-9270

MISSISSIPPI

Thomas S. Glasgow, M.D., 2161 S. Lamar, Oxford, MS 38655, (601) 234-2921

MISSOURI

Weldon L. Sportsman, M.D., 7504 N. Oak St., Kansas City, MO 64118,
(816) 436-7100
James W. Willoughby, M.D., P.O. Box 271, Liberty, MO 64068-0271, (816) 781-0902
Carleton Lee, M.D., 4104 St. Joseph Ave., St. Joseph, MO 64505, (816) 232-5493
Howard J. Aylward, Sr., M.D., 6651 Chippewa, St. Louis, MO 63109, (314) 647-8895
William T. K. Bryan, M.D., 9349 Parkside Dr., St. Louis, MO 63144, (314) 961-7414

MONTANA

Catherine H. Steele, M.D., Charles H. Steele, M.D., 2509 7th Ave., S., Great Falls,
MT 59405, (406) 727-3655
Ralph K. Campbell, M.D., Finley Point Rte., Polson, MT 59860, (406) 883-2232

NEVADA

Reed W. Hyde, M.D., 600 Shadow Lane, Las Vegas, NV 89106, (702) 382-8928
F. Fuller Royal, M.D., 6105 W. Tropicana Ave., Las Vegas, NV 89103, (702) 871-2700
Joseph F. Tangredi, M.D., 650 Shadow Lane, Las Vegas, NV 89106, (702) 382-3421
I. Marshall Postman, M.D., 1101 W. Moana Lane, Reno, NV 89509, (702) 826-4900

NEW JERSEY

Richard N. Podell, M.D., 29 South St., New Providence, NJ 07974, (201) 464-3800
Charles Harris, M.D., 20 Hospital Dr., Toms River, NJ 08753, (201) 244-3050
Faina Munits, M.D., 15 Rosemont Terr., West Orange, NJ 07052, (201) 736-3743

NEW MEXICO

Jacqueline Krohn, M.D., 5 Kiowa Lane, Los Alamos, NM 87544, (505) 662-9620

NEW YORK

James M. Miller, M.D., 40 Front St., Binghamton, NY 13905, (607) 722-0957

I-Tsu Chao, M.D., 1641 E. 18th St., Brooklyn, NY 11229, (718) 998-3331

Martin Feldman, M.D., 1695 E. 21st St., Brooklyn, NY 11210, (718) 744-4413

Doris J. Rapp, M.D., 1421 Colvin Blvd., Buffalo, NY 14223, (716) 877-8475

Rober M. Giller, M.D., 960 Park Ave., New York, NY 10028, (212) 472-2002

Jesse M. Hilsen, M.D., 1449 Lexington Ave., New York, NY 10128, (212) 861-1979

Karl E. Humiston, M.D., 104 E. 40th St. #906, New York, NY 10016, (212) 986-9385

Warren M. Levin, M.D., 444 Park Ave. S. (12th Fl.), New York, NY 10016, (212) 839-0950

Harold H. Markus, M.D., 161 Ave. of the Americas (14th Fl.), New York, NY 10013, (212) 675-2550

H. L. Newbold, M.D., 115 E. 34th St. #20K, New York, NY 10016-4631, (212) 679-8207

Joseph S. Rechtschaffen, M.D., 11 E. 68th St., New York, NY 10021, (212) 737-3136

Morton M. Teich, M.D., 930 Park Ave., New York, NY 10028, (212) 988-1821

Wellington S. Tichenor, M.D., 30 Central Park South, New York, NY 10019, (212) 371-8510

Sherry A. Rogers, M.D., 2800 W. Genessee St., Syracuse, NY 13219, (315) 488-2856

Miklos L. Boczko, M.D., 12 Greenridge Ave., White Plains, NY 10605, (914) 949-8817

Joseph S. Wojcik, M.D., 525 Bronxville Rd., Yonkers, NY 10708, (914) 793-6161

NORTH CAROLINA

R. Edward Huffman, M.D., 146 Victoria Rd., Asheville, NC 28801, (704) 253-3695

F. Keels Dickson, M.D., 485 N. Wendover Rd., Charlotte, NC 28211, (704) 366-0249

Bhaskar D. Power, M.D., P.O. Box 1132, Roanoke Rapids, NC 27870, (919) 535-1411

Walter A. Ward, M.D., P.O. Box 24039, Winston Salem, NC 27114-4039, (919) 760-0240

OHIO

Raymond S. Rosedale, Jr., M.D., 4150 Belden Village St., NW., Canton, OH 44718, (216) 492-2844

Richad B. Homan, M.D., 3444 Mooney Ave., Cincinnati, OH 45208, (513) 321-7333

Richard F. Bahr, M.D., 999 Brubaker Dr., Dayton, OH 45429, (513) 298-8661

David E. Brown, M.D., William D. Welton, M.D., 830 Fidelity Bldg., Dayton, OH 45402, (513) 223-3691

John W. Rechsteiner, M.D., 1116 S. Limestone St., Springfield, OH 45505, (513) 325-0223

OKLAHOMA

Clifton R. Brooks, Sr., M.D., 2114 Martingale Dr., Norman, OK 73072, (405) 329-8437

Howard E. Hagglund, M.D., 2227 W. Lindsey #1401, Norman, OK 73069, (405) 329-4458

John Lee Davis III, M.D., 3330 NW. 56th St., Suite 602, Oklahoma City, OK 73112, (405) 843-6619

Richard B. Dawson, M.D., 1117 N. Shartel, Suite 402, Oklahoma City, OK 73103, (405) 235-4421

Fannie Lou Leney-Hayward, M.D., 8555 S. Lewis, Tulsa, OK 74137, (918) 299-2661

OREGON

Joseph T. Morgan, M.D., 1750 Thompson Rd., Coos Bay, OR 97420, (503) 269-0333

John E. Gambee, M.D., 66 Club Rd., Eugene, OR 97401, (503) 686-2536

Donald C. Mettler, M.D., 2525 NW. Lovejoy St. #205, Portland, OR 97210, (503) 228-9497

G. A. Woodruff, M.D., 11110 SE. Main St., Portland, OR 97216-3550, (503) 255-4256

PENNSYLVANIA

Chin Y. Chung, M.D., 210 E. 2nd St., Erie, PA 16507, (814) 455-4429

George C. Miller II, M.D., Three Hospital Dr., Lewisburg, PA 17837, (717) 524-4405

Helen Fox Krause, M.D., 9104 Babcock Blvd., Pittsburgh, PA 15237, (412) 366-1661

Bernard Leff, M.D., 239 4th Ave. (2nd Fl.), Pittsburgh, PA 15222, (412) 281-8351

Harold E. Buttram, M.D., RD #3, Clymer Rd., Quakertown, PA 18951, (215) 536-1890

SOUTH CAROLINA

Allan D. Lieberman, M.D., 7510 Northforest Dr., North Charleston, SC 29418, (803) 572-1600

SOUTH DAKOTA

John W. Argabrite, M.D., Three East Kemp, P.O. Box 1596, Watertown, SD 57201, (605) 886-3144

TENNESSEE

Fred M. Furr, M.D., 9217 Park W. Blvd., Bldg. E., Knoxville, TN 37923, (615) 693-1502

Cecil E. Pitard, M.D., 403 Newland Professional Bldg., Knoxville, TN 37916, (615) 522-7714

Robert C. Owen, M.D., 210 25th Ave. N. #1016, Nashville, TN 37203, (615) 327-3291

Peter L. Ballenger, M.D., 1325 Eastmoreland, Suite 205, Memphis, TN 38104, (901) 725-6853

Richard G. Wanderman, M.D., 6584 Poplar Ave. #420, Memphis, TN 38138, (901) 683-2777

TEXAS

Richard Allan Berlando, M.D., R. W. Noble, M.D., 6757 Arapaho, Suite 757, Dallas, TX 75248, (214) 458-9944

Armando Lopez de Victoria, M.D., William J. Rea, M.D., Donald E. Sprague, M.D.,

8345 Walnut Hill Lane, Suite 205, Dallas, TX 75231, (214) 368–4132

Ralph E. Smiley, M.D., 3209 Rolling Knoll Dr., Dallas, TX 75234, (214) 241–0404

William H. Munyon, M.D., 4800 Albert, El Paso, TX 79905, (915) 533–3020

Charles R. Hamel, M.D., 3801 Hulen, Fort Worth, TX 76107, (817) 731–9531

Charles A. Rush, Jr., M.D., 7601 Glenview Dr., Fort Worth, TX 76118, (817) 284–9251

James C. Whittington, M.D., 1021 Seventh Ave., Fort Worth, TX 76104, (817) 332–4585

Vickey C. Halloran, M.D., 5629 FM 1960 W. #225, Houston, TX 77069–4215, (713) 370–6351

Jacob Siegel, M.D., 8300 Waterbury St. #305, Houston, TX 77055–3450, (713) 682–2553

William F. Andrew, M.D., 3716 21st St., Suite 202, Lubbock, TX 79410, (806) 797–3331

Lee R. Byrd, Jr., M.D., 4700 Lewis Dr., Port Arthur, TX 77640, (409) 982–3131

Harris Hosen, M.D., 2649 Proctor St., Port Arthur, TX 77640, (409) 985–5585

UTAH

Dennis W. Remington, M.D., 3707 N. Canyon Rd., Suite 8C, Provo, UT 84604, (801) 224–9000

VIRGINIA

Roger D. Neal, M.D., 176 W. Valley St., Abingdon, VA 24210, (703) 628–9547

Jack H. Eberhart, M.D., John W. Selman, M.D., 435 Commonwealth Blvd., Martinsville, VA 24112, (703) 638–3473

Henry J. Palacios, M.D., 8005 Algarve St., McLean, VA 22101, (703) 356–2244

WASHINGTON

George H. Drumheller, Jr., M.D., 1515 Pacific Ave., Everett, WA 98201, (206) 258–4361

David Buscher, M.D., 121 Third Ave., Kirkland, WA 98033, (206) 827–2151

Albert G. Corrado, M.D., 759 Swift, Suite 22, Richland, WA 99352, (509) 946–4631

John L. Carney, M.D., 1107 21st Ave., E., Seattle, WA 98112, (206) 324–8162

Daniel Pietsch, M.D., 11012 NE. Fourth Plain Rd., Vancouver, WA 98662, (206) 256–4118

Randall E. Wilkinson, M.D., Richard S. Wilkinson, M.D., 302 S. 12th Ave., Yakima, WA 98902–3176, (509) 453–5506

WEST VIRGINIA

Edwin M. Shepherd, M.D., 3100 MacCorkle Ave. SE. #606, Charleston, WV 25304, (304) 344–8039

WISCONSIN

Eleazar M. Kadile, M.D., 1901 S. Webster St. #3, Green Bay, WI 54301, (414) 432–2204

George F. Kroker, M.D., 2532 Edgewood Pl., La Crosse, WI 54601, (608) 782–2027
Melvin G. Apell, M.D., 555 S. Washburn, Oshkosh, WI 54901, (414) 231–5313
Wayne H. Konetzki, M.D., 403 N. Grand Ave., Waukesha, WI 53186, (414) 547–3055

WYOMING

Gerald L. Smith, M.D., 5320 Education Dr., Cheyenne, WY 82009, (307) 632–5589

VII. NATUROPATHY PRACTITIONERS

ALASKA

Patton Pettijohn, N.D., 502 E. Fireweed #4, Anchorage, AK 99502

ARIZONA

Mark James, N.D., 504 N. Humpreys, Flagstaff, AZ 86001
Steven Palley, N.D., 6 N. Leroux St., Flagstaff, AZ 86001
Meg Gilbert, N.D., 12236 N. 23rd St., Phoenix, AZ 85022
C. H. Junkin, N.D., 1800 E. Bell Rd., Phoenix, AZ 85022
Laurie Soloff, N.D., Valley Health Services, 3228 E. Indian School Rd. #103, Phoenix, AZ 85018
Clark Hansen, N.D., 8787 E. Mountain View Rd. #1099, Scottsdale, AZ 85258
Konrad Kail, N.D., 7119 E. Mercer Ln., Scottsdale, AZ 85257
Nancy Aton, N.D., R. Burke, N.D., 527 N. Tucson Blvd., Tucson, AZ 85716
Kenneth Blackman, N.D., 3002 E. Florence Dr., Tucson, AZ 85719
Don Canavan, N.D., 737 W. Altura, Tucson, AZ 85705
Cos Immel, N.D., 435 N. Tucson Blvd., Tucson, AZ 85716
Judy Patrick, N.D., 22 E. University, Tucson, AZ 85705

CALIFORNIA

Carol Doby, N.D., Berkeley Holistic Center, 3099 Telegraph Ave., Berkeley, CA 94705
Drew Collins, N.D., 5917 Chula Vista Way #3, Los Angeles, CA 90068
Jared Zeff, N.D., 2303 Midvale, Los Angeles, CA 90064
M. Rabinoff, N.D., 5901 Ross, Oakland, CA 94618
Arlen Brownstein, N.D., 126 Seale Ave., Palo Alto, CA 94301
Doug Rosenbaum, N.D., S.F. College of Acupuncture, 2409 19th Ave., San Francisco, CA 94116
Carl Hangee-Bauer, N.D., 610 Wisconsin St., San Francisco, CA 94107

COLORADO

Charles Cropley, N.D., 2885 E. Aurora, Suite 19, Boulder, CO 80303
Jody Shevins, N.D., 3770 Smuggler Way, Boulder, CO 80303
B. Shears, N.D., 115 N. Wahsatch, Colorado Springs, CO 80903

CONNECTICUT

Kathy Riley, N.D., 77 Cedar Dr., Danbury, CT 06811

Anne Mitchell, N.D., James Sensenig, N.D., 488 Whalley Ave., New Haven, CT 06511

David Filkoff, N.D., Nancy Mazur, N.D., 760 Farmington Ave., West Hartford, CT 06119

DISTRICT OF COLUMBIA

L. Bowen-Young, N.D., 2414 Perry St., NE., Washington, DC 20019

FLORIDA

Marion W. Cole, N.D., 1361 Pinebrook Dr., Clearwater, FL 33515
Stephan McKernan, N.D., 910 NE. 27th Ave., Hallandale, FL 33009
Lorna Murray, N.D., 1275 SW. 20th St., Miami, FL 33156
Julek Meissner, N.D., 1900 N. Orange Ave., Orlando, FL 32804
R. Barrows, N.E., 747 McIntyre Ave., Winter Park, FL 32789

HAWAII

Myron Berney, N.D., 2240A Pacific Hts. Rd., Honolulu, HI 96814
Paul Kenyon, N.D., 438 Ena Rd., Honolulu, HI 96815
Richard Rovin, N.D., 1750 Kalakaua Ave., Suite 2404, Honolulu, HI 96826
James Sankey, N.D., P.O. Box 1270, Honolulu, HI 96793
Jonathan Mather, N.D., 55–70 Wahinepee St., Laig, HI 96762
Collon Brayce, N.D., Island Health Center, 90 Central Ave., Wailuku, Maui, HI 96793
J. Dickens, N.D., 2119B Vineyard St., Wailuku, Maui, HI 96793

IDAHO

Ralph Day, N.D., 2768 Siesta Lane, Boise, ID 83704

ILLINOIS

L. Perz, N.D., 1040 Hibbard Rd., Wilmette, IL 60091

IOWA

A. Rothenberg, N.D., P. Herscu, N.D., 4430 N. 8th Ave., Carter Lake, IA 51510

KANSAS

W. Becker, N.D., 230 N. Dodge, Wichita, KS 67201
S. Beyrle, N.D., 2042 N. Arkansas, Wichita, KS 67203

MAINE

Paul Parker, N.D., 32 Essex St., Bangor, ME 04401
J. Marland, N.D., 148 East St., Yarmouth, ME 04096

MARYLAND

Michael D. Rabinoff, N.D., 4720 Montgomery, Bethesda, MD 20814
John Furlong, N.D., 813 Somerset Pl., Hyattsville, MD 20783
Gerald N. Douglass, N.D., 7524 Ardwick-Ardmore Rd., Landover, MD 20784

MASSACHUSETTS

Shivanath Barton, N.D., 42 Pleasant St., Arlington, MA 02171
Lisa Carberry, N.D., 1505 Commonwealth Ave., Brighton, MA 02135
Adam Sacks, N.D., 248 Green River Rd., Greenfield, MA 01301
Edward Ellis, N.D., 816 Merrimack St., Lowell, MA 01854

MICHIGAN

K. Carter, N.D., P.O. Box 72, Caro, MI 48723
Susie Gloriod, N.D., 680 Bear Lake Rd., North Muskegan, MI 49455
J. Casman, N.D., 16180 Oxley Rd. #102, Southfield, MI 48075

MINNESOTA

Helen Healy, N.D., 1365 S. Englewood Ave., St. Paul, MN 55104

MISSOURI

John Bailey, N.D., Applewood Medical Center, 9120 E. 35th, Independence, MO 64052

MONTANA

Russel Marz, N.D., 1321 8th Ave. N. #204, Great Falls, MT 59401
Michael Bergkamp, N.D., 25 S. Ewing, Helena, MT 59601
Amy Hayes, N.D., 321 SW. Higgins, Missoula, MT 59803

NEBRASKA

E. Bower, N.D., P.O. Box 404, Lincoln, NE 86334

NEW YORK

Deirdre O'Connor, N.D., 54^1/$_2$ Main St., Scottsville, NY 14546
K. Fuller, N.D., P.O. Box 343, Woodstock, NY 12498

NORTH CAROLINA

J. Massey, N.D., 109 Conner Dr., Suite 2102, Chapel Hill, NC 27514
Gil Alvarado, N.D., 80 New Life Clinic, 401 East Blvd., Charlotte, NC 28203
Stephen Barrie, N.D., Rt. 1, Box 7, Leceister, NC 28748

OHIO

Richard Liebman, N.D., Rt. 1, Rutland, OH 05775

OREGON

Stan Salimi, N.D., 905 W. Queen Ave., Albany, OR 97321
Richard Kirschner, N.D., A574 E. Main, Ashland, OR 97520
Martin Osterhaus, N.D., 450 Siskiyou Blvd. #1, Ashland, OR 97520
Terry Toth, N.D., 27 Third St., Ashland, OR 97520
Deborah Martin, N.D., 1185 Arthur St., Eugene, OR 97402

Stephen A. Messer, N.D., 910 Lincoln St., Eugene, OR 97401
T. Abshier, N.D., 8837 SE. Rhone St., Portland, OR 97266
A. Ackerson, N.D., 6704 SE. 122nd St., Portland, OR 97236
Merry Bern, N.D., 3939 SW. Springgarden, Portland, OR 97219
Richard Boggess, N.D., 3580 SE. 82nd Ave., Portland, OR 97266
Carlo Calabrese, N.D., 3134 SE. 111th St., Portland, OR 97266
Susan Delany, N.D., 12511A SE. Boise St., Portland, OR 97231
Raymond Diaz, N.D., 4416 SE. Madison, Portland, OR 97415
Paul Epstein, N.D., 332 NE. 156th St., Portland, OR 97230
Linda Herrick, N.D., 12224 NE. Hoyt, Portland, OR 97230
John Keilholtz, N.D., 2817 NE. Oregon St., Portland, OR 97232
Guru Sand Khalsa, N.D., 2539 SE. Madison, Portland, OR 97214
Susan Laier, N.D., 2148 NW. Irving, Portland, OR 97210
Richard Lounibus, N.D., 8885 SW. Canyon Rd., Portland, OR 97225
Brian McCoy, N.D., 520 SW. 6th St., Suite 806, Portland, OR 97203
Martin Milner, N.D., 2104 NE. 45th St., Suite 103, Portland, OR 97213
Fateha Moran, N.D., 1929 SW. Doph Ct., Portland, OR 97219
J. Neihaus, N.D., 13040 SE. Stephens, Portland, OR 97214
Patricia O'Bryan, N.D., 1904 SE. Pine, Portland, OR 97214
M. Rockwell, N.D., 7136 SE. Stark, Portland, OR 97215
Marvin Schweitzer, N.D., 2170 NE. Hancock #209, Portland, OR 97212
Joel Wallach, N.D., 20399 SW. Carlin Blvd., Portland, OR 97203

PENNSYLVANIA

Alan D. Horwitz, N.D., 2555 Huntingdon Pike, Huntingdon Valley, PA 19006
Michael Reece, N.D., P.O. Box 159, New Holland, PA 17557

TEXAS

John Hartman, N.D., 5547 Huisache St., Bellaire, TX 77401

UTAH

Cordell Logan, N.D., 1773 W. 7000 South, West Jordan, UT 84084

VERMONT

William Warnock, N.D., 70 Bartlett Bay Rd., South Burlington, VT 05401

WASHINGTON

Tom Ballard, N.D., 5312 Roosevelt, NE., Seattle, WA 98105
Felice Barnow, N.D., 5308 S. Hudson, Seattle, WA 98118
William Breznen, N.D., 1020 University #203, Seattle, WA 98105
Lyndon Capon, N.D., 19834 5th St., NE., Seattle, WA 98155
Judy Christianson, N.D., 204 NW. Bowdoin Pl., Seattle, WA 98107
Sharon Dermody, N.D., 518 First Ave., N., Seattle, WA 98109
Patrick Donovan, N.D., 7746 31st Ave., NW., Seattle, WA 98117
Kathrina Fennemann, N.D., 9507 Evenston Ave., N., Seattle, WA 98103
Mary Gallagher, N.D., 625 4th Ave., W., Seattle, WA 98119
Ann Gollin, N.D., 955 NW. 63rd St., Seattle, WA 98107

Kenneth Harmon, N.D., 1835 SW. 152nd St., Seattle, WA 98166
Pamela Houghton, N.D., 6303 Phinney Ave., Seattle, WA 98103
Herbert Joiner-Bey, N.D., 4718 11th St., NE. #12, Seattle, WA 98105
Sheryl Kipnis, N.D., 937 NW. 59th St., Seattle, WA 98107
Dan Labriola, N.D., 325 18th Ave., E., Seattle, WA 98112
Mark Lamden, N.D., 6204 8th Ave., NW., Seattle, WA 98103
Andrew Lange, N.D., 1438 Madrona Dr., Seattle, WA 98122
Francine Loeb, N.D., 911 29th St., S., Seattle, WA 98144
Nan Lopez, N.D., 3716 39th Ave., S., Seattle, WA 98144
J. Edward Madison, N.D., 5844 Woodlawn Ave., Seattle, WA 98103
Kathleen Naughton, N.D., 4112 Cascadia St., S., Seattle, WA 98118
Rick Posmantur, N.D., 5308 S. Hudson, Seattle, WA 98118
Carolyn Raleigh, N.D., 518 First Ave., N., Seattle, WA 98109
N. Sheinman, N.D., 144 NE. 54th St., Seattle, WA 98105
Fred Taub, N.D., 4733 W. Ruffner, Seattle, WA 98199
Dian Wagner, N.D., 3327 27th Ave., S., Seattle, WA 98144
H. Earl Moore, N.D., 3917 N. Monroe, Spokane, WA 99205
Todd Schlapfer, N.D., 511 S. Pine St. #517, Spokane, WA 99202
Daniel Patten, N.D., 116 S. 11th Ave., Yakima, WA 98902

ALSO BY GARY NULL:

The Complete Guide to Health & Nutrition
Gary Null's Nutrition Sourcebook for the Eighties
The New Vegetarian Cookbook
The Complete Handbook of Nutrition (with Steve Null)
The Complete Vegetarian (with Steve Null)
The Complete Question & Answer Book of General Nutrition
The Complete Question & Answer Book of Natural Therapy
Grow Your Own Food Organically
The Natural Organic Beauty Book